MAKING PEACE PREVAIL

SYRACUSE STUDIES ON
PEACE AND CONFLICT RESOLUTION

HARRIET HYMAN ALONSO,
CHARLES CHATFIELD,
LOUIS KRIESBERG
SERIES EDITORS

MAKING PEACE PREVAIL

PREVENTING VIOLENT CONFLICT IN MACEDONIA

Alice Ackermann

SYRACUSE UNIVERSITY PRESS

First Edition 1999
99 00 01 02 03 04 6 5 4 3 2 1

The paper used in this publication meets the minimum requirements of American National Standards for Information Sciences—Permanence of Paper for Printed Library Materials, ANSI Z39.48-1984 ∞

Library of Congress Cataloging-in-Publication Data

Ackermann, Alice.
Making peace prevail : preventing violent conflict in Macedonia / Alice Ackermann. — 1st ed.
p. cm. — (Syracuse studies on peace and conflict resolution)
Includes bibliographical references and index.
ISBN 0-8156-2812-9 (cloth : alk. paper). — ISBN 0-8156-0602-8 (paper : alk. paper)
1. Intervention (International law)—Political aspects Case studies. 2. Pacific settlement of international disputes Case sudies. 3. Conflict management Case studies. 4. Macedonia (Republic)—Politics and government—1992– I. Title. II. Series. JZ6368.A26 1999
327.1'7—dc21 99-32838

Manufactured in the United States of America

To A.
my best friend

ALICE ACKERMANN is assistant professor of international relations and conflict resolution at the University of Miami's School of International Studies in Coral Gables, Florida. She has published articles on conflict prevention and reconciliation in *Peace and Change, Security Dialogue, European Security, The Journal of Conflict Studies,* and *The International Spectator* (Rome). She also produced an award-winning video documentary on preventive diplomacy, *From the Shadow of History* (1997, with Sanjeev Chatterjee), which has been screened at educational institutions in the United States, Canada, Europe, New Zealand, and South Africa.

CONTENTS

ILLUSTRATIONS

Tables

Map

PREFACE

ALBERT CAMUS ONCE wrote that the twentieth century is the "century of fear." Having witnessed the carnage and destruction of World War II, Camus asked individuals to make a choice—to come out on the side of our "common humanity." Elements of Camus' thinking form the philosophical foundation of this book: namely, that wars and destructive conflicts are not part of humanity, that they are not inevitable—and that we can take action to prevent them.

For the Europeans, the violent disintegration of Yugoslavia and the continuing Yugoslav wars were deeply disturbing. No one had thought such carnage and brutality possible in a Europe that had experienced the excesses of World War II. It is perhaps not surprising therefore that when the violence escalated, Europeans reacted with helplessness, leaving the Yugoslav people to fend for themselves. Most discouraging was the lack of serious attempts to prevent the conflict from spilling over into Bosnia, where it destroyed not only much of the republic's beautiful architecture, but also the very multiethnic tapestry Bosnia-Hercegovina prided itself on.

My own thinking about conflict prevention was much influenced by what happened in Yugoslavia. I became intrigued by why the war did not spread into Macedonia, in the southernmost part of the former Yugoslavia, which also had a multiethnic society. This question motivated me to visit Macedonia four times in 1995 and 1996, and again in May 1999, and to explore in detail how it had succeeded in averting the fate of Bosnia.

What I saw when I first came to Macedonia in the late spring 1995 was much different from what I had expected to see. With the television images of Bosnia still fresh in my mind, I set about the task of discovering why peace had prevailed in this tiny country, wedged between the "Four Wolves"—Serbia, Albania, Bulgaria, and Greece. This book records my findings. Some of the conversations, preventive measures, analyses, and answers to questions that made their way into it can also be found in *From the Shadow of History,* a video documentary on preventive diplomacy in the Former Yugoslav Republic of

Macedonia that I produced with my colleague and friend Sanjeev Chatterjee in 1997. He is also the first person I wish to thank for his continued intellectual and personal support of this book and the documentary that accompanies it, both of which benefited from our numerous discussions and cooperative efforts.

I gratefully acknowledge funding by the United States Institute of Peace, the International Research and Exchanges Board (IREX), and also the University of Miami, which provided generous research support. I was fortunate to receive a Fulbright Research Scholarship to the Stiftung Wissenschaft und Politik (Foundation of Science and Politics) in Germany in 1996, where I was able to write portions of this book.

Louis Kriesberg deserves particular mention for reading the manuscript draft and providing comments and suggestions. I am also grateful to the manuscript's outside reviewer for the positive feedback I received on the book. The project would not have been possible without the Macedonian people from all ethnic groups whom I met and whose hospitality I enjoyed while conducting research. These include the many journalists to whom I spoke—particularly Branko Geroski and Gordana Stošic—ethnic leaders, government officials, and representatives from the United Nations, the Organization for Security and Cooperation in Europe (OSCE), and several nongovernmental organizations. In particular, I want to thank U.N. assistant secretary-general Henryk Sokalski, former UNPREDEP commander Juha Engström, OSCE ambassadors Tore Bøgh and Faustino Troni, and OSCE members Tatjana Seybbel and Julian Yates, as well as Violeta Beška, from the Ethnic Conflict Resolution Project, and Eran Fraenkel, of Search for Common Ground in Macedonia. I am also indebted to Ambassador Geert Ahrens and several individuals in the State Department and the OSCE—all of whom wish to remain unnamed. My special appreciation goes to Ljidia Dimova, my interpreter, translator, and guide in Macedonia. My colleague Michael Shin was kind enough to draw me a map of the Balkans in 1998. I thank doctoral students Paul Vicary, Shannon Curran, Liu Yang, and Ruth Reitan for their research assistance. I am grateful to those at Syracuse University Press who read the manuscript and provided editing and other substantive help; in particular I appreciate Jeffrey Lockridge's thorough editing of the manuscript and the encouraging support of Mary Selden Evans and John Fruehwirth. And finally, I thank my friends for being there. They all know who they are.

MAKING PEACE PREVAIL

Courtesy of Michael Shin, 1998

INTRODUCTION

IN DECEMBER 1991, only months before the outbreak of war in the former Yugoslav Republic of Bosnia-Hercegovina, its president, Alija Izetbegović requested that U.N. peacekeepers be deployed to his country in a preventive capacity.[1] Izetbegović's plea was rejected by the United Nations on the grounds that it was not established practice to send peacekeepers to an area before the outbreak of hostilities, and it was ignored, by the United States, despite the support of the U.S. ambassador to Yugoslavia, Warren Zimmermann.[2]

In November 1992, faced with a spillover threat of the war in Bosnia, the president of another former Yugoslav republic, Macedonia, made a similar appeal at the U.N. headquarters in New York. By then, the wars in Croatia and Bosnia had already exposed all their barbarity and human costs. Within less than a month, the Security Council authorized the first preventive deployment of peacekeepers in U.N. history.[3]

The Republic of Macedonia stands out as one of the relatively successful applications of preventive diplomacy. It is also unique. Several factors account for Macedonia's uniqueness. First, unlike other successful cases of preventive diplomacy such as Estonia or Slovakia, Macedonia was located in a war-torn region where the spillover of violence posed a credible threat. Second, external and internal sources of conflict were intricately linked in Macedonia; to be effective, preventive approaches were needed to address these sources simultane-

1. Earlier, in the summer of 1991, following Croatia's independence, Izetbegović had also asked the European Community (EC) for monitors, a request acceded to only in October, when the EC sent a handful of observers to Bosnia.

2. Warren Zimmermann was U.S. Ambassador to Yugoslavia from 1989 to 1992. Izetbegović asked that U.N. troops be sent no later than January 14, 1992, the day before the formal recognition of Slovenia and Croatia by the European Community (*New York Times,* December 24, 1991). Three years into the war, Ambassador Zimmermann (1995, 2–20) publicly expressed his regrets for not having backed Izetbegović's "innovative step" hard enough.

3. "Resolution 795, Adopted by the Security Council at Its 3147th Meeting on 11 December 1992," S/RES/795.

ously. Third, Macedonia's position within the southern Balkans was especially vulnerable, given the presence of hostile, more powerful neighbors, the lack of a military force, economic instability, ethnic tensions, and a political system in transition. Macedonia demonstrates that, despite its location in a war zone, a country can hold on to peace if it receives the help it needs in time.

Some of the actors providing that help were well-known third parties such as the United Nations or the Organization for Security and Cooperation in Europe (OSCE). Others, such as the Working Group of the International Conference on the Former Yugoslavia (ICFY), were less in the public eye but accomplished much through a "shuttle diplomacy" approach. Then there were those whose preventive efforts were directed toward building a sustainable peace through long-term conflict management projects on the societal level, and to initiate changes in the way individuals settle their differences. Finally, there were the domestic actors, who, despite conflicting agendas, abstained from playing the nationalist card and instead were willing to pursue political dialogue and accommodation, although this frequently involved sacrifices and frustrations on both sides.

Critical voices might claim that the Republic of Macedonia escaped a war not because of preventive diplomacy but because of other factors: an ethnic Serb population too small perhaps to motivate Serbia's intervention; the Yugoslav army's need to transfer troops stationed in Macedonia to the Bosnian theater of war; Serbia's need to use Macedonia to circumvent international sanctions; and the Greek government's need to avoid further destabilization of the region, which might lead to the creation of a Muslim state in Bosnia, a scenario far worse than a stable, sovereign Macedonia. While perhaps there is an element of truth to all these political and geopolitical considerations, they fail to explain why the Yugoslav war did not spread to Macedonia and why ethnic conflict did not break out there, as was feared in the early months of the country's independence.

The story of Macedonia and the success of conflict prevention there is a story that needs to be told. All too often, media accounts concentrate on violence and war, paying little or no attention to how conflict is managed through preventive efforts. The same is true for academic scholarship, with is overabundance of literature on the causes of war and its paucity of concrete studies on how wars have been and can be prevented. Thus members of the general public and students in international studies alike are left to believe that wars simply repeat themselves and little can be done to change that pattern. All too often, history itself, especially recent history, has given us grounds to fear this is so. The twentieth century, more than any other, has been the century of genocide, of mass refugees and displaced persons, and of countless wars in which the number of civilians killed has surpassed the number of those killed in combat. Indeed, in the words of Camus, ours is truly "the century of fear."[4]

To counteract that fear, we need to have hope. The study of conflict prevention provides us with such a prospect, although of course preventive efforts may not always succeed. Research strongly suggests that advanced violent conflicts are more likely to become intractable and defy successful third-party intervention than conflicts receiving preventive intervention in their early stages. Also, countries open to preventive measures stand a far better chance to build sustainable peace than those accustomed to resolving differences by force. Massive violence, bloodshed, and the expulsion of one group by another result in intense feelings of victimization, demonization of the "other," psychologically rooted trauma, and the need for revenge, making future violent conflicts much more likely.

The desire to change the Western image of the Balkans as a region of historical and ethnic animosities, war, and violence also propelled the undertaking of this study. In the early twentieth century, the Balkans were the site of two bloody regional wars fought in Macedonia. World War I was also triggered in the Balkans, and many lives were lost there during World War II. The Yugoslav conflict did much to revive the image of the Balkans as the powder keg of Europe. Despite the many speculations that Macedonia would fall victim to the Yugoslav wars of the 1990s, however, this newly independent country has defied its past and set an example for the future by demonstrating how peace can be maintained against all odds.

To the wider body of literature on ethnopolitical conflict and conflict management, this book brings a new focus on the concrete conditions under which conflict can be successfully prevented. Thus not only does it provide a comprehensive analysis of a case study, it also advances empirical research on conflict prevention, more commonly known as "preventive diplomacy," a subject that has produced few book-length publications. There is a clear need for more conceptual and empirical studies, including single-country case studies "to learn whether and how preventive action can work by doing [because] few have attempted to put this idea into practice, and even fewer have evaluated such attempts" (Rubin 1996, xi).

If we want preventive diplomacy to become a vital part of world politics, we need to learn more about how preventive action works and what makes it succeed. The purpose of this study is to explore the conditions under which preventive diplomacy can be successful, especially where a more complex pattern

4. This idea was expressed in his 1946 essay, *Neither Victims Nor Executioners* (27).

of conflict has emerged—one in which interstate and interethnic levels of conflict have become closely intertwined—and where external and internal conflicts must be dealt with at the same time to arrive at a peaceful outcome.

Although there is a wide-ranging body of research on conflict management and resolution, most studies (e.g., Bercovitch and Rubin 1992; Fisher 1995, 39–59; Kelman 1972, 168–204) focus on the advanced, violent stages of conflict and on the use of third-party intervention (mediation, negotiation, problem-solving workshops, conflict settlement) to mitigate or resolve them. Among the few scholarly works on conflict prevention, a recently published study by Michael Lund (1996a), former director of a preventive diplomacy research group at the United States Institute of Peace, provides a much-needed and detailed conceptual analysis of the subject. Lund identifies five generic factors that may determine the success of preventive diplomacy: third-party timing; multifaceted action; support from major players; moderate leadership; and state autonomy. Based on these factors, he proposes a series of generalizations that can guide case-specific studies, although few such studies exist.

The many deep-seated ethnic and nationalist differences that have persisted into the late twentieth century underscore the necessity for a systematic study of measures to prevent these differences from erupting into armed conflict or to contain such conflict in its early stages, before it becomes unmanageable and protracted. As we proceed from one armed conflict to the next, straining the capacities of international relief agencies and donor countries alike, there is growing interest in the dynamics of nonviolent peaceful settlement.

This study will help fill the void that exists in the area of empirical research on conflict prevention, and in particular, specific case studies. More empirical, single-country case studies on conflict prevention—whether successful or not—are needed so that we can identify what actually works or does not work in preventive diplomacy.

Following Lund (1996a), this book argues that, for preventive diplomacy to succeed, a combination of factors—concerted multifaceted action, moderate leaders, the support of major countries, and appropriate timing—must be present; and, further, that factors such as the ability of indigenous actors to abstain from an ethnic nationalist agenda, the absence of traumatic historical experiences (genocide, mass expulsion), a relatively low level of internal violence (sporadic rather than widespread), and moderation on the part of neighboring states are also conducive to conflict prevention.

Given what has happened in Croatia, Bosnia, and Serbia over the past several years, the relative success of preventive diplomacy in the Republic of Macedonia is of particular interest. Eight years have passed since Macedonia declared its independence from the former Yugoslavia. At the time, there was widespread speculation about the bleak future for this nascent democracy.

Pundits were quick to forecast a collapse of the new state, either through a spillover of war from adjacent states or through internal conflict. Yet today Macedonia continues on the path to democracy and economic transition despite its ethnic problems.

This book examines the different actors and instruments responsible for this outcome: statesmen, international and regional organizations, and nongovernmental agencies. Although it remains to be seen what long-term efforts will yield today, Macedonia continues to show the world that interethnic conflict can be satisfactorily managed through the respect of minority and other human rights, dialogue, negotiations, power sharing, compromise, statesmanship, and grassroots activism.

The overarching research questions guiding the present inquiry are, what made the Republic of Macedonia a successful case of preventive diplomacy, and what can we learn from this case? Several, more specific questions inform the inquiry: What has been the nature of conflict in Macedonia? What role have the leaders of conflicting parties played in preventing violence? What were the circumstances of third-party intervention? What role did third parties play in convincing leaders to opt for negotiation, compromise, and power-sharing arrangements? How did they carry out preventive actions? What role have the NGOs played? How has their role differed from that of regional and international organizations? What instruments and tools of prevention were used and proved most effective? What are the principal obstacles and limits to preventive diplomacy?

Chapter 1 argues that not only have ethnic conflicts been on the rise since the 1960s, as identified by Gurr (1994), but a more complex pattern of conflict has also emerged in which interstate and interethnic levels of conflict are often inseparably linked. It also discusses the historical and conceptual context of preventive diplomacy and how skeptics have cast doubts on the viability of preventive action.

Chapter 2 focuses on the successes and failures of preventive diplomacy in Africa, Eastern Europe, and the former Soviet Union. It contends that in two successful cases, in Slovakia and Hungary and in Estonia, the involvement of the Organization for Security and Cooperation in Europe and the OSCE high commissioner on national minorities was crucial for prevention; and that in two failed cases, or rather missed opportunities for prevention, Bosnia and Rwanda, factors such as the lack of political will to engage in multilateral action and the absence of moderate leaders largely accounted for the failure to prevent conflict.

Against the background of the disintegration of Yugoslavia and the wars in Croatia and Bosnia, chapter 3 explores the emergence of the Republic of Macedonia as a newly independent country and the internal and regional sources of conflict. It analyzes Macedonia's conflictive relationship with Serbia and Greece, as well as the tensions between ethnic Albanians, ethnic Serbs, and Slavic Macedonians. Chapter 4 examines the importance of a "preventive attitude" on the part of domestic leaders, arguing that external actors are more successful in their preventive actions if domestic leaders make a concerted effort toward power sharing, accommodation, and moderation, even in the face of public opposition. It explores preventive measures such as the Macedonian-Bosnian compromise of 1991 to avert the violent breakup of Yugoslavia, the Macedonian government's compromise with ethnic Serbs living in Macedonia, and its power-sharing approach adopted to prevent violent conflict with ethnic Albanians.

Chapter 5 highlights the role of international organizations such as the International Conference on the Former Yugoslavia and the United Nations; chapter 6, that of a regional security organization—the OSCE—arguing that although the OSCE was one of the earliest actors in Macedonia, the United Nations provided the most effective deterrent through its preventive peacekeeping force. Chapter 7 considers the ongoing long-term work of NGOs in conflict prevention, despite various obstacles and limits. Chapter 8 concludes by returning to the more generalized question of how violent conflicts can be prevented, and by offering an analytical, policy-oriented menu for the prevention of armed confrontations.

Research and writing for this book were carried out between 1995 and summer 1998, before the establishment of a new Macedonian government under Prime Minister Ljubco Georgievski, the United Nation's preventive deployment mission's removal, NATO's air strikes on Serbia, and the Kosovo refugee crisis. The analysis throughout chapters 3–7 therefore was completed before some of the recent events that have affected Macedonia's stability. Some updated information, often in footnotes, has been provided throughout these chapters wherever possible. An epilogue based on a visit to Macedonia in late April and early May 1999 reflects in more detail on these changes, their impact on Macedonia, and the prospects for preventive diplomacy. The epilogue's analysis was completed in early June 1999 and revised in August 1999.

The case of Macedonia demonstrates, above all, that conflict prevention requires not only good will but hard work by many actors, on many levels. A broad-based network of institutions coordinating their preventive efforts, the promotion of power-sharing provisions, and the political will to implement preventive action in a timely fashion were as important as a moderate leadership willing to pursue accommodative policies with respect to ethnic minorities and neighboring countries.

Although Macedonia's prospects look much better than those of its war-torn Balkan neighbors, in particular those of Bosnia, ethnic tensions are unlikely to disappear altogether. This is simply not a realistic outcome for any multiethnic country. Moreover, the conflict in nearby Kosovo and the refugee crisis posed a severe test to Macedonia and its ability to maintain a culture of peace. Despite ethnic tensions, however, and despite sporadic outbreaks of violence, as in February 1994 and the summer of 1997, we can hope that long-term preventive measures such as the integration of Macedonia into European institutions, the adoption of power-sharing practices, a constructive foreign policy approach toward its neighbors, and even the grassroots educational projects undertaken to change some of the attitudes and stereotypes the contending ethnic groups have of each other will over time build a sustainable peace in the Republic of Macedonia.

1

AN OUNCE OF PREVENTION . . .

AT THE DAWN of a new century, preventing the outbreak of violent conflicts remains one of our most difficult challenges. Multifaceted, consistent efforts, long-term international commitment, political will, and hard work will be required if peace is to prevail in a world where conflict remains the rule rather than the exception. Throughout the twentieth century, armed conflicts—both between and within states—have wreaked havoc not only on the contending parties but also on the global community. They have diverted resources, stifled economic development, militarized entire societies, and sustained high levels of political and social instability and poverty. From unprecedented levels of civilian deaths and genocide to mass expulsions and ethnic cleansing—an endless list of tragedies attests to the devastating consequences of unrestrained violence.

Individuals and organizations have increasingly called for a more preventive approach to armed dispute, in particular to civil wars, ethnic and other forms of communal violence, and humanitarian crises. In the early 1990s, the United Nations, the OSCE, the Organization of African Unity (OAU), many nongovernmental agencies (NGOs), various European countries, and the United States began to emphasize the need for preventive diplomacy. Much of the vocal support for preventive measures in the first Clinton administration came from Secretary of State Warren Christopher, National Security Adviser Anthony Lake, and Brian Atwood, director of the U.S. Agency for International Development (AID), all of whom emphasized the importance of resolving disputes before they became violent. Also, a small, yet growing body of literature on conflict prevention by international scholars continues to provide a much-needed focus on the practice of preventive diplomacy, particularly through the in-depth study of countries in which preventive action was successful in averting violence.

Despite these notably positive developments, unfortunately, preventive action still remains the exception whether from indifference, failure to view ethnic strife and other forms of internal conflict as threats to regional and global security, lack of political will, or the hesitancy of third parties to "intervene" through preventive instruments for fear such action might be too long-term, dangerous, and costly. What also impedes more concerted preventive efforts is the lack of a clear understanding as to what instruments to use, which of these are most successful for what particular conflicts, and how best to implement preventive action (Lund 1996a, 28–29).

Traditionally, states have remained indifferent to violent conflicts, relied on various means of conventional third-party intervention such as mediation or peacekeeping, or resorted to direct military action. A number of factors drive indifference to internal conflicts such as ethnic and civil wars, revolutions, and genocide. One is the reluctance of third parties to "meddle" in the internal affairs of sovereign states, a reluctance rooted in a long-established principle of international law, that of noninterference. Another explanation is that "unaffected" states are either unaware of or disregard the global ramifications of violent conflicts and the potential long-term threats these pose to international peace. This applies particularly to internal conflicts, which are often perceived as not affecting the security interests of outside states despite compelling evidence to the contrary. The unwillingness to commit resources for a cause beyond one's national interests, and the logistical difficulties involved in organizing and executing international action often delay any collective response, as does the unwillingness of parties in conflict to invite or accept external intervention. Moreover, outsiders do not always understand the root causes of conflict, particularly on the ethnic level. Needless to say, internal conflicts frequently produce reactions of "helplessness," stalling for time, or ignoring an imminent crisis for as long as possible—all of which impede the search for multilateral responses to those human tragedies that consistently play themselves out on the world stage.

In a study by the Carnegie Commission on Preventing Deadly Conflict, Alexander George and Jane Holl (1997, 16–17) contend that what we frequently witness at the threshold of violent conflicts are various types of "missed opportunities" to take appropriate action, especially if there is an impending communal conflict or humanitarian disaster. Among these missed opportunities are failure to respond to early warning indicators; inadequate analysis of early warning signs; inadequate, inconsistent, incomplete, and contradictory responses; and misused opportunities.

Third-party intervention has almost always come about after a dispute has become violent and protracted, most often after the warring parties have reached what I. William Zartman (1992) referred to in advanced civil wars as a "mutually hurting stalemate," a key component in a condition known as "ripeness for resolution." Third parties have sought to resolve conflict through a number of traditional means such as mediation, good offices, fact finding, arbitration, conciliation, peacekeeping, and sometimes coercive intervention, but usually after prolonged periods of warfare. International mediation in particular has a long-standing history (e.g., Mitchell and Webb, 1988; Mitchell 1993, 139–60; Rubin 1981; Touval and Zartman 1985; Young 1967), with third parties playing a crucial role in the negotiation and implementation of peace settlements (Fisher 1995, 39–62; Hampson 1996; Kriesberg 1996a, 1996b). For the most part, traditional third-party intervention occurs in the late stages of a conflict, when prolonged victimization and human sacrifice have erected psychological barriers difficult to remove.

The former Yugoslavia is a case in point, demonstrating the detrimental effects of third-party indifference and delayed intervention, resulting from incorrect and inadequate assessments of the sources of conflict, lack of political will, and diverging national interests, especially between Germany, France, Britain, and the United States. Early intervention to abort the escalation of violence was therefore beset with problems from the beginning. A crucial fallacy was to view the conflict as rooted in long-standing ethnic animosities predating Tito's regime, rather than in the emergence of nationalist leaders deliberately playing the ethnic card to mobilize their respective constituencies (Gagnon 1994/95, 130–66; 1995, 179–97; Woodward 1995). Western media also did much to reinforce the perception that the conflict was a replay of historically based ethnic hatreds, and thus reinvoked a popular nineteenth and early twentieth-century European image of the Balkans as a region of bloodshed, violence, and war. The Balkan's historical baggage, it was argued, would limit any international action because in such an ethnically driven conflict, external actors would lack the necessary leverage to mediate a settlement. The existence of several warring factions also discouraged any early third-party involvement, with the exception of the half-hearted efforts of the European Union, and later the peacekeeping and humanitarian efforts of the United Nations.

On the other hand, the many instances of ethnic and civil strife and the humanitarian crises unleashed in Croatia, Bosnia, Chechnya, Rwanda, and Somalia in the post–Cold War era have also given new impetus to policy makers and scholars alike to think about ways of how such violence can be prevented in the future. This notable interest in preventive diplomacy, which I have defined as "the conscious implementation of preventive measures by governmental and non-governmental actors at an early, or non-escalated stage of conflict" (Ackermann 1996), has also been made possible because of an improved international climate since the disintegration of the Soviet Union and the eclipse of communist ideology. More important, domestic and international constraints, including financial ones, dictate a proactive approach to managing future conflicts. Third-party involvement in the later stages of conflict, or in postconflict peacebuilding efforts, such as election monitoring, demilitarization, and reconstruction, and in long-term support of peace settlements is becoming an extremely costly liability. Finally that interstate and interethnic conflicts have become extricably intertwined dictates a preventive approach to violent disputes rather than a reactive one, as has been the case in the past. This suggests that it is no longer feasible or justifiable to let violent conflicts run their course until a "mutually hurting stalemate" brings adversaries to the negotiation table.

CONFLICT IN THE LATE TWENTIETH CENTURY

Despite the end of the superpower confrontation and the successful resolution of some regional conflicts, internal conflicts continue to plague the post–Cold War world. Although some before existed, many more seem to have come about with the demise of communist regimes, the fragmentation of formerly communist states into new, and most often multiethnic, entities, and the resultant struggle for state power. Data indicate, however, that internal conflicts were on the rise throughout the Cold War period (Gurr 1994). As of 1995, there were major conflicts or some form of political violence in 79 countries, 65 of which were located in the developing world; between 1989 and 1993, only 3 of 52 major conflicts were between states (United Nations Development Program 1995). The incidence of intrastate conflict continues to rise, as recent studies attest (e.g., Davies and Gurr 1998; Holsti 1996).

Indeed, since 1945, most armed conflicts have been intrastate and have taken place in developing countries. Because of their potential to spill over into neighboring territories, however, their threat to international peace and stability or the involvement of the superpowers, they often appeared to have interstate components as well (Ayoob 1996, 37–52; Holsti 1991; Kolodziej and Zartman 1996, 3–34; Rupesinghe 1992, 43–64). Most conflicts in Third World countries can be traced to decolonization, the formation of new states, and the subsequent struggles over political control, legitimacy, ideology, resources, and identity. More recently, the transition from authoritarian to democratic regimes has also resulted in increased levels of violence. Most conflict-prone was Africa, which became the battleground for 34 percent of all intrastate strife, with Asia and the Middle East accounting for 25 and 18 percent, respectively (Regan 1996, 336–59). Although interstate wars declined in the Cold War era, they did not become completely extinct, as the Arab-Israeli wars and the Iran-Iraqi War remind us. In fact, territorial issues remain a major source of large-scale hostilities for much of the postwar period.

Since the 1960s, the world has also witnessed the rise of what Gurr termed *ethnopolitical conflicts,* "in which groups that define themselves using ethnic and national criteria . . . make claims on behalf of their collective interests against the state, or against other political actors." Such ethnic criteria "may include common descent, shared historical experiences, and valued cultural traits." Claims advanced by ethnopolitical groups may range from political, economic, cultural, and religious demands, and "ethnopolitical groups organize around their shared identity" (Gurr 1996, 53). Kriesberg's term *communal conflicts* captures much of the essence of Gurr's ethnopolitical conflicts, but encompasses both conflicts between a state and a contending communal group and those between states distinguishing themselves on the basis of their communal identities (Kriesberg 1998b, 34).

According to Gurr (1993b), approximately 100 ethnopolitical groups were engaged in violent conflicts between 1945 and 1990, with at least 60 conflicts involving issues of autonomy. Of the 233 groups identified by Gurr, at least 200 have demanded or defended their collective rights between 1945 and 1989. Although not all of these struggles were violent, depending on the extent of demands and grievances and whether states were willing to accommodate them, Gurr demonstrates the potential of ethnopolitical differences to escalate into internal and regional conflicts with serious international consequence.

Developing countries are and will remain the epicenter of violent conflict. Some scholars (e.g., Blacker 1994, 42–62; Huntington 1993, 22–49) have argued that a new fault line between the stable center and the unstable periphery, which now includes post-Soviet states and parts of Eastern Europe, has been created in the post-Cold War era. This characterization of the emerging geographic pattern of conflict, however, does not sufficiently delineate the periphery, nor explain why some peripheral countries have succeeded in averting violence or in adopting nonviolent means to resolve their internal conflicts. What is evident, though, is that Eastern Europe and the former Soviet Union, once thought to be blessed with relative stability and few intrastate conflicts in the postwar era, have become the site of some of the more vicious wars and humanitarian crises.

The upward spiral of internal conflict in this region is likely to continue. Gurr (1996, 55), for example, lists 24 states in Eastern Europe and the former Soviet Union with 59 minorities that are "at risk," the second highest number after sub-Saharan Africa, where 28 states have 66 active minorities. Much of the violence in the post-Cold War era has been driven by the disintegration of states and the formation of new multiethnic countries, many of which have kindred communities across state borders. The most costly internal conflicts in Europe since the end of World War II—in terms of civilians killed, wounded, and displaced, and property destroyed—were caused by the violent breakup of Yugoslavia, where civil wars in Slovenia, Croatia, and Bosnia contributed to the demise of a multiethnic state.

In what some scholars describe as the internationalization of communal violence (Gurr 1993a, 3–26; Midlarsky 1993; Zartman 1993, 27–44) and others as the disappearance of the distinction between internal and external conflicts (Rupesinghe 1992, 43–64; 1995a, 65–92), intra- and interstate conflicts have become even more closely linked. Ethnopolitical groups in conflict often have members in neighboring countries, which complicates the task of conflict resolution. The potential for violent spillover requires a multilayered approach, in which intrastate and interstate components of the conflict must be addressed simultaneously.

Ethnic conflicts in Eastern Europe are a case in point. Here, ethnic groups constituting the majority of one state frequently live as minorities in others. One example is that of Albanians who reside in the Republic of Macedonia, the case explored in this study, in adjacent Kosovo, and in Albania. This interaction of external and internal factors of conflict is particularly potent in the Balkans, where several ethnic groups have "kin states," and makes preventive action an essential policy for responding to potential conflicts there.

Finally, ethnic strife is producing more and more refugees and displaced persons. In 1996, there were 14.5 million refugees and another 23 million people displaced by violent conflicts, bringing the total to more than 37 million (Dowty and Loescher 1996, 46). The number of refugees worldwide was 8.2 million in 1980; by 1990, it had more than doubled, to 17.2 million; and in both 1992 and 1993, it reached 18.2 million. The number of refugees generated by ethnic conflicts rose from 3.39 million in 1969 to 5.25 million in 1992, excluding Bosnian and Rwandan refugees. Most of the refugees are located in the world's poorest states. At the beginning of 1995, Africa had 5.9 million, the Middle East 5.5 million, South and Central Asia 1.8 million, and Europe and North America 2.6 million refugees (Weiner 1996, 5–42). In Africa for example, Guinea and the Ivory Coast took in 750,000 refugees fleeing from violence in Liberia. In 1994, within a two-month period following the genocide in Rwanda, almost two million people were internally displaced and another two million, mostly from the Hutu population, fled to Zaire, Tanzania, Burundi, and Uganda (U.S. Mission to the United Nation 1995, 23). Since then, many refugees have been forcibly resettled in Rwanda, have fled into inaccessible areas where they were cut off from all international humanitarian assistance, or have been massacred in the wake of Laurent Kabila's rebel army, as were Hutu refugees caught during the civil war in eastern Zaire (McKinley and French 1997).

Western Europe experienced the largest refugee flow since the end of World War II, with nearly 1 million refugees from the former Yugoslavia, excluding Kosovo (Weiner 1996). Although the U.N. High Commissioner for Refugees (UNHCR) has been able to resettle 9 million refugees between 1990 and 1995, the flow of refugees far exceeds the capacity to resettle them, a trend that will continue if more violent conflicts are not prevented (Dowty and Loescher 1996).

Conflict in the late twentieth century can thus be broadly characterized as follows: (1) the spread of armed conflicts into geographic regions once considered less prone to internal violence; (2) the continued upsurge of intrastate, especially ethnopolitical, conflicts; (3) the increased potential for internal violence to spill over into neighboring countries; and (4) the crushing burden the resultant refugee crises have imposed on many countries, primarily on poor, developing states. Conflict prevention, then, rests on a change in mindset, that is, a clear recognition that internal strife in any state puts at risk the security interests of all states.

WHAT IS PREVENTIVE DIPLOMACY?

The idea of preventing wars and violent conflicts is not new. Throughout the centuries, philosophers have thought of ways to eradicate war and to create a condition of permanent peace. In the spirit of the Christian tradition of the late Middle Ages, for example, models for peace were based on the creation of unified Christian states, as evident in the works of Dante. With the advent of the humanist tradition, which entailed a shift to the individual as the center of the political and social order, peace became associated with humanity as a whole, expressed in demands that the different religions be reconciled and harmony promoted between citizens from different countries (Fetscher 1972; Kende 1989, 233–47). Limiting war through crisis prevention captured the interest of diplomats and philosophers in the eighteenth century. In France, François de Callières explored how crises could be averted before they broke out and escalated into war (Lauren 1983, 31). In Germany, Kant proposed in his treatise *Perpetual Peace* that future wars be prevented by creating a confederation of sovereign democratic states, which over time would also lead to the emergence of a world citizenry with commonly shared interests and values.

Preventing future wars was also on the agenda of the Congress of Vienna in 1815, although the underlying objective was not so much to eradicate war as to limit its potentially disastrous consequences. Following the defeat of Napoleon, the victorious European powers sought to avert new crises and the eruption of large-scale wars by establishing a balance of power and rules of behavior, procedures, norms, and agreements. Europe's most skillful diplomats set out to prevent crises through mutual consultation, collective decision making, the creation of buffer or neutral states and demilitarized areas, the delineation of interests and areas of interests, the localization of regional conflicts, confidence-building measures, and the settlement of conflicts by peaceful means. Although Europe did experience wars in the nineteenth century, most notably the Franco-Prussian War of 1878, they remained limited in scope and did not destroy the domestic political and social order of the warring states, as had the Napoleonic Wars (Craig and George 1995, 25–31; Lauren 1983, 31; Weltman 1995).

In the postwar era of our century, conflict and crisis prevention as well as early warning measures formed the core of the national security agendas of the

SYRACUSE UNIVERSITY PRESS

1600 Jamesville Avenue, Syracuse, New York 13244-5160

20

DR SAMUEL TOTTEN
JOURNAL GENOCIDE RESEARCH
U ARKANSAS 107A/ PEABODY HALL
FAYETTEVILLE AR 72701

DR SAMUEL TOTTEN
JOURNAL GENOCIDE RESEARCH
U ARKANSAS 107A/ PEABODY HALL
FAYETTEVILLE AR 72701

MAR 00 REVIEW Sp 4th Class

1 MAKING PEACE PREVAIL (P) 24.95 % Free

SUB-TOTAL - .00

Free

CODE 7

$ .00

UNIVERSITY PRESS

Avenue, Syracuse, New York 13244-5160
Fax (315) 443-5545
Orders Only 1-800-365-8929
FID 15-0621510

ORIGINAL INVOICE

ACCOUNT NUMBER	PLEASE REFERENCE BOTH NUMBERS WHEN MAKING PAYMENT	INVOICE NUMBER
20		314452

MUEL TOTTEN
AL GENOCIDE RESEARCH
KANSAS 107A/ PEABODY HALL
TTEVILLE AR 72701

SHIP TO:
DR SAMUEL TOTTEN
JOURNAL GENOCIDE RESEARCH
U ARKANSAS 107A/ PEABODY HALL
FAYETTEVILLE AR 72701

E	CUSTOMER P.O. NUMBER	TERMS	SALES AREA	HOW SHIPPED	DATE SHIPPED
)	REVIEW	Gratis		Sp 4th Class	

QUANTITY	TITLE	LIST PRICE	DISCOUNT	AMOUNT
1	MAKING PEACE PREVAIL (P)	24.95	%	Free
	SUB-TOTAL -			.00
			SHIPPING/ HANDLING	Free

CODE 7

Please pay from this invoice. Service charge of **1-1½% per month (18% per annum)** on past due balances.

AMOUNT PAID	
BALANCE DUE $	.00

Zone:
Weight 1.05#

Qnan 1 | Free

0602 1 MAKING PEACE PREVAIL (P) 24.95

REVIEW 5P 4th Class

CUSTOMER P.O. NUMBER	HOW SHIPPED	DATE SHIPPED	PACKER
REVIEW	Sp 4th Class		

CODE	QUANTITY	TITLE	
0602	1	MAKING PEACE PREVAIL (P)	24.95

Quan 1

Weight 1.05#

Zone:

SHIPPING CHARGES	Free

SYRACUSE UNIVERSITY PRESS
1600 Jamesville Avenue, Syracuse, New York 13244-5160
(315) 443-2597 Fax (315) 443-5545
Orders Only 1-800-365-8929

PACKING SLIP

INVOICE NUMBER
314452

P.O.# REVIEW

SHIP TO:
DR SAMUEL TOTTEN
JOURNAL GENOCIDE RESEARCH
U ARKANSAS 107A/ PEABODY HALL
FAYETTEVILLE AR 72701

Sp 4th Class

CUSTOMER P.O. NUMBER	HOW SHIPPED	DATE SHIPPED	PACKER
REVIEW	Sp 4th Class		

CODE	QUANTITY	TITLE
0602	1	MAKING PEACE PREVAIL (P)

Quan 1

Weight 1.05#
Zone:

SHIPPING CHARGES Free

United States and the Soviet Union. The objective was to respond to superpower crises in a timely manner, to avoid surprise attack, and to prevent a nuclear confrontation (George 1983; Lund 1996a; Rupesinghe 1995a). Other structural and procedural arrangements set up in the immediate postwar era also served as conflict prevention measures. The Marshall Plan, implemented to alleviate economic and political instability in Europe and to prevent future disputes, channeled economic aid to the devastated countries of Western Europe, including a defeated Germany, and it stipulated that former enemies work together within an institutional framework—the Organization for European Economic Cooperation (OEEC)—to allocate collectively the amount of financial assistance to its various members.

The creation of NATO was also an important preventive mechanism, intended not only to provide a defensive system against the Soviet bloc but to overcome the individual security dilemmas of European states that had plagued their relations in the pre–World War II era. On the one hand, NATO served to contain Germany, security from Germany being as important to its European neighbors as security from the Soviet Union. On the other, by bringing former enemies together in collective decision making, bargaining, and compromise, it served to immerse West Germany in the democratic process.

Franco-German reconciliation was a major step toward preventing future wars among Western European states. It transformed an intractable conflict into a constructive relationship that helped establish the necessary norms and procedures for a number of common European institutions, later to evolve into the European Union (Ackermann 1994, 229–50; Feldman 1999, 1–22).

Despite the history of preventive measures and institutions, however, "preventive diplomacy" did not come into official use until 1960. Reflecting the limited powers of the United Nations during the Cold War, Secretary-General Dag Hammarskjöld defined *preventive diplomacy* as U.N. efforts aimed "at keeping newly arising conflicts outside the sphere of bloc differences," or "in the case of conflicts on the margin of, or inside the sphere of bloc differences . . . to bring such conflicts out of the sphere through solutions, aiming, in the first instance, at their strict localization [and to prevent] the creation of a power vacuum between the main blocs" (U.N. General Assembly 1960, 4). Thus preventive diplomacy at that time was primarily directed at preventing a wider confrontation between the superpowers, not at preventing armed conflicts altogether. As such, according to Hammarskjöld, it had largely succeeded—in the Suez, in Gaza, in Lebanon, in Jordan, in Laos, and in the Congo.

Although, in theory, one could argue that the United Nations always had as its primary objective the prevention of conflict, in practice, U.N. intervention was reactive. Thus peacekeeping forces were deployed only after the outbreak of hostilities. Ideological differences and the need to avoid superpower confrontations largely drove this reactive approach to violent conflict. Moreover, many of the instruments of prevention, such as deterrence, arms control or other cooperative agreements, as well as the creation of the United Nations and other international organizations after 1945 were intended to prevent interstate conflicts rather than intrastate strife (Holsti 1996; Nicolaïdis 1996, 23–72).

Some thirty years later, Secretary-General Boutros Boutros-Ghali (1992, 11), would redefine preventive diplomacy in an international environment freed from the constraints of the Cold War, making it a policy to prevent disputes from escalating to armed confrontations and from spilling over into other countries or regions.[1] According to Boutros-Ghali, preventive diplomacy is intended to fulfill three crucial objectives: prevention, nonescalation, and containment of conflict. He listed specific measures of preventive diplomacy: (1) confidence-building measures, such as the establishment of regional and subregional risk reduction centers and the systematic exchange of military missions; (2) fact-finding missions by senior U.N. officials or members of regional or nongovernmental organizations; (3) the strengthening of early warning networks, to include political indicators; (4) preventive deployment; and (5) the creation of demilitarized zones.

While Boutros-Ghali succeeded in drawing attention to the need for conflict prevention, there is as yet no consensus on the nature or scope of preventive diplomacy. What instruments or methods should preventive diplomacy entail? How should they be used, and in what types of conflicts? There is also no consensus over how preventive diplomacy differs from crisis management, peacemaking, and peace building, or even traditional intervention at different stages of conflict.

Criticizing Boutros-Ghali's conception of preventive diplomacy as too broad, Lund (1996a, 34, 37) suggests that its "conceptual core . . . has to do with keeping peaceable disputes from escalating unmanageably into sustained levels of violence and significant armed force."[2] Accordingly, Lund limits preventive diplomacy to a stage of "unstable peace," that is, a stage in the conflict spiral where massive violence has not yet occurred, or has manifested itself sporadically. For preventive diplomacy to be qualitatively different from conflict containment or management, it must occur at an early stage of conflict before the outbreak of full-scale hostilities.

1. Like Hammarskjöld, however, Boutros-Ghali (1992) stressed the need to include economic and social developments so as to eliminate the underlying causes of violence.

2. Lund (1996a, 37) goes on to define *preventive diplomacy* as action taken in vulnerable places and times to avoid the threat or use of armed force and related forms of coercion by states or groups to settle the political disputes that can arise from the destabilizing effects of economic, social, political, and international change."

For some scholars, however, preventive diplomacy is a narrowly defined alternative to coercive intervention, limited to diplomatic instruments such as mediation. Zartman (1983, 361–64) defines preventive diplomacy as providing diplomatic assistance in conflict situations, as a strategy to prevent renewed outbreak of hostilities, especially in conflicts that are protracted in nature. The problem with this definition is that it limits preventive diplomacy to diplomatic instruments of involvement, to be used only when there is a lull in the fighting to prevent the next round of warfare.

It is therefore helpful in defining preventive diplomacy to recall the distinction between traditional and crisis diplomacy. Traditional diplomacy is confined to states with stable interactions, whereas crisis diplomacy (or management) is undertaken when there is already a considerable level of confrontation with a high probability of war. Because preventive diplomacy corresponds best to the stage of an unstable or "negative" peace, when tensions may be high among contending parties and violence has not yet occurred or is only sporadic, is it thus situated between traditional and crisis diplomacy (Lund 1996a, 39–43).

For Kriesberg (1995, 92; 1997, 234; 1998b, 42–47), however, conflict prevention is not limited to averting violence or to preventing its escalation but also includes settling a conflict or eliminating conditions that led to the outbreak of violence in the first place. For this purpose, Kriesberg distinguishes between proactive policies, which reduce the underlying structural conditions of violence, and preventive policies, which address the more immediate sources of conflict.

In this study, following Lund, I define conflict prevention in the early, nonescalatory stage as the deliberate implementation of measures aimed at preventing violence before it has broken out or become widespread (see also Ackermann 1996, 409–24). Drawing also on Kriesberg and others (e.g., Leatherman et al. 1999, 8) I propose that the prevention of conflict can also be initiated in the postconflict phase, where measures such as rapprochement, reconciliation, and the building of common institutions and cooperative arrangements are designed to prevent conflict renewal. Such conflict prevention, whether in the preconflict or the postconflict phase, is part of a wider conflict resolution approach.[3] Table 1 illustrates this two-dimensional understanding of conflict prevention.

3. This conceptualization of conflict prevention as involving also "postconflict" prevention is rooted in my earlier research on reconciliation (Ackermann 1994). A similar observation is made by Raimo Väyrynen (1995, 8), who describes "three modes of prevention" corresponding to the stages of conflict: *conflict prevention,* defined as "preventing violent disputes from arising between parties"; *escalation prevention,* defined as "preventing both the vertical and horizontal escalation of hostilities"; and *post-conflict prevention,* defined as "preventing the emergence of disputes." See also Kolodziej and Zartman 1996, 27, and Leatherman et al. 1999, 8. *Preventive diplomacy, preventive action,* and *conflict prevention* are used interchangeably in this study.

Table 1
A Conflict Resolution Approach

Conflict Prevention	
Previolent/Low-Violence Stage	Postconflict Stage
Preventive Diplomacy	Postconflict Peacebuilding: Rapprochement, Reconciliation Institution-building

Preventive diplomacy encompasses an extensive list of instruments, including fact-finding and monitoring missions, the deployment of preventive peacekeeping forces, the creation of channels for communication among conflicting groups and their leaders, the provision of economic assistance, the implementation of long-term conflict management projects that address conflict at the grassroots level, conflict resolution training, problem-solving workshops, and more traditional third-party intervention mechanisms such as negotiation, mediation, and the use of good offices (Ackermann 1996; Evans 1993; Kriesberg 1998b, 43; Lund 1996a; Väyrynen 1995). Despite its name, preventive diplomacy is not confined to strictly "diplomatic" measures but relies on political, economic, military, and constitutional mechanisms, and includes efforts to convince warring groups to adopt power-sharing provisions that have alleviated tension in ethnopolitical conflicts (Horowitz 1985; Kriesberg 1997, 1998b; Lijphart 1977). Moreover, if the underlying sources of conflict are to be remedied, conflict prevention must include more long-term preventive policies such as the reduction of power inequalities, the amelioration of economic and social conditions, and the enhancement of shared identities (Kriesberg 1997, 240–46; 1998b, 43–48).

There is no exact measurement to determine which instruments work best under what circumstances because conflicts differ in their causes, escalation, and intensity of violence. Some scholars maintain that a distinction should be made between early and late preventive intervention. Early prevention—that is, intervention in the dispute stage—would rely primarily on nonmilitary instruments. Late prevention would set in at the threshold of an armed conflict, allowing the United Nations to resort to preventive deployment (Evans 1993; Peck 1996). The problem with this approach is that the dynamics of conflict are very complex, and it is often difficult to assess when a threshold has been reached. Also, as the case of Macedonia demonstrates, preventive deployment can be initiated in the earlier, dispute stage of the conflict, supported by a host of other political instruments, all of which complement each other. A better approach might be the one suggested by British Foreign Office Minister, Derek Fatchett, who called for a distinction between short-term operational conflict prevention and long-term structural prevention (U.K. Foreign and Commonwealth Office 1998, 8–11).

It is also difficult to determine in advance what kinds of coercive instruments should be applied because that again depends on the nature of the conflict. It has been suggested that room be left for a possible gradation of instruments, with softer preventive measures employed at first and more severe measures, including the threat or even use of force, on the immediate threshold of escalation (Munuera 1994). Other tools to prevent the outbreak of violence include confidence-building measures, demilitarized zones, arms embargoes, and preventive peacekeeping (Lund 1996a, 203). It remains unclear whether a limited show of force, which Lund includes in his preventive diplomacy toolbox, can still be considered preventive diplomacy. Väyrynen (1995, 111), Kriesberg (1998b), and Thompson and Gutlove (1994, 5) all rule out the use of force because it is likely to produce negative reactions on the part of warring parties and to increase the risk of escalation.

Although the existence of an early warning capacity, preferably within an international organization, is essential to preventive diplomacy, the relationship between early warning systems and preventive diplomacy also remains unclear. Proponents of early warning advocate creating a global system (Gordenker 1992, 1–14; Gurr 1993b; Moore and Gurr 1997; Rupesinghe and Kuroda 1992); those (e.g., George and Holl 1997, 3), who strongly favor establishing an integrated warning-response framework maintain that "missed opportunities" in preventive diplomacy are not failures to prevent, as critics often charge, but warning-response failures.

Besides the technical problems of implementing a global, integrated warning-response system, there are also the political problems surrounding early warning. Who is to be warned? Who does the warning? And how can governments be made responsive to possible internal conflicts and human rights violations, such as civil war and genocide, if they happen to be the perpetrators of such violence? There are a host of other issues: policy makers tend to put off preventive responses; information about conflicts may be misleading or false; interfering in the internal affairs of countries may raise legitimate concerns.

PREVENTIVE DIPLOMACY AND ITS CRITICS

Preventive diplomacy has not been without its critics. Despite its relative success in Macedonia and several other countries, those skeptical of preventive diplomacy have cast doubt on the effectiveness of intervention in the previolent stages of conflict. Much of this criticism is motivated by theoretical debate. Primordialists, who view ethnicity as innate in individuals and groups and therefore as resistant to change, see little sense in trying to prevent ethnic conflicts; instrumentalists and constructivists on the other hand, who view ethnicity as having a definite purpose and role to play in the political process and in human consciousness, are more likely to support preventive actions.

Criticism over preventive diplomacy is also motivated by policy and methodological considerations. Policy critics argue that its underlying premises are fallacious (Eyal 1994, 16; Stedman 1993, 1–16; 1995, 14–20), that it is all but impossible to predict when and where violence may occur next because some countries may be in a crisis mode for many years, and others for only weeks or months, before hostilities break out. Citing several cases of the failure of international involvement to prevent violent conflicts in their early stages, most notably in Yugoslavia, they insist that preventive diplomacy can never work because "to prevent the Bosnias of tomorrow demands major resources in situations where risks are high and success is in doubt" (Stedman 1995, 16). Methodology critics point out that it is impossible to accurately measure the success or failure of preventive diplomacy and to apply it systematically.

However well taken, these criticisms are shortsighted for several reasons. Although it makes use of traditional third-party intervention measures, such as good offices and observer or human rights–monitoring missions, preventive diplomacy also draws on strategies not found in traditional third-party engagement, such as preventive deployment, for a timely response to the potential outbreak of armed conflict. It is neither crucial nor possible to predict the occurrence of violent conflict on every occasion. Nicolaïdes (1996) suggests that, just as the medical approach to prevention is not to predict illnesses but to limit their occurrence, so the overarching goal of preventive diplomacy is not to predict violent confrontations but to limit their number.

Studies on preventive diplomacy do indeed defy rigorous methodology. It is difficult to evaluate the outcome of a particular conflict had preventive measures not been taken. To overcome these methodological shortcomings, it has been suggested that any assessment be based on counterfactual reasoning, similar to measuring the success or failure of deterrence, that success in preventive diplomacy be treated in relative terms (Ackermann 1996; Jentleson 1996). Kriesberg (1996b, 219) makes a similar argument in evaluating the effectiveness of mediation, where success may be "obscure," and where failure, though "easier to recognize than success," may also be "unclear and disputed in actuality" because, like success, it is relative to the ever-shifting objectives of the contending parties. Thus preventive diplomacy may be successful at first, but there is never any guarantee that its success will hold for years to come. Much depends on implementing long-term preventive conflict management measures.

Furthermore, we need to question whether the "failures" of preventive diplomacy are indeed failures, or simply missed opportunities to respond to conflicts in their early stages. There is a qualitative difference between failing at preventive action and failing to take any action at all, as has been more often the case. Critics of preventive diplomacy overemphasize failed cases but neglect to mention the relatively successful ones: Estonia, Hungary and Slovakia, the Ukraine, and Macedonia. While none of these countries constitutes a "perfect" case of preventive diplomacy, they are all "good enough," or what I call "relatively successful," to warrant further examination.

Preventive actions may not be risk-free, but no international involvement ever is. And preventive efforts certainly may not always result in a positive outcome for any number of complicated and unpredictable reasons involving the history, special dynamics inherent to each conflict, the varied circumstances, talents, attitudes, means, and capacities of the conflicting parties. But the same holds for intervention in the later stages of armed violence.

Moreover, there is little doubt that the material and human costs of preventive diplomacy are extremely low when compared to the costs of a protracted conflict, and the refugee crises and long-term humanitarian assistance that follow it. The Yugoslav wars provide an excellent example here. As of 1996, in Bosnia alone, more than 250,000 people were left dead or missing; the wars produced 3 million refugees, the largest refugee crisis in European post-World War II history, with 1 million fleeing to foreign countries, such as Germany or Austria or the United States. Postwar reconstruction costs for Bosnia alone, according to World Bank estimates, require external financing of about $5.1 billion over the next three to four years, with total damage estimated at $50–70 billion, not counting a 75 percent decline in GDP (World Bank 1996, 10, 61).

Some three million mines are still buried in Bosnia's soil, along with another three million unexploded shells. Close to 40 percent of the minefields are still unknown, which will make the rebuilding of Bosnia's agricultural capacity and infrastructure extremely dangerous. In addition, much of the reconstruction costs will have to cover the removal of these deadly devices.[4] Until these mines are removed or destroyed, civilians will continue to sustain injuries and death, even though the war is over.

The long-term humanitarian assistance needed in the aftermath of protracted violent conflicts, continues to drain the resources of national govern-

4. For example, international removal programs—such as those sponsored by the World Bank, the European Union, and individual countries—could cost as much as $40 million (O'Connor 1996). Military, economic, and humanitarian costs of the Bosnian and other conflicts are discussed in Brown and Rosecrance (1999).

ments and the international community. For example, following the Rwandan genocide in 1994, humanitarian relief efforts for a nine-month period amounted to $1.4 billion; between 1994 and 1995, $4 billion was spent on humanitarian assistance (Dowty and Loescher 1996, 44).

The intrinsic value of preventive diplomacy is that conflicts in their formative stages stand a better chance of being resolved by political means. Once fighting starts and atrocities are committed, once the security of the warring factions becomes threatened, the spiral of violence becomes never ending. Moreover, once the contending parties have sacrificed their members and matériel, it becomes more difficult for their leaders to seek a negotiated settlement.

Third-party involvement in the early phases of a conflict, when large-scale violence is still absent, is thus more likely to yield a favorable outcome. Moreover, countries stand a better chance to move toward sustainable peace if armed conflicts are not allowed to become protracted.

It needs to be stressed that conflict resolution in the post-Cold War era has become an increasingly selective and difficult task. This underscores the need for a systematic study of what types of preventive measures can best contain disputes before they escalate. The following chapters will explore why and how preventive diplomacy succeeds when it does.

2

PREVENTIVE DIPLOMACY: "SUCCESSES" AND "FAILURES"

MOST CONFLICTS DO not become violent immediately. Proponents of early warning and preventive diplomacy clearly make this point when they argue for more systematic assessments of impending crises or conflicts prior to their reaching a violent stage so as to enhance prevention (Birckenbach 1996b, 75–85; Davies and Gurr 1998; Gurr 1993b; Gurr and Harff 1994; Lund 1996a; Rupesinghe and Kuroda 1992). All successful cases of preventive diplomacy demonstrate that a proactive response must come in the early or formative stages of conflict, prior to the onset of violent confrontation. The case studies of Estonia and Russia and of Slovakia and Hungary, discussed in this chapter, attest to this, as does the case study of the Republic of Macedonia, which comprises the major focus of this book. In each of these cases, timely international involvement, the support of major countries or institutions, some form of multilateral initiative, and the moderate behavior of indigenous leaders were crucial to the successful outcome of conflict prevention.

Rwanda and the former Yugoslavia, the two "failed" cases analyzed in this chapter, are frequently cited as examples of the inability of the international community to intervene successfully in communal conflicts. Three strands of reasoning inform this argument. A primordialist strand holds that ethnic identity is innate and cannot be changed, that human beings are driven to defend their ethnic core, even by force. International efforts to prevent ethnic conflicts are therefore pointless. A second strand holds that ethnic conflicts are inevitable because of long-standing historical animosities among ethnic groups, often predating the formation of the state, while a third argues that communal conflicts are too complex for outsiders to resolve and pose unacceptable risks to third parties.

As the following narratives reveal, however, Rwanda and the former Yugoslavia stand out, not as failures of preventive action, but as failures to act preventively.

In both cases, the United Nations' peacekeeping abilities became tarnished and public confidence in collective action eroded. But as this study illustrates, U.N. peacekeeping efforts are only effective to the extent they are backed by major actors. Last-minute preventive efforts by the United Nations to stop the genocide in Rwanda were thwarted because of U.S. opposition to an international force. Deployment of a U.N. preventive force in Bosnia was rejected on the grounds that it might interfere with the ongoing peace negotiations in Croatia.

While ethnic tensions in Slovakia and Hungary and in Estonia remain an integral part of these multiethnic societies, the possibility for these tensions to escalate into violent conflicts has been largely removed, primarily with the assistance of preventive actors such as the OSCE. On the other hand, Rwanda and the former Yugoslavia, particularly Bosnia, remain unstable in the aftermath of the massive destruction and unspeakable horrors of the early 1990s.

From the four cases explored here, it also becomes obvious that the likelihood of achieving sustainable peace has been much higher where preventive action was taken than where it was not. Whether international or nongovernmental, preventive actors work to establish mechanisms and institutions that encourage political dialogue. Moreover, efforts to persuade political leaders to adopt accommodative policies, to work within the available democratic structures, and to convince a wider populace that peace among ethnic groups is to the benefit of the entire society, all contribute to the creation of a "culture of peace."

At first sight, the four cases do not seem to have much in common. They represent vastly different geographic regions—Eastern Europe and Africa—with vastly different historical, political, economic, and ethnic patterns. There are, however, a number of common elements that warrant a comparative analysis. First, the linkage pattern typical for conflicts in the late twentieth century is present in all four examples. Each of the conflicts has a certain level of complexity because interethnic and interstate components are so intricately intertwined. Hypothetically, each of the conflicts has also had the potential to escalate into a wider regional confrontation. In fact, the genocide in Rwanda indirectly triggered the overthrow of the Mobuto government in the former Zaire, which remains politically and ethnically divided.

In each of the two negative cases, Rwanda and the former Yugoslavia, third parties failed to respond preventively to the violence, although there had been ample early warning signs of impending conflict. Each of the two experienced horrendous destruction and gross human rights violations.

To analyze why preventive diplomacy succeeded between Estonia and Russia and between Slovakia and Hungary, and why, in Rwanda and in the former Yugoslavia violent conflict ran its course, we shall address the following specific questions:

- What is the nature of the conflict in each of the cases?
- What preventive actors and instruments were involved in those cases where preventive diplomacy was relatively successful?
- In what way did they shape the outcome?
- Why did third parties not prevent the violence in Rwanda and the former Yugoslavia?

SUCCESSFUL CASES OF PREVENTIVE DIPLOMACY

Case Study 1: Slovakia and Hungary

Nature of conflict. Although one may trace the conflict between Slovakia and Hungary back to the ninth century with the settlement of Magyars migrating from the Central Asian steppes to this region, it is the end of Communist rule in Central Europe that has triggered more recent tensions affecting the bilateral and ethnic relations of both countries. The annexation of Slovak territory by the Hungarian kingdom in the eleventh century, the carving up of Hungary following World War I, and the creation of Czechoslovakia in 1918, which incorporated the former Slovak territory, left not only a Hungarian minority in the newly formed Czechoslovak state, but also a Slovak population in Hungary, by then, much reduced in size.

In the crisis that developed between Slovakia and Hungary in the early 1990s, territory, water resources, and ethnicity were issues dividing the two states. The Slovak-Hungarian conflict first erupted in 1989 over the cancellation of the Gabcikovo-Nagyamáros hydroelectric project by Hungarian Prime Minister Antall Németh. The project, over a ninety-mile stretch of the Danube, which forms the border between the two states, had all the elements of a classical territorial dispute. Opposition from environmental groups who had supported Németh's election led the Hungarian government to renegotiate the Czech-Hungarian treaty that had launched the project in 1977. Although the rift occurred when Czechoslovakia was still an undivided state, tensions escalated during its breakup. Slovakia, to support its drive for independence in 1991 and 1992, rallied around the dam as a symbol of national pride. The Prague government also resisted the Hungarian decision to cancel, arguing that $3.5 billion had already been spent on the project and that the dam was essential to Czechoslovakia's flood control efforts. When negotiations broke down, Hungary annulled the treaty on May 7, 1992. Because two-thirds of the dam had been completed on the Slovak side, and because nationalist sentiments ran high in Bratislava, the Slovak capital, authorities proceeded with their construction plans, which included diverting the Danube.

Hungary used various tactics to halt the diversion. It accused Slovakia of violating the 1920 Treaty of Trianon and the 1947 Peace Treaty, both of which had settled the border between Hungary and Czechoslovakia. It also requested diplomatic intervention from the Danube Commission, the leaders of several states, and the CSCE. On October 23, 1992, a day before Slovakia was to proceed with the diversion, Hungary asked the CSCE to invoke emergency procedures and also vowed to bring the matter to the International Court of Justice. On October 24, the day the Danube was diverted, Hungary filed a protest with the U.N. Security Council. None of these organizations, however, responded to Hungary's attempts to defuse the crisis. It was the European Community that finally acted as a mediator in settling the dispute over the dam.

But the Gabcikovo-Nagyamáros Dam was not the only issue dividing Slovakia and Hungary in the early 1990s. Another persistent source of interstate tension was, and remains, the treatment of the approximately 600,000 Hungarians in Slovakia—roughly 11 percent of the population—whose situation has deteriorated since Slovakian independence. For a thousand years, Hungarians have been a presence in this region, which once belonged to the Hungarian kingdom. Following World War I, the Treaty of Trianon carved up Hungarian territory and incorporated its Slovak part into a newly created Czechoslovakia. But the treaty left a substantial Hungarian population in the southern parts of Slovakia, bordering Hungary. Budapest was able to seize that part of Slovakia during the Nazi occupation of the country, but lost the territory again as a result of World War II.

In the old Czechoslovakia, Hungarians simply made up another ethnic group, balanced between the two major ethnic groups, Czechs and Slovaks. With, however, the election in 1992 of Prime Minister Klaus Mečiar, a staunch Slovak nationalist, and with the division of Czechoslovakia into two separate states in January 1993, the position of ethnic Hungarians in Slovakia took a decided turn for the worse. Mečiar vehemently opposed granting cultural and language rights to ethnic Hungarians, fearing it might eventually lead to demands for secession. His controversial policies only served to escalate ethnic tensions, however. Hungarian names of villages, towns, and streets were changed into Slovak; it became difficult for ethnic Hungarians to use their Hungarian names in the civil registers. For their part, the ethnic Hungarians felt their cultural identity threatened by what they perceived as forcible attempts to assimilate them (Bugajski 1996; Cottey 1995; Lund 1996a; Munuera 1994; Rummel 1996, 197–235).

Having voted against Slovak independence on July 17, 1992, ethnic Hungarian parties then abstained from voting on the constitution and the government's program on minorities, finding these documents to be discriminatory. Although leaders of these parties have been cautious in voicing their demands, they have sought some form of cultural autonomy, primarily through local self-government. They have also insisted that they be granted the same rights as they had under the old Czechoslovak constitution. In particular, they have taken great offense to a clause in the Slovak constitution—"We, the Slovak nation,"—which was changed from the more ethnically inclusive phrase "We, the citizens of the Slovak Republic." Mečiar also refused to recognize the legitimacy of granting collective rights, claiming that the constitution's provisions on individual human rights also protects cultural and other minority rights.

Actors, instruments, and outcome. Preventive actors remained limited to European institutions, in particular the European Community (EC; after November 1993, the European Union or EU) and the Conference on Security and Cooperation in Europe (CSCE; after December 1994, the Organization for Security and Cooperation in Europe or OSCE). Given the specific linkage pattern of the conflict, preventive measures were directed toward the two levels of the dispute. On the interstate level, EC Commissioner Frank Andriessen suggested establishing an expert committee to assist with the Gabcikovo-Nagyamáros Dam, but this initiative failed because Slovak and Hungarian authorities refused to submit the matter to a third party. At the EC summit in Birmingham and again at the Visegrad-EC summit in London, member states stressed in no uncertain terms that their relationship with the two conflicting parties would be jeopardized if the dispute was not settled diplomatically. Finally, on October 28, 1992, both parties agreed to an EC-brokered protocol, which left open the project's termination date (to be negotiated later) but stipulated that Czechoslovakia redivert 95 percent of the Danube. In an EC-sponsored meeting on March 4, 1993, both parties further agreed to submit the matter to the International Court of Justice.

Preventive action on the part of the EC and the CSCE/OSCE resulted in a number of improvements in the Slovak-Hungarian relationship. In October 1992, the two countries signed a five-year military cooperation agreement, which included a number of confidence-building measures: the exchange of information on troop movement, the exchange of military observers, and the coordination of air defense systems. To facilitate economic cooperation, they also agreed to establish a joint bank and to set up three parliamentary committees to further study the Danube project. Most important, in March 1995, they negotiated and signed a bilateral treaty, agreeing to protect and promote the ethnic, cultural, religious, and linguistic identity of their minorities and recognizing that minorities form an integral part of the society of each state. Although similar in spirit to other bilateral treaties between countries having each other's national minorities, such as Germany and Poland or Hungary and Romania, the treaty has not resolved interethnic tensions within Slovakia over laws on language and the public advocacy of autonomy, over public funding of minority cultural organizations, and over minority rights such as the right to maintain contacts with kin across borders (OSCE HCNM 1996b). Indeed, ethnic tensions have turned out to be much more difficult to resolve than bilateral ones. While in office, Prime Minister Mečiar added to the difficulty, finding it politically convenient to play the ethnic card in mustering support for an independent Slovakia and to create the sentiment within the country that only a strong nationalist leader could guarantee Slovak nationalism.

But just as it had between the two governments, the EC intervened to mediate between Slovaks and Hungarians at the intrastate level. One way it did was through the Council of Europe, to which Slovakia had applied for membership. In reviewing Slovakia's application, the Council of Europe noted that Slovakia did not fulfil the requirements for the protection of human and minority rights in its treatment of ethnic Hungarians within its borders, and it proposed ten conditions under which Slovakia's admission to the Council of Europe would be considered.

Over Hungary's objections, Slovakia was admitted to the Council of Europe in June 1993. Although the Slovak government had not fully met the council's conditions on minority rights, member states made the convincing argument that more pressure could be exerted on Slovakia if it were also a member than if it were left outside in a vacuum (Bugajski 1996; Fitzmaurice 1996; Kasriel 1992; Lund 1996b; Munuera 1994).

Much more crucial at the intrastate level has been the role of OSCE High Commissioner on National Minorities Max van der Stoel, who, in 1993, recommended the creation of a three-member team of experts to study the situation of ethnic Hungarians in Slovakia and of ethnic Slovaks in Hungary. From September 1993 to May 1996, the expert team visited Slovakia and Hungary several times, concentrating on a number of concrete minority demands, such as cultural and educational rights, and investigating political representation of minorities in both countries. In Hungary, the team examined a recently adopted law on minority representation in Hungary's National Assembly and its impact on the ethnic Slovak population. In Slovakia, it studied a planned administrative reform and its impact on the Hungarian population; it also investigated language training facilities for Hungarian teachers at the Nitra pedagogical institute, and the introduction of Slovak as a language of instruction into ethnic Hungarian schools (OSCE Secretary-General 1994, 13).

During its fourth visit to Hungary in June 1995, accompanied by High Commissioner van der Stoel, the team discussed the parliamentary representation of minorities and examined the functioning of a Slovak national self-governmental body established earlier in the year; van der Stoel recommended appointing an ombudsman to mediate minority demands. In Slovakia on

January 8–10, 1996, van der Stoel met with Slovak and ethnic Hungarian leaders as well as the representatives of cultural organizations to obtain a firsthand account as to the implementation of a new law on state language and the government's cultural policy toward minorities. A visit to Budapest followed on January 11–13. In a series of meetings, van der Stoel asked government officials, members of the National Assembly, representatives of the Slovak national body of self-government, and other Slovak organizations about progress in the status of Slovak education in state schools, teachers' training, the promotion and development of Slovak culture, and the functioning and financing of self-governing bodies of the Slovak minority at the local and national levels (OSCE Secretariat 1996b, 5).

The fear that the Hungarian minority is more loyal to Hungary than to Slovakia and that some Hungarian groups may even seek secession continues to divide Slovak society. As part of the government's campaign to promote a strong national identity in Slovakia, the Law on the State Language, adopted on November 15, 1995, and in force since January 1, 1996, restricts minority languages and requires the use of Slovak in official settings. This new legislation has done much to bring ethnic tensions between ethnic Hungarians and Slovaks to the forefront. The law is generally seen as contradicting article 34 of the Slovak constitution, which permits minorities to use their languages. Even ethnic Slovaks are increasingly frustrated by the restrictiveness of the law, which has created havoc in the Slovak and regional media market (Fisher 1996, 14–16). The government's lukewarm commitment to its Hungarian minority mirrors the lack of public support for Hungarian cultural organizations and media, and is evident in the dismissal of ethnic Hungarians from positions in the educational sector. In his recommendations to the Slovak Foreign Minister Juraj Schenk in August 1996, High Commissioner van der Stoel noted that only 13 percent of all cultural projects for the Hungarian minority had been approved, compared to 75 percent of projects for other minorities (OSCE HCNM 1996b).

Despite the many efforts on the part of the OSCE and its high commissioner, respect for minority rights in Slovakia remains problematic. The language issue is particularly difficult to resolve, as will also be demonstrated in the case of Macedonia, because Hungarian ethnic identity and Slovak national identity (thus also the legitimacy of the Slovak nation) are both based largely on language.[1]

1. "In the case of the Slovaks and the Hungarians, language is integrally tied to the notion of nation, and as a result use and maintenance of language (or languages) is a crucial contested symbol in the nation" (Langman 1997, 126).

On a positive note, the OSCE's preventive actions have supported a more peaceful relationship between Hungary and Slovakia. And while Slovakia is still far from interethnic harmony, preventive diplomacy on the part of the high commissioner has kept pressure on the Slovak government to progress more significantly toward integration of the country's Hungarian population. Changes in the Slovak government in November 1998 were also expected to result in a more constructive approach toward minority rights as the new government vowed to reopen an interethnic dialogue and create a new office of Deputy Prime Minister for Human Rights and Minorities. Similarly, the high commissioner's engagement in Hungary has yielded positive outcomes on several occasions, including fulfilling some of the cultural demands of ethnic Slovaks.

Case Study 2: Estonia and Russia

Nature of conflict. The conflict between Estonians and Russians has its roots in Moscow's occupation and annexation of the Baltic state in 1940, and reoccupation in 1944, and in the ensuing forced collectivization, deportations, purges, and other forms of Soviet repression. Stalin's aggressive industrialization and colonization of this once virtually homogeneous country led to a large influx of Russian migrant workers in the post–World War II era. Three different waves of immigration would raise the proportion of Russians in Estonia from 8 to nearly 30 percent by 1995 (Ackermann 1993; Norkus 1996).

Moscow's objective was to change Estonians, only one of the many nationalities in the Soviet Union, into Soviet citizens. Its failure to do so was demonstrated by a 1986 study in which 90 percent of Estonians claimed Estonian as their dominant identity (Kirch 1994, 15). Russians in Estonia also enjoyed special privileges over Estonians, including better-paying jobs and housing. Russian language and culture were regarded as superior to that of Estonia's. Many Russian military officers assigned to Estonia retired there. The presence of these former military officers and their families became a significant source of tension when Estonia gained independence in August 1991.

Although in the capital, Tallinn, Estonians and other non-Russians make up 50 percent of the inhabitants, in the towns of the northeast, such as Narva and Kohtla-Järve, the Russian population is predominant. It is here that Estonian independence and the various laws on language, citizenship, and voting encountered the greatest resistance (Shafir 1995, 183).

The drive for independence further widened the division between the different ethnic groups.[2] In particular, ethnic Russians took offense to the citizen-

2. Of the 83 percent of eligible voters, 78 percent voted in favor of independence in the March 3

ship, voting, and language laws. Already in 1989, a language law declaring Estonian as the official language, stipulated that all persons in public positions demonstrate their ability in the Estonian language within a four-year period. In the same year, the Movement of Citizens Committee, created by the Estonian National Independence Party and the Estonian Heritage Society, declared that only pre-1940 citizens should have political rights (Ackermann 1993; Nørgaard 1996). A more inclusive concept, adopted in 1991, according to which Russians could receive citizenship by declaration, was abandoned soon after independence for a concept of citizenship based on ethnicity. Radical nationalists, arguing that Estonia needed to reestablish its national identity, supported a more restrictive citizenship policy, which led to adoption of the Estonian Citizenship Law in February 1992. Furthermore, Estonian citizens were deeply worried over the sharp decline in the proportion of Estonians, which in 1939 had been more than 90 percent but had fallen to nearly 65 percent in 1989 (Smith, Aasland, and Mole 1994, 181–206).

The Estonian Citizenship Law mandated that those who were citizens before June 16, 1940, and their descendants qualified for immediate citizenship. Those who took up residence in Estonia after 1940 could only acquire citizenship by meeting the four requirements for naturalization: a two-year residency beginning on or after March 30, 1990; a one-year waiting period after filing for naturalization; a knowledge of the Estonian language; and an oath of loyalty to the Estonian state. Former members of the Soviet military, security, and intelligence forces were ineligible for naturalization (Kask 1996, 193–212; Smith, Aasland, and Mole 1994, 181–206; Munuera 1994).

Although one could argue that Estonia's naturalization requirements were no more stringent than those of many other countries, their consequences were much more far-reaching and ethnically explosive. Thousands of ethnic Russians, more than 80 percent, were barred from participating in the presidential and parliamentary elections in September 1992, leaving them without national political representation.[3]

Apart from the tensions these policies were causing domestically, Russian-Estonian relations also became very strained. Russia, Estonia's immediate neighbor, protested against the citizenship law, arguing that it violated a January 1991 treaty between the two countries. Moscow undertook a series of retaliatory meas-

national referendum. Of the non-Estonians, most of which were Russian, at least 20 percent supported independence. In the northeast, ethnic Russians held their own referendum on March 17, voting overwhelmingly to remain in the Russian Federation (Shafir 1995, 183).

3. Earlier, on June 28, 1992, non-Estonians were barred from voting in a referendum on the constitution. In the same referendum, Estonians voted against giving non-Estonians who had applied for citizenship by June 1, 1992, the right to vote in the fall 1992 elections.

ures to force the Estonian government to change its discriminatory laws. In 1992, it slowed down the removal of Russian troops from Estonia. And in June 1993, when Estonia's Supreme Council passed the Law on Aliens, mandating that noncitizens residing in Estonia seek a residency permit and apply for Estonian citizenship or face expulsion, it threatened to suspend troop removal.

The Law on Aliens met with demonstrations and a demand for a referendum on secession by ethnic Russians, especially in Narva, and fueled anti-Estonian sentiments in Russia. President Yeltsin even referred to it as "ethnic cleansing" and "apartheid." Worse, the Presidium of the Supreme Soviet of the Russian Federation announced its intention to nullify the 1920 territorial treaty with Estonia—indirectly supporting secessionist demands from the Narva region, which fell under this treaty. Russia also halted its deliveries of natural gas, citing Tallinn's inability to pay outstanding debts. In return, Estonia accused Russia of waging an economic war on the resource-strapped country. The gas supplies were ultimately resumed, but only after Prime Minister Mart Laar publicly agreed to suspend the controversial law.

Actors, instruments, and outcome. As in the case of Slovakia, the OSCE helped keep the conflict tractable by preventing an escalation of tensions, primarily through its preventive diplomacy mission in Tallinn and the active involvement of High Commissioner van der Stoel.

At the request of Estonia, and following a Council of Senior Officials (CSO) meeting in Stockholm, a permanent CSCE preventive mission (for a six-month period, with renewal options) was officially established on February 15, 1993. Although the mission was not fully operational until April 1993, its six members immediately went to work. Their mandate was to promote understanding and integration among the ethnic communities, particularly between Estonians and Russians; to monitor and report on ethnic grievances, particularly over Estonia's citizenship, voting, and language laws, by creating contacts with governmental and nongovernmental institutions; and to assist in the creation of a civil society through facilitating dialogue and understanding (OSCE Secretariat 1996a; Törnudd 1994, 78–86).

The mission set about establishing and maintaining contacts with the Estonian government, representatives of political parties, trade unions, journalists, and Russian minority organizations, most notably, the Representative Assembly, founded in January 1993; the Union of National Cultural Associations, an umbrella organization representing 21 ethnic communities; and the more nationalist Russian Community of Estonia, founded in April 1993. They monitored implementation of the more accommodative measures on the part of the Estonian government, most of which were adopted as the result of CSCE/OSCE intervention. To serve the mostly Russian-dominated areas in northeastern Estonia, two additional CSCE offices were also set up in Kohtla-Järva and Narva (Törnudd 1994).

Since its inception, the mission has attended to several divisive issues: citizenship and residence laws, changes in the electoral law for local elections, language training for Russians, and procedures for non-Russians traveling outside of Estonia. It has also monitored local and parliamentary elections, in 1993 and 1995, and the implementation of a 1994 proposal to increase the number of Estonian language teachers and the efficiency of the National Language Centers Network in Estonia.

Citizenship and residency issues were among the most controversial problems affecting relations between Estonians and ethnic Russians. Tensions ran high in May 1993, when the Estonian Parliament amended the constitution to bar non-Estonian candidates from running for office in local elections. Nevertheless, the CSCE office urged non-Estonians to vote, placing advertisements in newspapers. And, to demonstrate its good will, the Estonian government granted citizenship to a number of moderate ethnic Russians so that they could run as candidates.

According to the CSCE mission and international observers who monitored the elections, voter turnout was substantially greater in northeastern Estonia than in other areas. In Tallinn, ethnic Russians gained 17 out of the 64 available seats in the city council. Thus the CSCE voter registration campaign succeeded in bolstering ethnic Russian participation in the local elections (Lahelma 1994, 87–99; Törnudd 1994)

The protest following the passage of the Law on Aliens created a major crisis in Estonia. Hundreds of signatures were collected in an effort to enlist the involvement of the CSCE mission. The crisis escalated when the city councils of Narva and Sillamäe called for a referendum on local autonomy. Although the Estonian authorities did not interfere with the referendum, held on July 16–17, 1993, they had the Supreme Court declare it illegal (Lahelma 1994).

Concerned over the explosive nature of the Law on Aliens, Estonian President Lennart Meri requested an expert opinion from the CSCE mission, the high commissioner on national minorities, and the Council of Europe. Their recommendations called for extending the deadline for registration of noncitizens, easing registration procedures, and expanding Estonian language training through special programs for ethnic Russians (OSCE Secretariat 1996a). Because of the crisis, High Commissioner van der Stoel visited Estonia twice in early July 1993, gaining assurances from the Estonian authorities that they did not seek the expulsion of non-Estonian citizens and that they would base decisions about residency for military members and their families on humanitarian considerations. As a result of this preventive involvement on the part of the CSCE mission and the high commissioner, the Estonian Parliament revised the law. The period in which non-Estonians could apply for residence permits was increased to two years. Non-Estonians who had resided in Estonia prior to July 1, 1990, were guaranteed residence and employment permits (Törnudd 1994).

The CSCE mission was also innovative in getting its voice heard on grievances by members of the former Soviet armed forces, a constant source of dispute between Russia and Estonia. Adding a new dimension to its mandate, on November 16, 1994, the mission appointed a CSCE representative to the Estonian Government Commission on Military Pensioners, thus permitting it to monitor fair implementation of social guarantees to Russian pensioners (OSCE Secretariat 1996a). The mission was also responsible for a government decision to grant travel documents to noncitizens, so that they could travel abroad, a problem that became most pressing to those whose old Soviet passports had expired and who did not want to apply for Russian citizenship (Chigas 1996, 25–97).

The OSCE Mission to Estonia continues to monitor the progress of development of a number of residency and language issues—and was responsible for inducing changes in several laws intended to restrict the movement of ethnic minorities. The mission and the high commissioner have closely monitored legislative debates on the revision of laws and the drafting of new ones (see, for example, OSCE Secretariat 1995b, 7). In March 1995, together with the Office for Democratic Institutions and Human Rights (ODIHR) and NGO representatives, the mission monitored the second parliamentary elections to take place since Estonia's independence, elections the ODIHR deemed to conform to existing electoral laws, despite the delay in granting citizenship to some non-Estonian voters (OSCE Secretary-General 1995).

The mission's contributions to dialogue, compromise, and accommodative policies, although limited in scope, would have been more difficult to achieve without the frequent follow-up visits by the high commissioner. A firm believer that ethnic conflicts are not inevitable but can be prevented through short- and long-term preventive instruments, Max van der Stoel has conducted numerous on-site visits to Tallinn and the northeastern part of the country, meeting with Estonian and Russian political leaders, making recommendations on legislation, such as the draft on the new Estonian law on citizenship on December 8, 1994, and exploring measures to overcome the difficulties many ethnic Russians have experienced with Estonian language training, an essential element for obtaining citizenship (OSCE Secretariat 1995b, 7; 1996a).

The high commissioner continues to press for more favorable requirements regarding citizenship, asking the authorities in December 1995 to consider simplifying the current language and constitutional examinations that every applicant must pass (OSCE HCNM 1996a). Although more than 43,000 individuals had passed the language examination as of October 1996, the perception is strong among many ethnic Russians that these citizenship requirements are intended to keep them out of the mainstream of Estonian society. The obstacles to learning the language are manifold: the absence of progressive teaching materials, the lack of affordable language schools, and the difficulty of Estonian itself, a non-Indo-European language with fourteen grammatical cases (Pettai 1996, 20–22).

But as in the case of Slovakia and Hungary, OSCE preventive actions have been successful thus far. Although relations between Estonians and ethnic Russians will probably continue to be marred by disagreements and disputes for some time, these are tractable. In February 1997, the OSCE Mission to Estonia noted that authorities had made significant progress toward changing the language examination, thus increasing the rate of those passing the examination (OSCE Secretariat 1997b, 5). Also, Ambassador van der Stoel continues to conduct his fact-finding missions to Estonia.

Integration of ethnic Russians into Estonian society is still far from becoming a reality. Yet much of the instability and the tensions witnessed in the early stages of Estonian independence have been addressed through adjustments in laws and practices discriminatory to Estonia's ethnic minorities. The withdrawal of Russian troops has much reduced the pressure on Estonia's security. A combination of different preventive activities such as monitoring the situation of ethnic Russians in the country, recommendations to the Estonian government to lessen the impact of controversial laws, and support for various mechanisms of interethnic dialogue, such as the Presidential Round Table, were all important ingredients to the successful implementation of preventive action. The active engagement of the high commissioner added an important diplomatic voice, which the Estonian government could not easily ignore. His series of recommendations induced the Estonian authorities to reevaluate their minority policies and make them more acceptable to the ethnic Russian population.[4]

Case Study 3: The Hutu-Tutsi Conflict in Rwanda

Nature of conflict. In 1994, Rwanda, a small state in central Africa with a predominantly agricultural economy, became one of the world's most gruesome sites of genocide. Following the death of Rwandan President Juvenal Habyarimana and Burundian President Cyprien Ntaryamira in an airplane crash on April 6, more than half a million Tutsis and moderate Hutus were killed over a period

4. For elaborate discussions on conflict and its prevention in Estonia, see Ackermann 1993; Barrington 1995, 103–48; Birckenbach 1996a; 1996b, 75–85; 1997; Kirch 1992, 205–12; Kirch and Kirch 1995, 439–48; Lund 1996a; Munuera 1994; Ott, Kirch, and Kirch 1996, 21–37; Park 1994, 69–87; Raun 1994, 73–80; Taagepera 1993; and Vetik 1993, 271–80.

of three and a half-months. Although the mass slaughter came immediately after the downing of the aircraft carrying the two presidents, U.N. sources suggest that the army and extremist Hutu parties had already planned the massacre of Tutsis and moderate Hutu leaders several months before.

Pregenocide Rwanda had a population of seven million people with three ethnic groups: Hutus, mostly farmers: 85 percent; Tutsis, predominantly livestock breeders: 14 percent; and Twas: 1 percent. Contrary to conventional interpretation, the Hutu-Tutsi conflict is rooted, not in ancient ethnic animosities of the region's precolonial past, but rather in a system of arbitrary classification created by the German, and reinforced by the Belgian, colonizers. In 1890, Germany consolidated the two neighboring kingdoms of Rwanda and Burundi into German East Africa and instituted a system of indirect rule rooted in existing local structures. Influenced by nineteenth-century rationalist thought, the Germans created ethnic labels to classify their various colonial subjects. The lighter-skinned Tutsis, considered more intelligent and closer to the Europeans than the darker Hutus, were treated with favoritism and allowed to govern through a Tutsi monarchy and a system of "chiefs."

Belgium, which administered the region after World War I, when Germany lost her colonial possessions in East Africa, reinforced these ethnic distinctions by specifying ethnic group status on identity cards (militant Hutus would use these cards to single out Tutsis during the mass killings), and by systematically favoring Tutsis in administrative positions and in the educational system (Adelman and Suhrke 1996, 295–304; Destexhe 1994–95, 3–17; 1995; Kuperman 1996, 221–40; Prunier 1995; U.N. Department of Public Information 1996a).

The "ethnic problem" created from above was further aggravated when, in the wake of a Tutsi-led independence drive, Belgium reversed its policy and actively encouraged the political participation of Hutus through representative councils. This "divide and conquer" principle allowed the Hutus to assert themselves politically. In 1959, with Belgian support, the Hutus overthrew the Tutsi monarchy, shortly after which the first massacres occurred. More than 20,000 Tutsis were killed and more than 120,000 were driven into exile into neighboring Uganda, Tanzania, Burundi, and Zaire (Destexhe 1995, 43; U.N. Department of Public Information 1996a, 9). Those who remained in Rwanda not only were excluded from the political process and educational institutions but increasingly became scapegoats as Hutu leaders played the ethnic card to maintain Hutu power. Rwanda finally achieved independence in 1962 but continued to be plagued by a series of massacres between 1959 and 1963, then again in 1973, 1991, and 1992, culminating in the genocide of more than half a million Tutsis and moderate Hutus in 1994.

Failure to respond preventively. Given the many early warning signs, the 1994 genocide in Rwanda should have been easy to predict and—because of an international peacekeeping presence in the country since 1993—also easy to prevent. Although no single factor explains adequately why prevention did not occur, the following analysis sheds some light on the early warning signs and discusses how the dynamics of internal and external circumstances hampered effective prevention.

Since Rwanda's independence in 1962, sporadic outbreaks of violence against Tutsis have plagued this African state, preventing any progress toward peaceful coexistence between Tutsis and Hutus. The asymmetrical distribution of political power between the two dominant ethnic groups, the one-party system, and Rwanda's economic problems, which intensified anti-Tutsi sentiment throughout the 1970s and 1980s, have also hindered any kind of reconciliation. In 1990, President Habyarimana's grudging movement toward political reform was interrupted when the Rwandan Patriotic Front (RPF, which included many of the descendants of Tutsis exiled in the early 1960s) launched an offensive from Uganda. A political and military movement founded in Kampala, Uganda, in 1988, the RPF had as its objectives to repatriate exiled Tutsis in Rwanda and to assume political power. Although Rwanda's army repulsed the attack, pushing the RPF across the Ugandan border, frequent RPF attacks destabilized the region further and led to the militarization of Rwandan society. The number of troops rose from 5,000 in 1990 to 30,000 in 1992; local militias with close ties to the Hutu-dominated Coalition pour la défense de la république (CDR, which opposed any dialogue with the RPF) sprang up throughout the country (U.N. Department of Public Information 1996a, 12). It is the widespread existence of militarized groups which made the 1994 genocide possible.

Growing concern over the political and ethnic instabilities and the gross human rights violations in Rwanda led to limited international involvement after a series of mass killings of Tutsis in 1991 and 1992 (Destexhe 1995; Prunier 1995). On July 31, 1992, the Organization of African Unity (OAU) brokered a cease-fire agreement between the Rwandan government and the RPF, establishing a buffer zone in Rwanda and sending about 50 OAU military observers to monitor the zone. An international team dispatched to investigate human rights violations in Rwanda reported in March 1993 that violations were indeed serious and cited the existence of death squads and plans for wholesale massacre of Tutsis (Destexhe 1995, 80).

In the aftermath of new outbreaks of fighting in early February 1993, and following requests on February 22, 1993 by Rwanda's and Uganda's presidents for a U.N. mission along the common border of the two countries, the Security Council authorized creation of the U.N. Observer Mission Uganda-Rwanda

(UNOMUR), whose mandate was to halt any military assistance to Rwanda.[5] Also in 1993, the European Community, France, Belgium, and the United States resorted to economic pressures, which resulted in the Arusha Accord, signed on August 4, 1993, between the Rwandan government and the RPF. The accord called for creating a transitional government, integrating the RPF, fusing Tutsi and Hutu military forces, demilitarizing Rwanda's capital, Kigali, and establishing a U.N. peacekeeping presence in Kigali to monitor the cease-fire and provide some security assistance.

On October 5, 1993, the Security Council authorized creation of the U.N. Assistance Mission in Rwanda (UNAMIR), totalling 2,500 soldiers and military observers.[6] Deployed to Rwanda on November 1, 1993, and with its mandate renewed on July 29, 1994, UNAMIR was to oversee implementation of the Arusha Accord. But the peace process stalled when political leaders failed to agree on representation in the interim institutions (U.N. Department of Public Information 1996a).

When the first massacre began near Kigali's airport, within half an hour after news of the deaths of Rwandan President Habyarimana and Burundi President Ntaryamira on April 6, 1994, UNAMIR was in fact present in Rwanda. One could therefore logically argue that the prevention of the killings should have been possible. Various authors attribute the responsibility for failing to intervene in the early stages of the genocide either to the United Nations (e.g., Destexhe 1994–95, 1995) or to the downplaying of the crisis by the United States, which seriously impeded any efforts for an effective and more timely U.N. intervention (e.g., Burkhalter 1994, 17–21; 1995, 44–54). Although neither actor can be singled out, they can certainly be said to share some blame for not containing the carnage, even if they were unable to prevent the killings when they first began.

Instead of preventing further escalation in the first few weeks of the genocide, the Security Council passed a series of resolutions calling for, not an increase, but a reduction in UNAMIR forces, from 2,500 to 270.[7] Moreover, the mandate of the UNAMIR peacekeepers prohibited them from intervening through the use of force (U.N. Department of Public Information 1996a). Secretary-General Boutros-Ghali, in a strongly worded protest on April 29, 1994, urged the Security Council to reconsider its decision so that the killings might be

5. "Resolution 846, Adopted by the Security Council at Its 3244th Meeting on 22 July 1993," S/RES/846.

6. "Resolution 872, Adopted by the Security Council at Its 3288th Meeting of 5 October 1993," S/RES/872.

7. "Resolution 912, Adopted by the Security Council at Its 3368th Meeting on 21 April 1994," S/RES/912.

stopped in Rwanda. It was not until May 17 that the Security Council responded to the violence, calling for an end to the massacres, expanding UNAMIR's mandate to protect unarmed civilians, and agreeing to increase the reduced contingent of 440 peacekeepers to 5,500 troops, renamed "UNAMIR II".[8]

Direct calls for intervention came for the first time in June 1994, nearly two months after the first massacre began. It was France which announced on June 11 that it would consider humanitarian intervention in cooperation with other European states. This announcement drew the support of Secretary-General Boutros-Ghali, and the Security Council authorized France and other interested states to take "all necessary means" for the protection of the population and the organization of food and relief assistance.[9] Named "Operation Turquoise", French intervention established a temporary security zone in the southwestern part of Rwanda, which helped save the lives of thousands of Tutsis.

The puzzling question remains, why was the international community so slow in responding to the conflict, and why did it respond only halfheartedly? There is broad agreement that the mass killings could have been prevented, especially because there was already a U.N. presence in the country. Alain Destexhe, secretary-general of Médecins sans Frontières, a nongovernmental organization providing medical assistance in Rwanda, for example, argued that early third-party intervention should have been forthcoming and would have made a difference to the outcome of the crisis (Destexhe 1994–95, 1995).

One reason the United Nations responded too little and too late is that it lacked sufficient backing from countries in a position to assert leadership in the crisis. Because of domestic politics, the United States was unwilling to become a spokesperson for a collective humanitarian effort in the aftermath of Somalia; indeed, at first it rejected expanding UNAMIR's mandate and called for the complete withdrawal of U.N. soldiers from Rwanda (Burkhalter 1994). Secretary of State Warren Christopher, the Pentagon, and President Clinton himself failed to demonstrate any serious interest in the mass killings, thereby depriving the United Nations and other proponents of intervention of the leadership needed to initiate collective intervention.[10]

8. "Resolution 918, Adopted by the Security Council at Its 3377th Meeting on 17 May 1994," S/RES/918.

9. "Resolution 929, Adopted by the Security Council at Its 3392nd Meeting on 22 June 1994," S/RES/929.

10. Washington's unwillingness to lead any international action was supported by the release of Presidential Decision Directive (PDD) 25 on May 5, 1994. Announced during the middle of the Rwandan crisis, PDD 25 stipulated that any U.S. participation in U.N. peacekeeping must be classifiable as a response to a threat to international peace, must advance American interests at acceptable risks, and must have an exit strategy and an adequate command and control structure. The

International intervention was also delayed because of disagreements over the classification of the violence in Rwanda. The U.N. Human Rights Commission on May 25, 1994, determined that "acts of genocide" had been committed and that a U.N. special rapporteur be appointed to investigate this possibility. The rapporteur's report clearly stated that "the massacres were systematic and spared nobody," that there were "lists drawn up by the public authorities with the aim of identifying Tutsi, after which they were immediately executed," and that "the term 'genocide' should henceforth be used as regards the Tutsi" (U.N. Department of Public Information 1996b, 569–92). However, the U.S. ambassador to Rwanda made a statement rejecting these conclusions noting that "as a responsible government, you don't just go around hollering 'genocide'" (Jehl 1994).

The only two international engagements forthcoming, although too late to be preventive, were the French-initiated Operation Turquoise and the humanitarian "Operation Hope," in which the United States played a leading role. French military involvement, although having obtained the support of Boutros-Ghali and the Security Council, was for many reasons an unfortunate choice. First, the French had been supporters of the Habyarimara government, which had fomented ethnic violence to remain in power. Moreover, France had provided military assistance to President Habyarimara during his struggle against the RPF in the early 1990s. France also lacked credibility in being motivated simply for humanitarian reasons, given French policy to intervene militarily in its former African colonies. American involvement came only after the mass exodus of Hutu refugees to Tanzania and later Zaire, when the RPF was already on the verge of assuming control over Rwanda. On July 26, 1994, the U.S. government announced Operation Hope, a U.N.-supported humanitarian intervention, which was easier to justify politically than a military engagement to stop genocide.

The failure to intervene early in the conflict had long-term consequences, beyond the immediate mass exodus of Hutus from Rwanda. Directly related to the exodus was a refugee crisis that resulted in the death of many more Hutus from disease, especially in the Goma refugee camps in Zaire. Refugee camps became the base of operation for most of the Hutus who had taken part in the killings in Rwanda. Through violent tactics, they prevented many of the refugees from returning, forcing international aid organizations to supply the camps for

directive, which came in the aftermath of the Somalia crisis, was designed to keep the United States from getting enmeshed in conflicts outside its national interests or from having to bail out U.N. forces when operations in such conflicts faltered, as in the case of Somalia (Burkhalter 1994; Destexhe 1995).

more than two years. Moreover, Hutu guerrillas used the camps to place pressure on the new government in Kigali and were directly responsible for the fighting that broke out in eastern Zaire in late 1996, when several groups opposed to President Mobuto, including members of Zaire's Tutsi population, fought against the country's leader, deposed him, and took over the country. Renamed the Democratic Republic of Congo by the rebel leader Laurent Kabila, the former Zaire remains politically and economically unstable and beset by civil war. Worse, human rights organizations and the United Nations have maintained that Kabila's forces were responsible for the killing of thousands of Hutu refugees. This comes again largely as the result of inaction of countries like the United States, despite U.N. calls for an international rescue mission.

Because the Rwandan army was not able to screen all returning refugees, many of the militia members were able to slip back into the country where they stepped up their offensive against the Kigali government. Since 1997, hundreds of Rwandans, mostly civilians, have been killed in random acts of violence in cases where Hutu guerrillas have targeted Tutsi villages. In January 1997, more than 200 people were murdered, especially in the northwestern part of Rwanda, which is a Hutu stronghold. Hutu insurgents also began to target members of aid organizations and human rights monitors employed by the United Nations. In an attempt to combat the guerrillas, the Rwandan government adopted a counterinsurgency strategy, which resulted in the deaths of innocent Hutu civilians as government forces swept through neighborhoods and villages in search of Hutu militants (McKinley 1997). Before Kabila's takeover, Zaire's military allegedly recruited and armed Hutu militias in an attempt to defeat Kabila's troops, who first took control over eastern Zaire before consolidating their hold over the rest of the country.

Whether the two groups can ever be reconciled will be left to the Rwandan government that took over after the genocide. The key will be its ability to rebuild a political, economic, and legal system and to continue a process of reconciliation. Whether Rwanda's society can heal the wounds from 1994 is not yet clear—it will be a difficult and long-term process.

Case Study 4: The Yugoslav Wars

Nature of conflict. When civil war broke out in Yugoslavia in 1991, many were quick to point an accusing finger at the Balkan's bloody history and its alleged deep-seated ethnic hatreds. Of the underlying and immediate causes that triggered the violence, none is related to historical animosities. All have been extensively discussed in the literature, and therefore a short summary will suffice here. Prominent among the various causes for the wars are the disintegration of governmental authority and the political and civil order after the death of Tito; the failure to resolve the debt crisis, and the resultant growing economic deterioration; the failure to move toward market reform, democratization, and political decentralization, and the ensuing constitutional crisis; the rise of nationalism throughout the 1980s, especially in Serbia and Croatia; and ultimately, the failure to negotiate a compromise solution for a more loosely organized political structure (Cohen 1993; Duncan and Holman 1994; Gagnon 1995, 179–97; Glenny 1994; Munuera 1994; Steinberg 1993, 27–76; Woodward 1995; Zametica 1992).

The immediate trigger of the war was the declaration of independence by Slovenia and Croatia in June 1991, which unleashed the first armed confrontation when the Yugoslav National Army (YNA) tried to prevent the breakup of the country. But there were also a number of early warning signs that the constitutional crisis in Yugoslavia might escalate into violence. In January 1990, the Yugoslav Communist Party collapsed after Slovenia's delegates opted to walk out of the party congress, followed by the members from the Croatian delegation. Slovenia's bold initiative led to the first multiparty elections in all the republics throughout 1990. In Slovenia, Croatia, Bosnia-Hercegovina, and Macedonia (where reformed Communists remained in a coalition), non-Communist, nationalist leaders were brought to office, whereas in Serbia, the Communist Party maintained its control under the leadership of President Milošević. When attempts to negotiate a compromise for a more loosely organized Yugoslav confederation failed by early 1991, referenda were held in Slovenia and Croatia in which popular support favored independence. Because Croatia had a substantial Serbian minority, especially in the region of Krajina bordering Serbia, local Serbs boycotted the referendum and proclaimed that they would seek an independent republic of Krajina. Skirmishes following independence eventually escalated into war as Serbia provided YNA support to local Serb militia fighting in Croatia, and later in Bosnia.

While the violent conflict lasted only ten days in Slovenia, leading to the withdrawal of YNA troops, Croatia was less fortunate. With the help of the Yugoslav army, the Serbs in Croatia seized about one-third of the country's territory, including the Krajina and Slavonia. Bosnia-Hercegovina also was not spared the horrors of war. Although President Izetbegović tried to avert war in this multiethnic republic, made up of Bosnian Muslims (44%), Serbs (31%), and Croats (12%), by supporting a confederation rather than the disintegration of Yugoslavia into fully independent states, his preventive approach failed for several reasons. The first of these is that by late 1991, it was obvious that Slovenia and Croatia could not be forced back militarily into a rump Yugoslavia, especially after the European Community's decision, reached in December 1991, to recognize the independent status of the breakaway republics by January 1992. These events left Bosnia with only two options: it could seek independence or it could remain in a rump Yugoslavia under Serbian dominance. But the second option was problematic because Bosnia's Croats sought to become part of Croatia, and its Serbs, part of a "Greater Serbia."

Following a referendum held in February 1992, and boycotted by Bosnia's Serbian population, Izetbegović's government also declared independence in March 1992.[11] EC recognition came in early April 1992, along with the proclamation of a Serbian Republic of Bosnia-Hercegovina. By that time, however, the sporadic skirmishes taking place since the referendum had turned into a full-fledged war, with atrocities that would surpass in scope even those committed in Croatia.

Failure to respond preventively. Several factors explain the failure to respond preventively in the former Yugoslavia. To begin with, responsibility rests with the individual republics and their leaders, especially Slovenia, which started the war, but also Croatia and Serbia, which played the nationalist card to promote their own interests regardless of the bloodshed, and whose leadership was willing neither to resolve their differences without force nor to influence the behavior of their ethnic kin across their own borders. Another important factor is that regional and international organizations and the individual governments of Europe and the United States did not heed the many early warning signs, including the outcome of the 1990 Yugoslav elections, the inability of the constituent republics to adopt common strategies to resolve the economic crisis, and the failure among the republics' leaders to seek, much less reach, political accommodation. By the time external actors became involved diplomatically to prevent armed conflict, polarization was already advanced, making mediation more difficult.

Although various regional and international organizations participated in conflict mediation, after they failed to prevent the initial outbreak of hostilities, a collective approach to contain and end the violent confrontations was hampered by differences in opinion about the origins of the war, differences in goals, and differences in strategies to end the war (Woodward 1995, 7–10). Because there was a consensus, however, that regional institutions should carry the primary responsibility for the management of conflicts in Europe and because the United Nations was reluctant to interfere in what it considered to be an internal affair, the CSCE and the European Community found themselves initially to be the dominant actors. This had serious repercussions. In 1991, the CSCE

11. Of the 66.4 percent of Bosnians who voted, 99.7 percent were for independence, with Bosnian Muslims and Croats voting overwhelmingly for an independent Bosnia-Hercegovina (Commission on Security and Cooperation in Europe 1992, 23).

was still in the process of developing its various conflict prevention mechanisms, while the European Community was preoccupied with negotiations over the upcoming Maastricht Treaty and was structurally incapable of providing the necessary political, let alone military, resources to respond to the violence. Moreover, a lack of U.S. leadership accounted for the failure to consider any serious political or military response in the early stages of the conflict. Washington simply refused to view the conflict as a threat to its national interests and other geopolitical concerns (Woodward 1995, 7).

On the European side, three crucial phases of EC involvement can be identified: (1) the conduct of diplomatic and monitoring missions and the mediation of cease-fires and negotiation attempts between the warring parties; (2) the establishment of a peace conference and an arbitration committee; and (3) the shift from nonrecognition to the recognition of the Yugoslav republics as independent states (Giersch and Eisermann 1994, 91–125).

In the summer and fall of 1991, the European Community launched a variety of diplomatic initiatives. In early July 1991, it sent its first "Troika" mission—consisting of the foreign ministers of Luxembourg, the Netherlands, and Italy—to Belgrade to negotiate a cease-fire. Although this mission failed, the Troika soon thereafter scored its first mediation success when it brokered the Brioni Accords, which called for a cease-fire and a three-month moratorium on implementing Slovenia's and Croatia's declarations of independence, to allow the conflicting parties time to search for a political solution. In July, the European Community also agreed to ban arms sales and to freeze EC assistance to Yugoslavia, as well as to dispatch EC monitors to Slovenia and Croatia, who were to oversee the withdrawal of YNA forces from Slovenia and to monitor hostilities in Croatia. Although the EC Monitor Mission (ECMM) was successful in both regards, its mandate was limited. As the fighting escalated in Croatia, the EC mediation efforts soon faltered. By August, the European Community shifted from mediation to arbitration, when it set up a peace conference in The Hague under the chairmanship of Lord Carrington, and an arbitration committee chaired by the French lawyer Robert Badinter.

Ruling on the complex legal problems that the conflict had unleashed, the Badinter Commission noted on November 29, 1991, that the disintegration of the Yugoslav state constituted a dissolution rather than a series of secessions because the republics had expressed the wish for independence either through a referendum or through a sovereignty resolution ("Opinion of the Arbitration Committee" 1991, 17–19). The Yugoslav presidency refuted the commission's opinion on December 8, 1991, arguing among other positions, that the "right to self-determination and secession is the right of nations and not the right of republics, . . . that Croatia's Serbian population had not opted for independence, that Bosnia-Herzegovina's Serbian population by referendum had expressed the wish to remain part of Yugoslavia, and that Macedonia, although in favor of independence in its referendum, had really wanted an association with a union of sovereign Yugoslav republics" ("SRFY Presidency Views" 1991, 19–24).

The Hague Conference, convening for the first time on September 7, produced what was called the "Carrington Plan," which recommended a loose confederation of the former republics, patterned after the European Community, with a council of ministers, a court of justice, and a parliament (Steinberg 1993, 243). The plan proposed autonomy guarantees, including provisions for self-administration, for regions where national ethnic minorities constituted a majority, and called for an international observer mission to monitor its implementation. Moreover, it recommended a special court on human rights consisting of legal experts from the republics and the European Community, who were to function as arbitrators in case of disputes over the autonomy status (Giersch and Eisermann 1994, 110).

For all that, the Carrington Plan failed in early November 1992, about the time the United Nations, whose engagement had been limited to the support of the arms embargo, assumed a wider role. U.N. Special Envoy Cyrus Vance was able to convince Serbia and Croatia to accept a U.N. peacekeeping force in Krajina and Slavonia to monitor the cease-fire and the withdrawal of YNA units. At this time, the European Community also shifted its roles, moving from mediator to regulator, when Germany, Denmark, Italy, and Austria challenged the existing EC policy supporting the territorial integrity of Yugoslavia to lobby for the recognition of the independent former republics. The United States and the United Nations, both of which favored preservation of the Yugoslav state, as well as EC President Hans van den Broek, advised against recognition, warning that it would worsen the conflict and sabotage any political settlement. But pressures within the European Community increased, with Germany and some of the smaller European states, pushing the cause for recognition. At a meeting of foreign ministers in mid-December 1992, the EC agreed to recognize all the republics as of January 15, 1993, but stipulated that they fulfill certain conditions, including adherence to human and minority rights and support for the continuation of the Yugoslav conference to negotiate a political settlement to the conflict.

Although it is difficult to determine in the aftermath of the Bosnian war whether the European Community's shift in policy caused the widening of the conflict to Bosnia or whether Serbian paramilitary forces would have fought over Bosnian territory at any cost, it can be argued that early recognition of the breakaway republics cut short the time given for implementation and monitoring of minority rights, particularly in Croatia and Bosnia. The EC's contradictory reasoning on the shift only made things worse: whereas it had justified its earlier refusal to recognize Bosnia on the basis that recognition would cause war, the EC now justified recognizing Bosnia on the basis that it would *prevent* war (Ackermann 1995).

Conflicting opinions among the primary external actors as to what caused the hostilities resulted in conflicting strategies on how to terminate them. In the United States and Europe, two contending perspectives on the origins of the war best exemplify the widely held assumptions. According to one view, the wars in the former republics of Yugoslavia were an act of aggression, instigated by Serbian President Slobodan Milošević with the assistance of the Yugoslav army. The wars grew out of Milošević's objective to create a Greater Serbia, and thus followed a particular pattern by which first Slovenia, then Croatia, and finally Bosnia became a battleground. The second interpretation was that the revival of ethnic hatreds caused the war, whether as the result of the death of Tito, the vacuum created over the collapse of Communism in Eastern Europe, or both (Woodward 1995).

Those who saw the conflict as an act of Serbian aggression advocated a cease-fire agreement, whereas those who viewed the war as the revival of ethnic enmity, especially after fighting in Croatia spilled over into Bosnia, argued for recognition of Bosnia and its partition into three cantons. But the international community, according to Woodward, failed to prevent the war in Bosnia-Hercegovina in three respects: "either by putting an early stop to the war in Croatia before it could spread to Bosnia-Herzegovina, by persisting in the negotiation of a comprehensive settlement for the entire country, or by not repeating earlier mistakes when the Bosnian war did explode" (Woodward 1995, 274).

Apart from the incompatible views on the causes of war and how to end it, opportunities for prevention were missed because of the lack of leadership and a strong political and military commitment on the part of the United States in the earlier phases of the conflict. Like Britain and France, the United States initially supported the territorial integrity of Yugoslavia and resisted pressures to recognize the individual republics. The United States also welcomed the involvement of the EC and the CSCE in conflict management because, it argued, the crisis in the Balkans did not affect its national security concerns and should therefore be left to the European institutions. After the Bosnian war erupted in 1992, the United States shifted its policy stance, calling for the recognition of Bosnia, and, under the Clinton administration, a territorial settlement that would do justice to the security concerns of Bosnian Muslims.

Because of the widely held perceptions in the United States and in Europe that the European Community had failed in its efforts to obtain a political settlement and because of the unwillingness of the United States to assume a leadership role for ending the war, the United Nations was called on to fill the void. It did so through monitoring countless cease-fire agreements in Croatia, providing humanitarian assistance to the Bosnian population, and creating safe areas, some of which U.N. peacekeepers were incapable of defending because of their limited mandate and firepower. In response to European pressures for a more concerted American role, to prevent the deployment of U.S. ground troops, and to counter the drive for a more effective intervention that might lead to a political settlement, the United States resorted to the use of NATO air power to end the hostilities. By that time, however, all of Bosnia had become a battleground, and the Serbs had succeeded in gaining control of close to two-thirds of Bosnian territory. Also, by the time of NATO intervention, limited air strikes proved problematic as an instrument of intervention because of the U.N. forces on the ground, primarily French and British, and the need to obtain authorization for the use of air power from U.N. commanders (Woodward 1995, 274).

Finally, the legal dilemma over upholding the principle of territorial integrity, on the one hand, and upholding the right to self-determinaiton, on the other, was partly responsible for the failure to prevent armed conflict. With the shift toward recognition of the breakaway republics, the international community overturned a long-standing practice of withholding recognition from secessionist territories.

In summary, several equally significant factors explain why the United States and Europe failed to prevent the violent disintegration of Yugoslavia: the failure to heed and respond to early warning signs; the presence of too many third parties with incompatible national interests and strategies to terminate the war; the absence of leadership necessary for any collective action; a military intervention that came after existing territorial arrangements had been significantly altered; and contradictory positions regarding the inherent dilemma posed over the primacy of self-determination versus state integrity.

ANALYSIS

What emerges from the exploration of the relatively successful cases is that a proactive approach was crucial to the nonviolent outcome of conflict management in Estonia and in Slovakia and Hungary. In each of these case studies, the CSCE/OSCE and its high commissioner on national minorities made a critical contribution to prevention through fact-finding missions, mediation, and recommendations to the appropriate authorities in an attempt to change restrictive policies into more accommodative ones.

Backing by the EC and OSCE member states in the case of Slovakia and Hungary and by OSCE countries in the case of Estonia was an important factor as well to ensure a positive outcome. Moreover, leaders were moderate enough and could be persuaded by the OSCE to adopt more responsible positions toward the minorities in their countries. Also, involvement early on in the conflict was important because it created opportunities for political dialogue before the onset of any form of serious confrontation.

But while significant progress has been made in resolving disputes over minority rights, with changes in the laws on citizenship, education, and cultural rights, none of the conflicts in the positive cases above has been completely settled. For example, in Estonia, citizenship requirements remain a source of tension even though they have undergone significant changes. Ethnic Russians still object to the difficulty of passing language examinations and of obtaining the necessary language qualifications. And ethnic minorities have not been fully integrated into Estonian society.

Of course, one may argue that settling conflicts is not the primary objective of preventive diplomacy. It is more important that contending parties learn how to address differences in a peaceful manner rather than let tensions run unchecked. In that sense, preventive diplomacy certainly has been a success in the positive cases discussed in this chapter.

I call these cases, including the more lengthy study of Macedonia, "relatively successful" to acknowledge that their conflicts are still ongoing and far from being completely resolved and to reflect the limits that preventive diplomacy has set for itself. Preventive diplomacy does not attempt to resolve conflicts in their entirety, an unrealistic goal, particularly where multiethnic societies are concerned, but rather to help countries, especially those with only limited democratic experience and resources, set up the appropriate institutional mechanisms needed to advance peaceful solutions to conflicting positions. What is needed in these countries, and as the case of Macedonia demonstrates as well, is that preventive diplomacy be followed by long-term conflict management, which means that third parties, whether international or nongovernmental organizations, must remain engaged beyond implementing the initial preventive measures.

The former Yugoslavia and Rwanda are tragic cases of the failure to take preventive action early enough. Although there were attempts to find a peaceful solution to the conflict among some of the leaders of the Yugoslav republics and by EC member states, these measures came too late, especially in the case of Bosnia-Hercegovina. Equally important was the determined nature of the nationalist leadership in Croatia and Serbia, in light of which the credible threat, or even the show of force, was needed to prevent the war from spreading to Bosnia. Once sporadic violence had turned into large-scale force, attempts to negotiate peace settlements for the two countries became futile. Unfortunately, the failure to prevent the war in Croatia and then in Bosnia, and the war's prolonged duration there, have given considerable support to the pessimists who believe that armed conflicts can only be settled after they have significantly progressed and reached a "hurting stalemate," that warring factions cannot be forced to the negotiation table until they have exhausted their resources and military forces.

The tragedy that befell Rwanda in 1994 is by far the most serious failure of the international community to initiate preventive action. Not only did this failure unleash a three-month-long genocide in which close to half a million men, women, and children were gruesomely murdered, but it had serious long-term consequences for Rwanda and its neighbors. The case of Rwanda demonstrates that preventive efforts on the part of international organizations and governments remain selective, with little done to intervene in massive violations of human rights, genocide, and the massive displacement of people across borders.

The next four chapters undertake an in-depth analysis of preventive actors, their instruments, and the outcome of preventive action in the case of the Former Yugoslav Republic of Macedonia, which represents one of the best working cases of successful preventive diplomacy. Although conflict between Slavic Macedonians and ethnic Albanians continues to dominate the country's political and social life, Macedonia stands out as being the only place where extensive preventive measures were implemented, including the deployment of a preventive force for the first time in the history of the United Nations. Macedonia also serves as a potent lesson on how countries at the brink of armed confrontation can manage to prevent bloodshed and violence.

3

MACEDONIA AND THE BALKANS

A SMALL, LANDLOCKED country of approximately 26,000 square kilometers (about the size of Vermont) and 2.1 million inhabitants, Macedonia gained its independence from the central Yugoslav government in September 1991. It captured international attention in the early 1990s with the outbreak of war in Slovenia, Croatia, and Bosnia, in large part because of the fear of a spillover of armed conflict into this southernmost republic of the former Yugoslavia.

Had it not been for the outbreak of war in the former Yugoslavia, perhaps few would have been interested in this tiny country, in which various ethnic groups still coexist, much as they had in the old Yugoslavia and centuries before that. Macedonia is home to Slavic Macedonians (66.5%), ethnic Albanians (23%), and ethnic Serbs (2%), as well as Turks, Rom, Vlachs, and others (8.5%).[1] Residing primarily in the mountainous region of western Macedonia, along the border with Albania and Kosovo, ethnic Albanians form the largest and politically most vocal ethnic minority. Having been subjected to discrimination, especially throughout the 1980s, ethnic Albanians initially reacted to Macedonia's independence in 1991 with suspicion, largely because of concerns over their status in the new state. Since then, ethnic tensions have been a constant as a source of conflict.

Whereas the other former Yugoslav republics have gone to war, however, Macedonia has kept on the path of peace. Relying on the skills of its own political leaders and those of third-party actors, the Republic of Macedonia has preserved its multiethnic society as it proceeds toward democracy and economic reconstruction.

That Macedonia has become one of the best case studies for successful preventive diplomacy is largely due to the preventive efforts of various actors,

1. According to the official 1994 census figures, there were, in round numbers, 1.3 million Slavic Macedonians, 443,000 ethnic Albanians, 77,000 Turks, 44,000 Rom, 39,000 ethnic Serbs, and 8,500 Vlachs (Republic of Macedonia Statistical Office 1994b, 40).

including Macedonia's political and ethnic leaders, international and regional organizations, and nongovernmental institutions. This chapter explores the specific contributions domestic players have made to the peaceful management of ethnic and regional tensions through the use of political dialogue, policies accommodative to the country's ethnic populations, and the deliberate rejection of a nationalist agenda for the country. The example of Macedonia illustrates that third-party involvement and domestic efforts must go hand in hand to prevent the outbreak of armed hostilities.

This chapter first traces the historical fault lines that characterize the Balkans, and specifically Macedonia. It then explores the emergence of the Republic of Macedonia as a newly independent state in the early 1990s, and the domestic and regional context of conflict, played out on intra- and interstate levels, both of which were addressed by preventive action. Supporting the argument that preventive measures cannot be limited to third-party actors alone, it shows how Macedonia's political and ethnic leaders assumed a major role in conflict prevention, particularly through dialogue and accommodation.

THE PAST AS VIOLENT CONFLICT

Macedonia has a long history of violence and external domination. It is perhaps for this reason that in the early 1990s the very name "Macedonia" conjured up once more the image of the region as a center of intractable conflict, and of the "Macedonian Question," which had preoccupied European statesmen in the nineteenth and early twentieth century. Arising over the territorial ambitions of Macedonia's neighbors, Bulgaria, Serbia, and Greece, as they tried to carve out their share of a territory the Ottoman Turks had occupied since the fourteenth century, the Macedonian Question had a destabilizing impact on the entire region, and the struggle for control over Macedonia ended in two bloody Balkan Wars. The question was finally settled with the end of World War II, largely as the result of the victory of the Yugoslav partisans under Josip Broz-Tito and the creation of a separate Macedonian nation as part of the new Communist Yugoslav state. Even though in 1991 some observers feared a revival of the question (Pettifer 1992, 475–86), Macedonia's peaceful secession from Yugoslavia and its successful avoidance of armed conflict demonstrates that history has its own dynamics and does not necessarily repeat itself.

Macedonia's history is as complex as the histories of other Balkan countries. An ancient land first settled by Illyrians, Peonians, Thracians, Dacians, and Moseians, the contemporary Republic of Macedonia was part of the Macedonian Empire in the fourth century B.C. under Philip II (reigned 359 B.C.–335 B.C.) and his son, Alexander the Great (reigned 336 B.C.–323 B.C.). The Macedonian Empire was a vast geographic area that included most of the present-day Republic of Macedonia, Kosovo, Albania, southern Bulgaria, Greece, Turkey, Egypt, and Iran.

After the death of Alexander the Great, the empire was divided into three parts—Macedon, Syria, and Egypt. In 148 B.C., Macedon became a Roman province, when it reverted once more to a border region "marking the zone between Latin- and Greek-speaking cultures, and between the western and eastern halves of the empire" (Poulton 1995, 16). In the fourth century A.D., Macedonia became part of the Eastern Roman Empire; from the sixth century, Slavic peoples began to move into the region. In the ninth century, two Greek missionaries, Cyril and Methodius, undertook the conversion of the Slavs to Christianity, and also developed the first written Slavic language, Church Slavonic or Old Bulgarian.

Before it was annexed by Ottoman Turks in the fourteenth century, Macedonia came variously under the rule of the Bulgarians, the Byzantines, and the Serbs. After the defeat of the Serbian Kingdom in 1389 at Kosovo Polje, the Ottoman Turks extended their rule to Macedonia, and many Albanians, Rom, and Slavic speaking peoples converted to Islam. Five centuries of Ottoman rule left a distinct oriental imprint on the country, still visible today in the fifteenth-century Turkish baths of the capital, Skopje, and in the mosques of in western Macedonia.

However repressive and exploitive, Turkish rule was also a time of peaceful coexistence. Turks, Slavs, Albanians, Greeks, Vlachs, Jews, and Rom often lived together in multiethnic communities. With the decline of the Ottoman Empire, however, and the emergence of the modern nation-states of Greece, Serbia, and Bulgaria, Macedonia fell prey to the territorial ambitions of its neighbors. Although still under Turkish rule, these new states staked out claims to Macedonian territory, justifying them on historical, linguistic, and ethnic grounds.

At the end of the Turkish-Russian War in March 1878, a large part of Macedonia was ceded to Bulgaria, with the blessing of Russia, which preferred a Greater Bulgaria to counter Austrio-Hungarian influence over the region. Four months later, at the Congress of Berlin, the Great Powers returned the area to the Ottoman Turks. This led to a concerted effort on the part of Greece, Bulgaria, and Serbia to regain some influence over the territory through their national churches. The Internal Macedonian Revolutionary Organization (VMRO), founded in 1893, fought against Turkish domination.[2] In its most renowned uprising, the Ilinden Rebellion on August 2, 1903, the VMRO proclaimed the Republic of Kruševo, only to be crushed by the Ottomans who then killed many Macedonians in reprisal. The revolutionary movement had, how-

2. The Macedonian abbreviation VMRO is being used throughout this study.

ever, lacked broad popular support because of internal divisions—some favored a separate Macedonian state; others, a Greater Bulgaria—and because of the severe consequences of failed uprisings.

To liberate Albania and Macedonia from Turkish rule, Serbia, Montenegro, Bulgaria, and Greece formed a union, which defeated the Turks in the First Balkan War (1912–13). Fighting over the spoils, however, led immediately to the Second Balkan War (1913), in which Bulgaria faced a Greek, Serbian, Montenegrin, and Romanian alliance. Under the Treaty of Bucharest, Bulgaria received approximately one-tenth (Pirin Macedonia), Greece one-half (Aegian Macedonia), and Serbia the remaining two-fifths (Vardar Macedonia) of Macedonian territory, with each occupier bringing its own administration and national influence to the divided land.

During World War I, Bulgaria was successful in occupying Vardar Macedonia—the geographic unit that is now the Republic of Macedonia—but saw its claims to the territory overturned at the Peace of Neuilly in November 1919, under which Vardar Macedonia—some 26,000 square kilometers—became an integral part of the Kingdom of Serbs, Croats, and Slovenes, or what would later be known as "Yugoslavia." Greece received roughly 35,000 square kilometers of the larger Macedonian territory (Aegian Macedonia), now part of its northern province Macedonia, and Bulgaria kept 6,800 square kilometers (Pirin Macedonia). During World War II, Macedonia was again occupied, this time by German, Italian, and Hungarian forces, with Bulgaria given part of its territory as a reward for joining the Axis powers. Only in 1944 did the fragmentation of Macedonia at last come to an end. Macedonia was created and recognized as a separate republic within the Yugoslav federation, having a distinct Macedonian identity and its own national language. Through this political move, Tito intended not only to undermine Bulgarian claims to Macedonia but also to combat Serbian ambitions to make Macedonia part of a Greater Serbia, especially because, in the first Yugoslav state, the Serbs had categorically referred to this territory as "Southern Serbia" (Danforth 1995; Errington 1990; Perry 1994a, 31–58; Poulton 1995; Schevill 1991; Völkl 1993, 218–25).

After the war, the ideal of a multiethnic Yugoslav state was realized under the leadership of Tito, who broke with Soviet-style Communism and helped found the nonaligned movement. This second Yugoslav state included six republics, and two autonomous regions—Kosovo and Vojvodina. Postwar Yugoslavia was not held solely together by Tito's charisma or his authoritarian leadership style, but rather also by an intricate political system of federalism, social and economic equality, and group and national rights, including "shared sovereignty among its many nations" (Woodward 1995, 22). It seemed that in those postwar years, the Yugoslav experiment was finally succeeding because of the constructive balance it kept between the country's national groups.

MACEDONIA AND THE YUGOSLAV WARS

The wars in Yugoslavia count as the bloodiest in post–World War II European history. Like so many armed confrontations, their underlying and immediate causes were manifold. Although the immediate triggers were the declarations of independence by Slovenia and Croatia in June 1991, and Belgrade's decision to use force to secure a unified Yugoslavia, the literature has also identified a wide range of underlying causes. These include the failure of institutional mechanisms such as the Federal State Presidency after Tito's death;[3] the breakdown of central authority; growing nationalist sentiment in the republics; Belgrade's assertion of control over Kosovo, following several years of ethnic unrest; diverging political agendas, in which Belgrade's more centralized approach became pitted against the republics' demand for a decentralized system and other political and economic reforms reflecting the changes taking place in Central and Eastern Europe; the severe economic crisis and disagreement among the leaders of the republics on how to resolve that crisis; the mobilization of ethnic groups by political leaders; and ultimately, the collapse of the political and social order (Cohen 1993; Gagnon 1994–95, 130–66; 1995, 179–97; Glenny 1994; Woodward 1995).

Why, after what appeared to be a peaceful transition in 1990, did disputes in the former Yugoslav republics escalate into violence? And how did Macedonia, although similar to Croatia and Bosnia in its multiethnic composition, avoid armed confrontations? To answer these questions, one has to revisit the crucial year of 1990, when it appeared that Yugoslavia, like other former Communist states in Central and Eastern Europe, would shift toward a pluralist system.

In the late 1980s, Slovenia and Croatia were among the first republics to call for economic and political reforms. Mounting disagreement over the direction of change among the republics' leaders, however, blocked the reform process. Slovenia, in particular, insisted on democratization and a multiparty system, whereas Serbia argued for a recentralization as a way to overcome the crisis. A major split among the republics occurred at the Fourteenth Extraordinary Congress of the League of Communists in January 1990, when Slovene delegates left the congress after failing to obtain a majority for reforms

3. The Federal State Presidency's powers, including the command of the army, were spelled out in the 1974 constitution. It had eight members, one each from the six republics and the two autonomous provinces, with each member rotating every year in heading the Presidency. The system was designed to decentralize power and also to provide the republics and provinces with political weight. After Tito's death, the Federal State Presidency functioned as Tito's successor. In 1991, the system began to break down when Serbia blocked the rotation of the Croatian representative to head the Presidency. See Rogel 1998, 24.

giving more autonomy to the individual republics and ensuring closer cooperation with western European institutions. In February 1990, Slovenia's Communist Party seceded from the League of Communists, and then renamed itself the "League of Communists of Slovenia–Party of Democratic Reform." The Croatian Communist Party and the Macedonian Communist Party did likewise. Slovenia's and Croatia's decision to hold multiparty elections in the spring 1990 compelled other republics to follow suit, and brought more nationalist-oriented leaders into power (Cohen 1993; Woodward 1995).

Macedonia held its first multiparty elections in November and December 1990, in which the Macedonian National Front, a coalition of four nationalist, proindependence parties, under the leadership of the nationalist Internal Macedonian Revolutionary Organization–Democratic Party for Macedonian National Unity (VMRO–DPMNE or simply VMRO) became the strongest party in the National Assembly. The VMRO captured 37 out of the 120 seats available. It was followed by the reformed communists, who in May 1992, renamed themselves the "Social Democratic Union of Macedonia" (SDUM), a party that officially supported a Yugoslav federation at the time of the 1990 elections but that was increasingly favoring independence. The SDUM won 30 seats. Another major party, the Party for Democratic Prosperity (PPD), supported mainly by ethnic Albanians, won 24 seats. Out of the 17 parties participating in the elections, several smaller parties won a few seats in the National Assembly, including the National Democratic Party (NPD), the Socialist Party of Macedonia (SPM), the Reformist Forces of Macedonia–Liberal Party (RFM–LP), and the Party for the Complete Emancipation of Romanies in Macedonia (Perry 1993c, 31–37).

A party with a pronounced nationalist agenda, the VMRO was led by a twenty-four-year-old self-styled poet, Ljupco Georgievski, who with a group of young people founded the party—the last of the 17 Macedonian parties to be established—only four months before national elections. Georgievski borrowed the name from the nineteenth-century nationalist revolutionary movement that unsuccessfully attempted to liberate Macedonia from Turkish rule. The VMRO was quite outspoken on its political objective of an independent Macedonia. Believing that there could be a peaceful breakup of Yugoslavia into sovereign states, the VMRO ran on a political platform that advocated four crucial objectives: (1) independence for Macedonia; (2) the withdrawal of the Yugoslav National Army and the establishment of a Macedonian defense force; (3) an independent currency; and (4) international recognition as a sovereign state (Georgievski 1996a). The party's message was that Macedonia was only for Macedonians, which produced widespread resentment among the republic's ethnic minorities.

Macedonia's reformed Communist Party, first renamed the "Social Democratic Union of Macedonia" (SDUM), and with the 1994 elections, the

"Social Democratic Alliance of Macedonia" (SDSM), took a much more cautious approach to the political crisis unfolding in Yugoslavia. The SDSM stressed the need for a compromise solution whereby Macedonia would be part of a union of sovereign, quasi-autonomous Yugoslav republics. Given that none of the Macedonian political parties obtained a clear majority, to provide for a moderate domestic and foreign policy, a government of "experts" was created, in which only a few of the cabinet members had a party affiliation, although it took until March 1991, to assemble such a government. Also included among the "experts" were three ethnic Albanian ministers, a sign of the government's early commitment to power sharing. Although Georgievski's party had captured a slight majority of votes, the National Assembly, on January 27, 1991, appointed Kiro Gligorov, a former senior Communist official, as president. Georgievski was offered the vice presidency, and Nikola Kljusev, a professor of economics, became prime minister. VMRO's confrontational stance toward an independent Macedonia was feared to be too aggressive a policy for this southern republic, which had also been strongly dependent on the central government in Belgrade, and which now feared Serbian intervention. Also, not all of Macedonia's citizens favored an independent Macedonia. A poll in April 1991, for example, indicated that 60 percent of Macedonia's population preferred a restructured Yugoslavia of sovereign republics. Moreover, as the Yugoslav crisis progressed in the months of spring and early summer, it became increasingly clear that a leader with nationalist sentiments could easily lead Macedonia down the path of Slovenia and Croatia.

Liberal forces were crucial in the decision to make Kiro Gligorov the helmsman of Macedonia. Although appointed by the National Assembly elected in 1990, the choice of Gligorov as president had not been left to coincidence. A group of liberal politicians and intellectuals, referred to as the "Young Lions," which included individuals such as Branko Crvenkovski, who later became Macedonia's prime minister, and Vladimir Milcin, a playwright, theater director, drama professor, and later the executive director of the Open Society Institute, invited Gligorov to run and nominated him for the presidency. Intent on averting the spread of extreme nationalism, a war with Serbia, and an ethnic war at home, this group worked tirelessly to ensure that ethnic tensions in Macedonia did not escalate into violence, as they had in Slovenia and Croatia (Milcin 1996).

President Gligorov turned out to be a wise choice. A moderate who favored reform in the late 1980s, Gligorov maintained close ties with U.S. Ambassador Warren Zimmermann and, through him, with the United States (Milcin 1996). The multiparty political system that emerged in the 1990 elections under Gligorov's leadership proved crucial in September 1991, when independence was proclaimed, in averting a crisis with Serbia and in pursuing accommodation and power sharing among Macedonia's contentious ethnic groups.

As Yugoslavia unraveled in the early months of 1991, President Gligorov and President Izetbegović of Bosnia vigorously pursued a compromise solution by which bloodshed could be avoided (Cohen 1993; Poulton 1995; Perry 1996, 113–17; Woodward 1995). Their proposal was to transform Yugoslavia into a union of federal states. But the breakdown of negotiations and the subsequent secession of Slovenia and Croatia on June 25 tied the hands of Bosnia and Macedonia, which had been much more dependent on Belgrade than the northern republics. Macedonia was left with only two options—to seek independence or to remain part of a rump Yugoslavia under Serbian dominance. In a referendum held on September 8, 1991, 68 percent of Macedonians voted for independence (Bugajski 1994, 124). On September 17, Macedonia became an independent state.

A second crucial factor in staying on a nonviolent, less nationalist course was the voters' rejection in 1994 of the VMRO platform, which took a confrontational approach toward Serbia and ethnic Albanians in Macedonia. Macedonian citizens made a critical contribution to accommodation and prevention by reelecting a moderate government. Elections yielded a victory for the Alliance for Macedonia, a coalition of the Social Democratic Alliance of Macedonia (SDSM), the Socialist Party of Macedonia (SPM), and the Liberal Party (LP), which formed a government with the PPD, again under Gligorov's leadership (Perry 1995, 40–45).[4] The coalition's victory was a third crucial factor in maintaining a moderate and pragmatic foreign policy toward Macedonia's neighbors—Serbia, Greece, Bulgaria, and Albania—all of which had conflictive relations with Macedonia, and an accommodative and integrative domestic policy toward ethnic Albanians.

INTERNAL AND REGIONAL SOURCES OF CONFLICT

Three sources of potential violent conflict in the Republic of Macedonia since independence are (1) tensions between Slavic Macedonians and ethnic Albanians, and between Slavic Macedonians and ethnic Serbs living in Macedonia; (2) conflictive relations with Serbia, including the fear of a spillover of war from Bosnia and from Kosovo; and (3) the Greek-Macedonian dispute.

Domestically, social peace also continues to be threatened as Macedonia undergoes privatization and economic reform, which have created significant social dis-

4. In the 1994 elections, the SDSM obtained 58, the SPM 8, the LP 29, and the PPD 10 seats. The use of initials for the various Macedonian political parties mentioned in this chapter and throughout the study is problematic as not all of them match their English names. I have therefore used initials as they appear in translated official Macedonian publications. The exception is the ethnic Albanian parties, for whom I have used the Albanian initials (see footnote 7 to this chapter).

locations. A weak economy has exacerbated ethnic tensions, with each ethnic group fearing it will be excluded from already scarce resources. These tensions, albeit not violent, are likely to persist into the future and need to be addressed through long-term preventive efforts and conflict management education.

Much of the more explosive conditions for violent confrontation between Macedonia and Serbia, but also between Macedonia and Greece, have been removed since the signing of the Dayton Accord and the Greek-Macedonian agreement in 1995. Nevertheless, an analysis of conflicts since Macedonia's independence is essential to understand the extent of preventive efforts directed toward these two different conflicts.

Given the multiple layers of conflict, neither the Macedonian government nor the external actors alone could have achieved the formidable task of averting violence. The relative success of preventive diplomacy in Macedonia has been determined by the interplay of preventive actors and their varied instruments at all levels.

The Ethnic Dimension

Two of Macedonia's ethnic groups have been most problematic for the government in terms of their demands and political mobilization. Ethnic Serbs, who live in towns and villages near the Serbian border, seized on the occasion of Macedonian independence to proclaim their own Serb republic, modeling their action on that of Croatia's Serbian population in the Krajina region. However, with the assistance of the International Conference on the Former Yugoslavia, the Macedonian government quickly resolved this crisis by meeting most of the demands of ethnic Serbs, as we shall see in chapter 4. Because tensions between ethnic Serbs and the Macedonian government are no longer an issue, the investigation into the ethnic dimension of conflict in Macedonia will be limited to ethnic Albanians.

Relations remain volatile between Slavic Macedonians and ethnic Albanians, whose political and cultural demands are much more substantial than those of ethnic Serbs. Indeed, ethnic Albanian grievances fall into four overlapping areas of concern: (1) group status; (2) language rights; (3) educational rights; and (4) discriminatory practices.

Group status. Ethnic Albanians protest their status as a minority group and demand to be recognized as a constitutive nation, as they were under the old Yugoslavia.[5] In particular, ethnic Albanians resent the wording of the preamble

5. The term *national minority* was replaced with *nationality* in the 1974 Yugoslav constitution, which allowed ethnic Albanians and ethnic Turks to call themselves a "constituent national-

of Macedonia's 1994 constitution, which declares that "Macedonia is established as a national state of the Macedonian people," in which Albanians, Turks, Vlachs, Romanies and other nationalities have "full equality as citizens." Macedonian legislators have argued that the Macedonian constitution is explicitly directed toward "citizens of the Republic of Macedonia," which includes ethnic Albanians (Kitanovski 1995). Granting ethnic Albanians the status of a nation would therefore change nothing and only exacerbate ethnic tensions because other groups would also demand to become constitutive nations.

Grievances over group status are closely linked to disagreements over the number of ethnic Albanians in Macedonia. To obtain accurate numbers, the Macedonian government conducted a population census in the summer 1994 with the assistance of international observers.[6] Having boycotted a 1991 census because census forms were not printed in Albanian, ethnic Albanians contested the results of the 1994 census (Antonovska 1995). They continue to insist that they constitute between 30 and 40 percent of the population, instead of the official figure of 23 percent. Slavic Macedonians have argued that some of the ethnic Albanians living in the Republic of Macedonia are not Macedonian citizens but recent immigrants from Kosovo. Ethnic Albanians, on the other hand, have accused the government of passing deliberately restrictive citizenship laws that have discriminated against ethnic Albanians from Kosovo and other parts of the former Yugoslavia.

Finally, ethnic Albanians resent that Macedonia's constitution does not provide them with territorial autonomy. Concerned over their status as a minority in an independent Macedonia, ethnic Albanians boycotted the referendum on independence in 1991 and instead held their own referendum on territorial autonomy on January 11–12, 1992, where 74 percent of roughly 280,000 ethnic Albanians (92 percent of eligible voters) favored autonomy. Although the Macedonian government declared the referendum illegal, fearing it to be a step toward secession, it signaled to many Macedonians that ethnic Albanians were not willing to coexist in a common state (Perry 1994a, 36; Schmidt 1995, 22–30; Stosič 1995). By 1996, more vocal ethnic Albanian politicians such as

ity" of Macedonia, along with the Macedonian "nation." The term *ethnic group* was reserved for Vlachs and Rom to indicate that they had no national status beyond the borders of Yugoslavia. In the 1991 constitution, the status of Turks and ethnic Albanians was changed to "citizens," removing the designation of "nationality" (Friedman 1993, 81–82). According to Eran Fraenkel (1996a, 129, n.3), at present, Slavic Macedonians refer to themselves as "nation" (*narod*) but refer to ethnic Albanians, Turks, or Serbs as "nationality" (*narodnost*), and to Rom or Vlachs as "ethnic group" (*etnička grupa*) or "community" (*zaednica*). Ethnic Albanians in Macedonia demand classification as a "constituent nation" (*narod*), which would give Albanian the status of a second official language.

6. For a personal account on the 1994 census, see Friedman 1996, 81–128.

Arbën Xhaferi, leader of the Party for Democratic Prosperity of Albanians (PPDsh)—now renamed the "Democratic Party of the Albanians" (PDsh)—which split off from the PPD in 1994, however, reframed the quest for territorial autonomy into "internal self-determination," with structures more representative of ethnic Albanians.[7]

Language rights. The demand for equal status with ethnic Macedonians is also reflected in the disputes over language rights, especially because article 7 of the constitution declares Macedonian the official language of Macedonia. Although article 7 also mandates that, in matters of local self-administration where there is a "majority" or a "considerable number of inhabitants belonging to a nationality," the language and alphabet of that nationality can be used as official language in addition to the Macedonian language, ethnic Albanians have long argued that this is not sufficient. Much of their discontent over language rights can be traced to the National Assembly's delay in implementing the local self-administration laws regulating language use. There is also considerable confusion over implementation of the government's more general language policies. Ethnic Albanians demand the officially recognized right to use their language freely, the use of Albanian in public settings being closely linked in their minds to equal status with the Slavic Macedonian nation.

Educational rights. Although ethnic Albanians are guaranteed instruction in their mother tongue on the primary and secondary school levels, university education is available only in the Macedonian language. Ethnic Albanians have therefore demanded their own Albanian-language university. This demand reflects concerns over the lack of training institutions for Albanian teachers, the wish to replace Priština University in Kosovo, which has now become inaccessible to Macedonian Albanians, and more significantly, the need for institutions that maintain Albanian culture in Macedonia. In other words, an Albanian-language university is part of ethnic Albanians' effort to promote and maintain cultural autonomy.

7. The Albanian-language abbreviation PPDsh, which stands for Partia Për Prosperitet Demokratik Shquiptarëve, is used here. The party is referred to in Macedonian as the PDP-A. The PPD split in February 1994, during its second party congress, following the resignation of the fifteen-member PPD leadership in December 1993, when Menduh Thaci took over the Gostivar branch of the party. In February 1994, the old leadership remained with remnants of the PPD, and the new PPD under the leadership of Arbën Xhaferi founded the PPDsh. Although both parties claimed to be successors to the PPD, in the 1994 elections, only the PPD under its new leader, Abdurrahman Aliti, was recognized as the legal successor to the original PPD (Poulton 1995, 189–90; Schmidt 1995, 28). By October 1998, the PPDsh renamed itself the Democratic Party of the Albanians (PDsh). For the sake of simplicity, however, PPDsh will be used throughout this book.

Fadil Sulejmani, a former professor at Priština University who left Kosovo in 1991 when Serbia cracked down on the province, has led the struggle for the creation of an Albanian-language university. When, in February 1995, acting without government approval, Sulejmani and his supporters attempted to open the university in Tetovo, a city in western Macedonia with a majority of Albanian-speaking inhabitants, the police moved in and one ethnic Albanian was killed (Hope 1995, 4; Rusi 1995, 8). In their search for a compromise, the Macedonian government made various concessions to defuse tensions.[8] Over the widespread objections of Slavic Macedonians, in 1997, it reinstituted the Pedagogical Institute in Skopje for the training of Albanian teachers, an institution abolished in the 1980s, when anti-Albanian sentiments were widespread.

Discriminatory practices. Since 1990, the government has appointed from four to five ethnic Albanians to any given cabinet and has allowed ethnic Albanians to form their own political parties and to operate their own television, radio, and newspapers. Nevertheless, many ethnic Albanians claim that they continue to be underrepresented, particularly in the armed forces, in the police, in the legal professions, and in political office. For example, only 3 percent of police officers, and only 7 percent of military personnel are ethnic Albanian. However, the government continues to take positive steps toward integration, appointing two ethnic Albanian justices to the Constitutional Court (out of nine) and increasing the number of ethnic Albanians on the Supreme Court from one to four (out of sixteen). In addition, one ethnic Albanian was promoted to general in the army and three ethnic Albanians were appointed ambassadors (Munuera 1994, n. 104). The proportion of ethnic Albanian cadets at the military academy also increased from 2 to 12 percent, and the proportion of ethnic Albanian officers in the military rose from an overall low of 0.1 percent in 1992 to 3 percent in 1995 (Rubin 1996, 72). Despite these efforts, ethnic Albanians continue to demand wider representation in all areas of Macedonian society.

National versus cultural identity. Ethnic Albanians and Slavic Macedonians have distinct cultural, religious, and social attributes, and there is sometimes little daily interaction between the two groups. Although most ethnic Albanians, especially those who have resided in Macedonia for generations, speak Macedonian and Albanian, the same cannot be said for Slavic Macedonians.

8. When the Macedonian authorities offered to raise the number of ethnic Albanian students admitted to the St. Cyril and Methodius University in Skopje, Sulejmani objected (Rusi 1995); when they then tried to create an Albanian-language track in all disciplines taught at the university, the university's administration objected.

The highly visible existence of two distinctly different alphabets in the everyday life of western Macedonia creates a sense of two distinctly different societies, as does the presence of ethnic Albanians from Kosovo and other parts of the former Yugoslavia who lack Macedonian language skills and who therefore must resort to Serbo-Croatian in their interaction with Slavic Macedonians. This infuriates many Slavic Macedonians, who interpret such behavior, however justified objectively, as unwillingness on the part of ethnic Albanians to learn the Macedonian language. Moreover, a common perception among Slavic Macedonians is that Albanian is an inferior language, a language of peasants, lacking its own literature and poetry (Milcin 1996).

From the interviews I conducted and my own observations during extensive visits to Macedonia in 1995 and 1996, I have collected a number of persistent stereotypes and misperceptions Slavic Macedonians and ethnic Albanians hold about each other. For example, Slavic Macedonians frequently express concern over the higher birthrate of ethnic Albanians, especially of those still living in the countryside, and the immigration of more Albanians from Kosovo, many of whom are perceived as "troublemakers." Any increase in the ethnic Albanian population, whether real or imagined, is believed to tilt the demographic balance in favor of Albanians, eventually allowing them to assume political power over the country. Two censuses in the eight years since independence and the continued contesting of census results by many ethnic Albanians testify to the sensitivity of demographics in Macedonia. To claim a higher percentage of the total population is a crucial strategy in the struggle of ethnic Albanians for recognition as a constitutive nation.

Each group perceives the other as more aggressive, although psychological tests have revealed no such differences; in fact, test scores from both ethnic groups revealed traits of nonaggressiveness (Beška 1996a). Nevertheless, each group believes itself more peaceful than the other. Xhaferi, for example, considers peacefulness to be part of the spiritual heritage of Albanians, who have historically manifested a sense of responsibility for others as well as for themselves. When asked who should take most of the credit for the fact that there was no war in Macedonia, Xhaferi did not hesitate to answer that the responsibility for peace rests solely with the Albanians (Xhaferi 1996b).

Much of the suspicion between Slavic Macedonians and ethnic Albanians is driven by ignorance of each other's culture. This is particularly the case for Slavic Macedonians living in regions with few or no ethnic Albanians. While there seems to be a general willingness on the part of Slavic Macedonians to live peacefully with ethnic Albanians, most interviewees admit to little actual contact (Ackermann and Chatterjee 1997). Ethnic separation thus remains an obstacle in building a multiethnic community. According to psychology professor Violeta Beška, most ethnic Albanians and most Slavic Macedonians have retreated into their respective ethnic groups, which remain highly mistrustful of each other (Beška 1996b, 133–46).

There is also considerable misinformation as to whether ethnic Albanians are committed to a Macedonian state. Slavic Macedonians claim that ethnic Albanians give conflicting messages as to their willingness to live in one state. Much of this is owing to the fact that in the early years of Macedonia's independence, different factions of ethnic Albanians espoused the hope for territorial autonomy, whether within a federation, as a separate territory within Macedonia, or through secession. Although even when the more nationalist ethnic Albanian leaders speak now of "internal self-determination," they mean some form of cultural rather than territorial autonomy, Slavic Macedonians still cling to the image of ethnic Albanians as a monolithic bloc in pursuit of a single objective—the breakup of Macedonia (Milcin 1996).

There is much in the recent collective memory to sustain the perception of ethnic Albanians as "noncommitted citizens" posing a potential threat to Macedonia: the boycott of the referendum on independence in 1991, the ethnic Albanian referendum on territorial autonomy in January 1992, which many Slavic Macedonians perceived to be the first step toward secession, the boycott of the census in 1991, and the contesting of the internationally monitored census in 1994. Then there were several other incidents: the November 1992 Skopje market riot, in which four people died after the police accosted a fifteen-year old marketeer; the November 1993 discovery of what the media referred to as an "Albanian paramilitary organization" (later considered to have been an Albanian self-defense unit organized to resist a possible Serbian incursion into Macedonia), in which an ethnic Albanian deputy defense minister was implicated; and the unauthorized opening of Tetovo University in February 1995, in which the police killed one ethnic Albanian and arrested a number of university administrators. More recently, on July 9, 1997, ethnic Albanians hoisted an Albanian flag on a public building in Gostivar, near the Albanian border, and two were killed by police.

As the country and its inhabitants struggle with the demands of statehood and the search for a Macedonian national identity, ethnic tensions will inevitably increase, especially because there has never been an independent Macedonian state to fall back on for national symbols and markers of national identity. Even the Macedonian language is claimed to be, not a genuine national language, but a variant of Bulgarian, although Slavic Macedonians uniformly object to this.

What Macedonia can draw on instead is a long history of coexistence among its various ethnic groups and of domination by outsiders including Serbs, Bulgarians, Greeks, and Ottoman Turks, all of whom left their imprint on the country. When Tito accorded Macedonia the status of a constituent republic in the second Yugoslav state, and the Macedonian language and culture were allowed to flourish, Belgrade encouraged a Yugoslav rather than Macedonian identity so as to avoid associating the Yugoslav state with any particular "national" (ethnic) group.

The process of constructing a national identity inevitably clashes with the need of Macedonia's ethnic minorities, especially the ethnic Albanians, to maintain their cultural identity. The more Slavic Macedonians assert their cultural identity, the more ethnic Albanians feel the need to assert theirs, leading to a vicious circle. Thus forming a national identity, so essential to building a state, becomes a stumbling block to building an integrated, multiethnic society (e.g., Csepeli and Örkény 1992, 45–51; Kürti and Langman 1997).

In forming a national identity, Macedonia faces several challenges. The first of these is to prevent the rise of an extreme Slavic Macedonian nationalism at the expense of other ethnic groups—and the rise of an extreme ethnic Albanian nationalism in response. Thus far, the country has been able to nurture this complex balancing act although the most critical challenge remains—to create an identity of "citizen" that allows for the expression of ethnic identities. It is for this reason that emphasis is given to the "Macedonian citizen." President Gligorov is optimistic that a national identity built on citizenship rather than on ethnicity can eventually overcome the ethnic tensions in the country. When asked in an interview whether Albanians are willing to be integrated into Macedonian society and whether the "us" could include ethnic Albanians and Slavic Macedonians alike, President Gligorov struck a positive note:

> We are all Macedonians. We are all citizens of this country and Albanians have a long-term interest to integrate themselves in this country. This does not mean that they should lose their national, cultural, and linguistic characteristics. On the contrary, they should have all the prerequisites to nurture their special characteristics. Yet, at the same time, we expect them to be good citizens of this state. In the Balkans, people have learnt to live together regardless of their national, cultural, and religious differences. In the ethnically-mixed Balkans, it is impossible to create compact national states in which only members of one nation can live. This is an absurdity which can hardly be realized in Europe, where ethnic intermingling is high and where such a solution would only lead to new and endless wars. Perhaps one nation could win a victory here and there but then this would only lead to revanchism on the part of the others, and thus, there would never be an end [to warfare]. (Reuter 1995, 512)

A way to overcome the dilemma of competing national identities on the part of the political leadership is to create an alternative identity, namely, that of the

"European citizen." It is one of the reasons that Macedonia has been eager to become a member of several European institutions.

It is important to remember, however, that most ethnic Albanians in Macedonia have lived there for generations—they consider Macedonia their home, and themselves Macedonian citizens. This was poignantly revealed in an interview with Nusret Jakupi, a military officer in the Macedonian army: "I, as an Albanian, feel I am in my country. I haven't come from another country. I am living in the same place where my grandfather, my great grandfather, and generations before have lived" (Ackermann and Chatterjee 1997).

Although there is no evidence of ancient ethnic hatreds between Slavic Macedonians and ethnic Albanians, there is nevertheless the need to overcome past discrimination and past inequalities. Ethnic Albanians are particularly sensitive to perceived attempts to assimilate rather than to integrate them into Macedonian society (see Xhaferi 1996a). There is also a sense on the part of the more nationalist ethnic Albanian leaders that they have already made a significant concession by giving up the right to secession which they claim to have had in the former Yugoslavia, in favor of "internal self-determination rights," to include cultural and language rights (Xhaferi 1996a).

Tetovo University. Nowhere is the conflict between ethnic Albanians and Slavic Macedonians more pronounced than over the issue of Tetovo University. Perceived by Slavic Macedonians as an attempt to create parallel institutions, or worse, as a step toward separatism, the Albanian-language university remains one of the most divisive issues in Macedonian society. Not only does it form a major element in the debate over language and educational rights, but for nationalist ethnic Albanians it is also a central institution for the promotion of Albanian culture, language, and national values. Tetovo University draws strong support from a broad spectrum of ethnic Albanians, including those in the diaspora.

The conflict dates back to early June 1994, when ethnic Albanians officially requested the creation of an Albanian-language university, to be part of the Macedonian educational system. Defying the disapproval of the government, Tetovo University was established in private houses donated by ethnic Albanians in Tetovo. During the opening ceremony on February 17, 1995, government officials overreacted, and in trying to prevent the university from holding its first classes, Macedonian police killed one Albanian and wounded many others. More than fifty students were arrested, as were seven professors, most of them university administrators. Many foreign and domestic observers were worried as to the consequences of such confrontations and began to speak of an increasing polarization of relations between ethnic Albanians and Slavic Macedonians ("Ethnische Spannungen" 1995, 5; Hope 1995, 4; Rusi 1995, 8).

Various forms of protests accompanied the closing of the university and the arrest of its administrators. Ethnic Albanian parliamentarians boycotted the National Assembly in Skopje, although PPD leaders called upon Albanian citizens to keep calm and not allow themselves to be provoked ("Zunehmende Spannungen" 1995, 5). But Albanian factions, perceived as more radical by Slavic Macedonians, such as the PPDsh, threatened to declare autonomy (Hope 1995) or to create autonomous institutions, like those in Kosovo. This led to speculation in the international press that Macedonia was heading toward the kind of secession witnessed in Croatia's Krajina or in Bosnia's Serb-dominated region. In Albania, authorities referred to the killing of an ethnic Albanian by Macedonian police as a "chauvinistic act"; and in Kosovo, ethnic Albanian leader Rugova demanded that Gligorov open the Albanian-language university ("Zunehmende Spannungen" 1995).

Although the authorities argued that a separate Albanian-language university violates article 48 of the Macedonian constitution, which guarantees the right to education in the languages of the majority on the primary and secondary school levels, they pursued several compromise solutions, some of which have already been mentioned here. Although the government continues to resist a separate Albanian-language university, it has demonstrated flexibility in discussing and implementing alternatives, such as an Albanian-language curriculum at the Pedagogical Institute. Despite efforts to discourage attendance at Tetovo University, by declaring its diplomas invalid, there have been few efforts to physically close the university. Instead, Macedonian authorities continue to pursue alternative means for providing Albanian-language university education, means they hope will be acceptable to a less radicalized Albanian student population. The OSCE's high commissioner on national minorities and the Open Society Institute in Skopje have also suggested several compromise proposals, including the creation of a multilingual institution for business administration.

Tetovo University continues to exist, although in physical appearance it resembles less of a regular university campus than the parallel institutional structures that characterized Kosovo's educational and social system. During a tour of the "campus" of Tetovo University, accompanied by Professor Sulejmani, I was amazed at the elaborate teaching and administrative facilities set up in the past few years, which include three buildings with fifteen classrooms, an administrative building, a small bookstore, and a cafeteria. All facilities are located in private houses, where basements and even entire first or second floors have been donated to accommodate students, professors, and administrators. According to Sulejmani, as of the summer 1996, approximately 1,300 students were enrolled, of which half were female, with total enrollment projected to increase to 2,500 in 1997.[9] There are also approximately 150 professors, most of whom are ethnic Albanians from Macedonia, who taught at Priština University or other parts of the former Yugoslavia, and who lost their teaching jobs when the country disintegrated (Sulejmani 1996b). While these numbers are difficult to verify, the campus tour revealed well-attended classrooms, enthusiastic professors, and "departments" for the study of music, economics, philology, philosophy, art, law, and the natural and computer sciences. Albanian citizens, both in Macedonia and the diaspora, finance the university, donating one deutsche mark per month per person in support, this in addition to the facilities, which are donated by ethnic Albanians residing in Tetovo.

That the creation of Tetovo University coincided with the return of ethnic Albanian professors from the rest of Yugoslavia may provide one explanation as to why a separate Albanian-language institution has been pursued so vigorously. Certainly Macedonia's two major universities would not have been able to absorb such a significant number of teaching staff. However, there are at least three other reasons for an Albanian-language university: the scarcity of training facilities for teachers of ethnic Albanian primary and secondary schools, the absence of equality among ethnic groups in obtaining a superior education (equal educational opportunity had been guaranteed in the old Yugoslavia), and the lack of a significant quota for ethnic Albanians at the university level (Sulejmani 1996b; Xhaferi 1996a, 1996b; Ibrahimi 1996a).

But there is a more crucial argument for the university, one that goes beyond the demand for equal rights to education, ethnic identity, and language. It is the principal demand expressed by prominent ethnic Albanian leaders such as Xhaferi—to have institutions for the development of Albanian culture in Macedonia. Because currently Macedonian institutions represent mostly what is perceived as the dominant Macedonian culture, ethnic Albanians in Macedonia find themselves in a marginalized position (Xhaferi 1996b). In Xhaferi's view, an Albanian-language university is essential for cultural autonomy, which is the basis of internal self-determination.

Although ethnic Albanian leaders argue that the university is not a political but an educational issue, and although they continue to see the issue as a broader cultural controversy, the Albanian-language university has strong political undertones and has indeed been the subject of a political battle. For more liberal ethnic Albanians, such as Teuta Arifi, a former journalist working for the Macedonian government, the university is an issue on which both sides assumed extreme positions and failed to communicate with each other.

9. As of May 1999, an independent observer put the number of Tetovo university students at 6000.

Although the Macedonian authorities were insensitive to the specific needs of ethnic Albanians, who had lost access to Priština University, ethnic Albanians were equally insensitive in refusing to openly discuss those needs. In Arifa's opinion, however, what is principally at stake is not the university itself but whether Albanian will become an official language in Macedonia (Arifa 1995).

For ethnic Albanians, the perception prevails that the Macedonian government is not opposed to the university as an institution, especially because its founders had requested that it be part of the university system in Macedonia. Rather, Macedonia's leadership is opposed to Tetovo University because it would elevate Albanian to the status of an official language, which, in turn, would legitimize the status of ethnic Albanians as a nation (Xhaferi 1996b).

Meanwhile, the controversy remains much alive and is a persistent source of conflict between Slavic Macedonians and ethnic Albanians. Even though Sulejmani (1996b) expressed the view that the conflict was between the government of Macedonia and ethnic Albanians, and not between the ethnic Albanians and Slavic Macedonians, few Slavic Macedonians are convinced of that. A more widespread perception is that ethnic Albanians are out to isolate themselves within Macedonian society. Because many Slavic Macedonians hold a deeply rooted fear that a separate university is the first phase toward secession, there is little public tolerance for political dialogue on the subject. In the words of one Slavic Macedonian interviewed in our documentary:

> Why do they [the Albanians] think that in a country of two million one has to have a separate language in universities where every little group will be able to study in its own language? We won't be able to have verbal communication, not to mention other communications such as economic or cultural. Should we put up a fence and stare at each other as enemies? (Ackermann and Chatterjee 1997)

Another perspective was even more hostile:

> Today the Albanians, but tomorrow, maybe the Turks will want to learn only Turkish, the Rom Romany, and the Vlachs, Vlach. In that case they will have turned to self-isolation which will lead to their own self-destruction. Since a third of the population are minorities and have chosen to destroy themselves, then I don't see why the government should even bother to resolve the issue. (Ackermann and Chatterjee 1997)

Despite such antagonistic remarks on the part of some Slavic Macedonians, the authorities continue with the dialogue because of their commitment to guarantee minority rights, their foreign policy objective to pursue a "European option," and their fear of violent ethnic conflict, which has torn apart other former Yugoslav republics. International actors, such as the OSCE spillover mission, the OSCE's high commissioner, and, previously, UNPREDEP's chief of mission, all have stressed the need for maintaining dialogue and a policy of accommodation. Chapter 4 will explore the government's efforts in those and other aspects of conflict prevention.

The Regional Dimension

Macedonia is wedged between four regionally powerful neighbors—the "Four Wolves"—Serbia to the north, Bulgaria to the east, Greece to the south, and Albania to the west. Although Serbia, Bulgaria, and Greece occupied and laid claims to various parts of the Macedonian territory until the creation of a second Yugoslav state after World War II, since 1991, only Serbia and Greece have constituted a major problem to the Republic of Macedonia with violent conflict expected to emanate only from Serbia, especially until 1994. Greece's obstructive foreign policy, although destabilizing to Macedonia as a fledgling independent state, was not anticipated to trigger violent actions. Within the region, the conflict potential has decreased in intensity because of three diplomatic developments: the 1995 Dayton Peace Accords on Bosnia; the 1995 accord between Greece and Macedonia; and the 1996 agreement between Serbia and Macedonia. Initial difficulties between Macedonia and Albania and between Macedonia and Bulgaria following Macedonia's independence have been largely resolved in the diplomatic realm, and conflictive differences now center on nationalist concerns and sentiments.

Regional instability remains, however, with Kosovo still overwhelmed by violent conflict—its consequences for Macedonia to be assessed in the epilogue. Moreover, conditions in the former Bosnia-Hercegovina, now divided into the Serb Republic and the Croat-Bosnian Federation, are still volatile.

Because preventive efforts were taken largely as a means to avert Serbian aggression and to avoid a spillover of the Bosnian war into Macedonia, and because Greek-Macedonian relations were a major source of conflict during the first few years of independence, it is essential to understand how the actions of these regional players put Macedonia on the brink of violence and instability.

Bosnia and Kosovo. Until the Dayton Peace Accords were signed in December 1995, one of Macedonia's primary security concerns was that the Bosnian war might spill over. President Gligorov's request for a U.N. preventive force was largely directed toward averting such a fate. Gligorov's successful negotiations for the withdrawal of the Yugoslav National Army were crucial in denying Serbia launching bases for a possible military move against Macedonia. On the other hand, it also left the country defenseless because the Yugoslav army removed all weaponry. One of the major tasks for U.N. peacekeepers was to guard Macedonia's border with Serbia and to deal with the border encroachments, which happened frequently prior to the signing of the 1996 agreement between Serbia and Macedonia.

Serbia's calling Macedonia an "artificial nation" was much resented (Perry 1996, 114); its close alliance with Greece during the embargo was viewed with suspicion. In 1992, Milošević suggested that Macedonia be carved up between Greece and Serbia (Ackermann 1996, 413). During a visit by the Greek foreign minister to Belgrade in November 1993, he suggested there might soon be little left of Macedonia to recognize (Munuera 1994, 51, n. 122). Information gathered from interviews with government officials indicates that Milošević had plans to arrest Macedonia's political leadership immediately following independence and to replace it with politicians loyal to Serbia.

Moreover, in 1994, Serbian military forces temporarily seized a small area on the Macedonian side of the border drawn by the United Nations (Perry 1996, 115). Of nineteen border incidents reported on the Macedonian-Serbian border from April to June 1994, twelve involved Serbian incursions onto Macedonian territory, or clashes between U.N. troops and Serbian border patrols ("Dangerously Escalated" 1994).

Although, in an attempt to weaken the Macedonian state, Milošević demanded self-determination for Serbs living in Macedonia, much of the danger of ethnic Serb unrest was removed with the involvement of the International Conference on the Former Yugoslavia (ICFY) Working Group, which brokered a negotiated compromise settlement between President Gligorov and the ethnic Serb leadership in Macedonia, and with Gligorov's accommodative policy. Serbia did not recognize the Republic of Macedonia until 1996, when the two countries signed an accord.

A continuing, serious threat to Macedonia's security is the situation in Kosovo, a former autonomous region in Serbia, whose population before recent events was 90 percent ethnic Albanian. In 1990, following widespread riots, Serbia dissolved the provincial government and rescinded Kosovo's autonomous status. Resisting Serbian repression, Kosovo Albanians set up alternative political and social institutions as a major element of their strategy of nonviolent resistence and noncooperation (Salla 1995, 89–100). By early 1998, after Ibrahim Rugova—the elected president of Kosovo—failed to obtain critical international support, a group of militant Kosovo Albanians, calling themselves the "Kosovo Liberation Army," engaged Serbian police and military forces in combat. It was followed by countless retaliatory acts against Kosovo's ethnic Albanian civilian population, the mass murder of hundreds of people, and the forced expulsion of more than 800,000.

Although the United States and Europe finally intervened, first by negotiating with President Milošević for the withdrawal of Serbian forces and the introduction of 2,000 OSCE monitors, and when that failed, by launching round-the-clock air strikes against Serbia, the danger for Macedonia remains as long as there is no viable political settlement to the Kosovo issue.

The Greek embargo. The conflict between Greece and Macedonia also dates back to the country's independence. Although there was no imminent threat of war, Greece's obstructive foreign policy vis-à-vis Macedonia was politically and economically destabilizing.

To the Greeks the adoption of the name Macedonia, the name of their northern province bordering the Republic of Macedonia; the use of the Star of Vergina (a symbol used by Alexander the Great in the fourth century B.C.) on the Macedonian flag; and the use of what the Greeks claimed was the White Tower (a landmark in Thessaloniki) on Macedonian coins—a claim Macedonia rejected—all, demonstrated the expansionist ambitions of the new republic.

Athens also objected to article 49 of the 1991 Macedonian constitution, which stipulated: "The Republic is concerned with the situation and the rights of adherents of the Macedonian people who live in neighboring countries and emigres from Macedonia."[10] The Greek government claimed that article 49 encouraged territorial ambitions toward the Greek province of Macedonia, which has an unrecognized Slavic Macedonian minority. To assuage Greek concerns, on January 6, 1992, the Macedonian legislature passed two amendments to the constitution, renouncing "territorial claims against neighboring states, and stating that "the borders of Macedonia could be changed only in accordance with the Constitution . . . and generally accepted international norms," (amendment 1) and that the country would "not interfere in the sovereign rights of other states and their internal affairs" (amendment 2).

None of these confidence-building measures, however, seemed sufficient to the Greek government. Until September 1995, when the interim agreement was signed, followed by the lifting of the embargo in mid-October 1995, Athens practiced a policy of obstruction vis-à-vis Macedonia. Greece refused to recognize the new republic unless it renounced the name Macedonia. Although the Badinter Commission—in its report issued on January 11, 1992 stated that of the former Yugoslav republics, only Slovenia and Macedonia had made the most

10. The revised article 49 in the 1994 Macedonian constitution reads as follows: "The Republic cares for the status and rights of those persons belonging to the Macedonian people in neighboring countries, as well as Macedonian expatriates, assists their cultural development and promotes links with them."

progress toward the protection of minority rights, and, were thus worthy of EC recognition, Greek pressures on its EC partners stalled this process.[11] A compromise solution on Macedonia's name finally opened the way to admission into the United Nations in 1993, thus giving the economically strapped country long-awaited access to international loans. Macedonia entered the international community with the cumbersome name of the Former Yugoslav Republic of Macedonia (FYROM).

Unfortunately, this did not resolve the conflict between Greece and Macedonia. In May 1993, Greece rejected U.N.-sponsored confidence-building measures negotiated under Cyrus Vance. On February 16, 1994, the newly elected Papandreou government imposed an embargo on the Republic of Macedonia, after the United States and Russia bestowed recognition on the country.[12] The embargo was an economic disaster for Macedonia, especially because it cut off much-needed oil supplies.[13] Estimates put Macedonia's losses at $40 million per month (Perry 1995, 41).[14] Because Macedonia had been greatly dependent on using the Greek port of Thessaloniki, and because it lacked alternative transit routes, the country's economic activities became severely curtailed. Moreover, U.N. sanctions against the former Yugoslavia created further economic losses, for which Macedonia received no compensation. With the assistance of the United States and the United Nations, Greece and Macedonia reopened negotiations. An agreement signed in September 1995 lifted the embargo and stipulated that Greece and Macedonia negotiate compromises on their outstanding differences and work toward the improvement of bilateral relations (Kraft 1995, 385–412; Varvaroussis 1995, 358–64).

Conflict with Albania. Although Macedonia's relations with Albania have not produced the same level of anxiety among the Macedonian leadership as those with Serbia and with Greece, there have been concerns in Macedonia over

11. The Badinter Commission advised the European Community against recognizing Croatia because of its unsatisfactory progress in the protection of minority rights. Ironically, the EC recognized Croatia on January 16, 1992, along with Slovenia, but withheld recognition from Macedonia.

12. Russia recognized Macedonia on February 4, 1994, under the name "Republic of Macedonia." The United States recognized the country on February 9, 1994, under the name "Former Yugoslav Republic of Macedonia" (FYROM).

13. The Greek government had imposed already an earlier embargo in August 1992 which lasted three months. For a discussion on the Greek embargo, see Lefebvre 1994, 711–33. The Soros Foundation was crucial in providing loans for the purchase of oil supplies.

14. According to Assistant Minister of Industry at the Ministry of Economics Branko Ivanov (1995), the losses incurred by Macedonia from the Greek embargo amounted to $52 million per month.

Albania's intentions in supporting ethnic Albanians in neighboring states. Albania's role in the region is certainly a complex one because of Tirana's close links with ethnic Albanian leaders in Kosovo and in Macedonia. The relationship between Albania and Macedonia began to improve once Tirana moved away from its irredentist nationalism to pursue a more moderate foreign policy. In June 1992, President Gligorov and Albanian President Sali Berisha met to discuss a new course in Albanian-Macedonian relations, followed by the opening of an Albanian diplomatic mission in Skopje in 1993 and the signing of a treaty on mutual cooperation. In 1994, during the Greek embargo, Tirana also made its port in Durres available to Macedonia.

However, on issues affecting ethnic Albanians in Macedonia, Tirana does not hesitate to voice its concerns, as it did for example in 1993 with the arrest of members of the "All-Albanian Army." In early 1995, Albania announced it would reassess its foreign policy toward Macedonia if authorities there did not carry out the promises they had made in meeting the demands of ethnic Albanians ("Albania to Reconsider" 1995). But despite its rhetoric and diplomatic meddling, Albania is also aware that Macedonia's stability is crucial for the region and that moderation needs to be exercised in its relations with Macedonia.

Conflict with Bulgaria. Like Albania, Bulgaria is also interested in maintaining stability in the region. Although one of the first countries to recognize the Republic of Macedonia as an independent state, Bulgaria has officially denied the existence of a separate Macedonian nationality, for reasons having largely to do with Bulgaria's national history and nationalist sentiments. Macedonian officials view this denial more as a nuisance than a serious foreign policy problem. Indeed, President Gligorov referred to it in 1995 as "a typical Balkan irrational dispute, as is the conflict with Greece over the name Macedonia and the symbols that go with it." Underlining the point that Macedonian was different from Bulgarian, a claim the Bulgarians reject, the president noted that "every nation has the right to the language it speaks." Gligorov went on to state that "this reality must be recognized; otherwise it represents a Balkan syndrome of fighting against windmills" (Reuter 1995, 511).

Apart from the issues of nationality and language, however, relations between the two countries are cordial. Bulgaria has officially declared that it has no territorial ambitions toward Macedonia, and trade between the two neighbors has increased as more transportation and communication lines connect Sofia and Skopje.

Although Macedonia's external relations are now such that they can be managed in a constructive and peaceful manner, its ethnic problems remain potentially explosive. Chapter 4 examines the actions taken by the domestic actors to prevent the outbreak of violence in Macedonia and of a wider war in the Balkans.

4

THE DOMESTIC POLITICS OF PREVENTION

EVEN THE BEST preventive efforts are not successful without the support and the responsible behavior of the leaders of contending parties. Although the literature on communal conflict emphasizes the importance of leaders for the expression of collective grievances and for the effective mobilization of group members (e.g., Gurr 1993b; Kriesberg 1998a), the role of domestic leaders in preventive diplomacy remains virtually unexplored (but see Lund 1996a; Thompson 1997). It is often assumed that governments undertake preventive measures, not of their own free will, but only when pressured to do so by third parties. Although third parties can indeed exert pressure on domestic leaders through various incentives for moderation, carrot-and-stick approaches, or even coercive measures, the effectiveness of such pressure varies widely. Domestic leaders, however mindful of state interests and ethnic concerns, are also driven by their own political and personal agendas. It is therefore more appropriate to view prevention as a two-way process more likely to succeed with the simultaneous support and commitment of both external and domestic actors.

In the case of Macedonia, domestic political leaders from various contending parties—whether President Gligorov or moderate ethnic Albanian and Slavic Macedonian politicians—all deserve credit for averting violent confrontations. It is political leaders who decide whether their parties or states pursue an exclusionary nationalist agenda that appeals to ethnic differences or an inclusionary, citizen-based agenda that transcends those differences.

This chapter explores the contributions Macedonia's domestic actors have made to conflict prevention. It highlights measures taken by political and ethnic leaders to prevent (1) the violent breakup of Yugoslavia; (2) violent interethnic conflict in Macedonia; (3) the spillover of the war from Bosnia; and (4) the escalation of instabilities induced by Macedonia's neighbors into serious interstate confrontations.

DEALING WITH THE YUGOSLAV BREAKUP AND EXTERNAL THREATS

Macedonian-Bosnian Compromise of June 1991

From the time of escalating tensions in the spring of 1991 to the outbreak of war in Slovenia and Croatia, Macedonia's leadership assumed a critical role in the search for a compromise that would de-escalate the political crisis. Their efforts were largely driven by pragmatic politics and the need for a peaceful resolution of the conflict. Unlike Slovenia and Croatia, Macedonia was poor and dependent on Belgrade for its commercial ties and security needs, thus in no position to make demands. Moreover, hostile confrontations between these more powerful republics would certainly hurt Macedonia, whose ethnic situation somewhat resembled that of Croatia. There ethnic Serbs, concentrated in a single geographical region, the Krajina, had mobilized against the Tudjman government. In Macedonia, ethnic Albanians were largely concentrated in a single area of western Macedonia, which made secession practicable—thus that much more likely. Macedonia's ethnic situation also somewhat resembled that of Bosnia-Hercegovina, with its many ethnic groups, although Macedonia's ethnic Serbian population was substantially smaller in number and proportion. Macedonia's leadership also feared the growing nationalist sentiment in its own republic, where nationalist parties, such as the VMRO, and several smaller parties, were already promoting the idea of a Greater Macedonia. Finally violent disintegration of Yugoslavia was most certainly going to lead to war in Bosnia-Hercegovina. There was widespread speculation that the hostilities would inevitably spill over to Macedonia and that Serbia and Greece, perhaps even Albania and Bulgaria, would then become involved in a wider regional war ("Jugoslawiens Vielvölkerstaat" 1990, 5). A political compromise was therefore the only way to ensure Macedonia's political and territorial survival.

Even as late as July 1991, after armed confrontations had confirmed the secession of Slovenia, President Gligorov and Bosnia's President Izetbegović urged the contending parties to find a compromise solution (Gligorov 1991). Much of their mediation attempts focused on renegotiating a new constitutional structure for Yugoslavia. But conflicting visions between the more powerful republics, Serbia and Croatia, interfered with finding a nonviolent solution to the crisis. During an interview in 1997, Gligorov gave his perspective on the search for a compromise:

> When the Yugoslav crisis did come to the surface and when various accusations started being cast, as to who was to blame for this crisis

> and whether this solution for Yugoslavia was becoming more and more apparent, we gave a number of initiatives, to reach some kind of agreement between the representatives of the six republics. To maintain what could be maintained, to keep the ties that could be kept. And if we decided not to live together anymore, as a people who had lived together for seventy years, to try to resolve our problems not by way of war, but to separately go our own way peacefully. Our initiative, however, was not accepted. (Ackermann and Chatterjee 1997)

For President Gligorov, who in a 1995 interview, placed primary responsibility for the violent breakup of Yugoslavia on internal factors and domestic players, the most crucial question was how to prevent the war from spreading into his country (Reuter 1995, 509).

Once violence had erupted between Serbs and Croats in Croatia, a negotiated compromise became less likely. In the first three weeks of March 1991, tensions among the republics rose dramatically as leaders were unable to agree over the political reorganization of Yugoslavia. On one side, Serbia favored the continuation of a unitary, centralized federation, on the other, Croatia, supported by Slovenia, pushed for a confederation.

It became increasingly clear that Yugoslavia was on the verge of a breakup. On March 2, 1991, Croatian police clashed with Serbian police reservists in the Croatian town of Pakrac, fueling debate among members of the Federal State Presidency over whether to deploy Yugoslav National Army units to restore order. On March 9, the YNA was sent to Belgrade to quell riots between students, oppositional forces, and the police, resulting in two deaths and the injury of more than 200 protesters. Serbian Yugoslav State President Borisav Jović called for the use of armed force to prevent further violence. Unable to gain support, Jović resigned from the Federal State Presidency on March 15. Two other members—from Montenegro and Vojvodina—followed suit. On March 16, the remaining five members, including Macedonian member Vasil Tupurkovski voted against the use of force, instead declaring their commitment to a democratic solution and to dialogue in order to manage Yugoslavia's political crisis.

For his part, Serbian President Milošević accused the Federal State Presidency of sabotaging efforts to preserve Yugoslavia and threatened not to recognize its decisions. The crisis was further deepened when also on March 16, the Krajina region declared its intention to secede from Croatia.

On March 18, the Kosovo member of the Federal State Presidency, who had voted against the emergency measures, was removed by Serbian directive, and on March 19, the Kosovo provincial state presidency was abolished. Serbia justified its actions by stating that Kosovo had cast a negative vote because it sought to promote ethnic Albanian separatism.

Macedonia now seized the initiative. Tupurkovski called Serbia's removal of the Kosovo member unconstitutional; he called on the Federal State Presidents and the presidents of the republics to meet for summit talks. The first of six summits, referred to as the "Yu-summits," was held in Split on March 28, with Yugoslav Prime Minister Ante Marković and the president of the Federal Assembly also in attendance. The focus of the meeting was a ten-point document, prepared in early March by a commission of constitutional and economic experts, that included plans for a Yugoslav common market, similar to that of the European Community.

The presidents of Bosnia-Hercegovina and Macedonia proposed establishing a Yugoslav common market both as a compromise solution to avert violent conflict and as alternative for the smaller, more multiethnic republics to the reorganization plans favored by Serbia and Croatia (Frankland 1995, 336). The common market idea promised, at least theoretically, to be the most suitable compromise between confederation, supported by Croatia and Slovenia, and federation, vehemently defended by Serbia and Montenegro.

After the Split summit, five more rounds of talks followed, with each republic serving as the host (Woodward 1995, 142).[1] But the meeting between Presidents Tudjman and Milošević in late March on the reorganization of Yugoslavia within a two-month period gave a clear message that the center of action had now shifted from the federal state presidency to the presidents of the republics, and that Croatia and Serbia had become the dominant players in the negotiations over the restructuring of Yugoslavia.

The crisis appeared to have been averted when, on June 6, 1991, the six presidents of the republics meeting in Sarajevo announced that the June 3 compromise proposal submitted by Macedonia and Bosnia-Hercegovina had been accepted by all of them as the basis on which to negotiate Yugoslavia's future.

The compromise proposal called for the creation of a loose federation along the lines of the European Community in four common areas of interests—human rights, economic affairs, foreign affairs, and defense. Yugoslavia would remain within its current administrative borders and would maintain a common foreign policy, a common parliament, and a common military. There would be a single market and a single currency, as well as a collective head of state. However, in other areas, the republics were to have complete autonomy, including the right to establish independent diplomatic missions. In other words, there would be sovereignty for the republics, as in the con-

1. The other five Yu-summits were held in Belgrade on April 4, 1991; in Brdo, near Kranj, Slovenia, on April 11; in Ohrid, Macedonia, on April 18; in Cetinje, Montenegro, on May 29; and in Stojč, near Sarajevo, on June 6 (Woodward 1995, 142).

federation supported by Croatia and Slovenia, and there would be state sovereignty, as in the federation demanded by Serbia. Crucial was also the support voiced by the European Community after the visit of EC Commissioners Jacques Santer and Jacques Delors with Presidents Gligorov and Izetbegović on May 30.

Acceptance of the June proposal, it was widely believed, would provide the framework for settling the dispute between Serbia and Croatia over the constitutional structure of Yugoslavia. This soon proved to be an illusion, however. Croatian police contingents and Serbian paramilitary units staged frequent incursions into Bosnia, fueling fears among leaders in Bosnia-Hercegovina that Serbia and Croatia wished to partition their country. Although a consensus had been reached at the Sarajevo meeting to resolve the crisis by holding further negotiations, it became increasingly clear that the Macedonian-Bosnian proposal would be difficult to implement given the rising tide of nationalist feelings in Slovenia, Serbia, and Croatia.

In the end, the compromise solution came too late to check the growing violence that was now breaking out. In April and May 1991, Croatian police and ethnic Serbs clashed in Croatia over attempts to dismiss Serbs from police and military units. The situation was made worse when Serbia blocked Croatian member Stipe Mesić from assuming the chairmanship of the Federal State Presidency, a confrontational move intended to demonstrate that Serbia would not yield its political power to Croatia. Then, in separate referenda on May 12 and on May 19, Krajina's Serbian population voted to become part of Serbia, and Croatia voted for independence.[2] On June 21, Croatia and Slovenia proclaimed their independence from Yugoslavia, proclamations met by force, with the Yugoslav National Army moving first against Slovenia and later against Croatia.

Although in Slovenia, armed confrontations lasted only ten days, largely because of EC mediation efforts and because the republic was less ethnically divided than its neighbor, in Croatia, the fighting became more violent and protracted. Sporadic violence between Croatians and Krajina Serbs had already erupted in 1990. By March 1991, it had escalated into widespread armed clashes between police, paramilitary groups, and citizens, especially in towns where populations were ethnically mixed, and finally a full-fledged war involving Croatian forces, the YNA, and Serbian paramilitary units. In January 1992,

2. In the May 12 referendum, 99.8 percent of Krajina Serbs voted to remain within the Yugoslav state. In the May 19 referendum, the voter turnout was 84 percent. Of those, 93 percent voted for Croatia's independence (Cohen 1993, 212–13).

the United Nations mediated a cease-fire and deployed peacekeepers into specially designated areas. The deployment brought stalemate but not an end to the war. Worse was to come, when in early April 1992, violence also erupted in Bosnia-Hercegovina, which had hoped to avoid the fate of Croatia. All eyes were now fixed on Macedonia, and predictions ran high that this former Yugoslav republic would also be consumed by violence (Andrejevich 1991a, 1991b; "Beharren auf Bundesstaat 1991; Cohen 1993; Meier 1991a; "Nach Sarajewo" 1991; "Die Präsidenten der sechs jugoslawischen Teilrepubliken 1991; Ramet 1992, 1996; Woodward 1995).

Macedonian-Serbian Agreement of February 1992

With the war in Croatia, warnings that Bosnia and Macedonia would be next became widespread during the summer and fall of 1991. In early September, Radio Free Europe journalists filed reports speculating that for now the two republics "remain somewhat on the sidelines," but that this situation "could change quickly at any time" (Moore 1991). Unfortunately, the situation changed rather rapidly for Bosnia; and when it did, the repercussions for this multiethnic republic surpassed even the direst predictions.

Following the armed confrontations in Croatia, a spillover of the violence into Macedonia seemed all but inevitable. Three scenarios were put forward: (1) spillover of the Kosovo conflict, perhaps even involving Albania; (2) escalation of internal conflict between ethnic Albanians and Slavic Macedonians, facilitated by growing ethnic Albanian nationalism; and (3) invasion by Greece, Bulgaria, and Serbia in yet another attempt to establish their dominance over the breakaway republic.

When Macedonia had declared independence and asserted its sovereignty on September 17, 1991, it had kept open the option of joining a union of independent Yugoslav states, a measure intended to signal to Serbia that Macedonia was still amenable to a compromise solution. Moreover, Yugoslav National Army units were still stationed in the country, making it that much easier for Serbia to move militarily against the secessionist republic. Indeed, Belgrade reacted to the Macedonian declaration of independence by hinting that it might use force to prevent secession (Bugajski 1994, 156).

Although concerned over a potential military invasion, Macedonia nevertheless took an assertive stance against the policies of the rump Yugoslavia. On October 17, 1991, it refused to abide by the decisions of the Federal State Presidency, which had been controlled by Serbia, Montenegro, Kosovo, and Vojvodina since October 3, and announced its intention to defend its sovereignty and territorial integrity ("Mazedonien erkennt" 1991). On November

17, Macedonia's National Assembly adopted a new constitution, and on November 21, Macedonia proclaimed itself to be an independent state.[3]

In those early months following independence, fear of a possible Serbian intervention and potential violent unrest among its Serbian and ethnic Albanian populations dominated Macedonia's day-to-day existence. With the war in Croatia in full swing, Macedonia continued to live with YNA units on its territory, although it was negotiating their withdrawal. Although the government had officially adopted a policy of "active neutrality" as far as the conflict between Serbia and Croatia was concerned, this was no guarantee that Macedonia would not also be drawn into the war. Also problematic was the continued presence of Macedonian soldiers in the Yugoslav National Army. As a first demonstration of its "active neutrality" ("Mazedoniens behutsame" 1991), the Macedonian government stopped sending new soldiers into the YNA and called on its young men not to enlist. Popular pressure had been building for the recall of all Macedonian soldiers from the YNA since May 1991, when Croatian demonstrators had killed a Macedonian soldier serving in Split.

Negotiating the withdrawal of 60,000 YNA soldiers was one of Gligorov's first major hurdles in keeping the country out of war. Although the YNA had already transferred weaponry and troops to the north at the beginning of the war in Croatia, leaving at least 50 percent of the control posts along the border with Greece, Albania, and Bulgaria unoccupied, there was considerable concern about the remaining YNA units, concern that grew with rumors that military positions in Macedonia were actually being reinforced rather than reduced (Bugajski 1994, 105).

On February 4, 1992, in a letter rejecting Serbia's demand that negotiations could only be conducted with the Federal State Presidency, Gligorov argued that the withdrawal was a military, not a political, decision, and that he considered the Federal State Presidency an illegal institution. Two days later, an agreement was reached whereby Gligorov would directly negotiate with YNA representatives. The agreement also guaranteed the protection of Macedonia's borders during the time of the withdrawal. First withdrawals of military units came on February 17, when 300 military vehicles with equip-

3. In December, the European Community announced that it would recognize any former Yugoslav republic meeting the Badinter Commission criteria, which included the guarantee of political, territorial, and minority as well as other human rights. Although Macedonia was considered to have made the most progress in this direction, the EC withheld recognition after Greece objected to Macedonia's use of what Athens claimed were Greek national symbols and to the prospect of an irredentist, independent Macedonia at its borders.

ment departed from Macedonia. On February 21, an agreement was signed in Skopje setting April 15 as the deadline for complete withdrawal. Under the agreement, the Yugoslav military was required to leave behind equipment and territorial defense weapons. A joint commission was created to resolve disputed issues.

The withdrawal proceeded in various stages throughout March. On March 18, for example, nine posts on the border with Albania were vacated and handed over to the Macedonian Territorial Defense units. Also, YNA units were withdrawn from Skopje and Prilep, and the army training grounds near Kavadarci were closed. The military airport was handed over on March 20. The withdrawal was completed on March 26, 1992, and Gligorov and General Uzelac, the commander of the Third Military District to which Macedonia had belonged, signed a final document on Macedonia's takeover of YNA military facilities.[4]

Although the YNA withdrawal was greeted with relief in Macedonia, the country was now left without a viable defense capacity. Macedonia's own territorial defense units were small in number and lacked modern military equipment. The situation was made worse because the YNA had removed equipment and supplies President Gligorov deemed vital for a properly armed military force. Also, much of the weaponry had been withdrawn to neighboring Kosovo, a development that alarmed Macedonia further.[5] Letters to U.N. negotiator Cyrus Vance, the European Community and the ambassadors of the United States, Canada, and Russia protesting the "rough and uncivilized way" in which the YNA removed or dismantled "complete sets of equipment, modern electronic devices and systems, and reserves of food and medicines" as well as machinery belonging to Macedonia had little effect.[6]

Nevertheless, the withdrawal of the Yugoslav army was Gligorov's first victory in ensuring the survival of his country—a victory made crucial because it came only two weeks before the outbreak of war in Bosnia-Hercegovina. Gligorov continued to worry, however, that the war in Bosnia could easily spill over into Macedonia, especially if Serbia quickly gained the upper hand. It was then that Gligorov decided to appeal for international assistance.

4. In a 1995 interview, President Gligorov noted that the negotiations with Serbia on the withdrawal of the Yugoslav National Army were also successful because the army was allowed to "make a dignified exit without the harassment suffered by [YNA] units in Croatia who were besieged inside their barracks at the start of the war in 1991, and jeered at as they left" (Robinson and Hope 1995, 35).

5. I thank Professor Örjan Sturesjö of Uppsala, Sweden, for providing this information on the deployment of YNA weaponry from Macedonia to Kosovo.

6. Reconstructed from Foreign Broadcast Information Service sources.

An Appeal to the United Nations

It is widely accepted that the U.N. Preventive Force (UNPREDEP) played a crucial role in averting the much-feared spillover of the war from the other republics into Macedonia. Symbolic as that preventive force may have been—no more than 1,000 peacekeepers from the Scandinavian countries and the United States—it nevertheless proved to be an effective deterrent. In particular, the inclusion of U.S. soldiers in UNPREDEP gave a strong signal to Milošević that the United States was committed to preventing a spillover of war. Even though the U.N. mandate was limited to monitoring, reporting, and preventive deployment, and did not include defending Macedonia should Serbian troops invade, over time, Macedonians came to see U.N. peacekeepers as a substitute for the defensive forces they lacked.

Gligorov appealed for a U.N. preventive force as early as December 1991, two months after Macedonia proclaimed independence, in a meeting with U.N. Special Envoy Cyrus Vance. It was a highly volatile time for the country. Yugoslav forces were still stationed in various parts of Macedonia, including Skopje, its capital; images of a war-torn Croatia flashed daily across television screens; tensions ran high as ethnic Albanians, having boycotted the referendum on Macedonian sovereignty, prepared for their own referendum on territorial autonomy. It was widely believed that Macedonia faced the possibility not only of war with Serbia but of secession of its western territory, following the example of Croatia, where ethnic Serbs had seceded by referendum. In a 1997 interview, Gligorov described the thinking behind his appeal to the United Nations in November 1992:

> When the first incidents started in Croatia, and before that in Slovenia, after which in Bosnia, it became obvious to us that there could be a spillover in the southern part of the Balkans as well. That was a signal to us, and made us think of how we could prevent it. We had no army to speak of. All the arms had been taken by the Yugoslav army. We didn't have any neighbors that would help us defend our country. That's when we decided to put forward a proposal before U.N. Secretary-General Boutros Boutros-Ghali. We suggested a preventive mission. (Ackermann and Chatterjee 1997)

Although aware that a U.N. preventive force could not defend the country, Gligorov recognized its deterrent potential: "Merely their presence in Macedonia, especially the American participation . . . was a signal enough for all future aggressors telling them who will be awaiting them should they decide to cross the border" (Ackermann and Chatterjee 1997). Although U.N. troops were never put to the test at Macedonia's borders with Serbia and Albania, their very presence in the country constituted one of the most effective preventive measures against Macedonia's external threat.

DEALING WITH INTERNAL THREATS

One way in which Macedonia addressed its ethnic problems—particularly those with ethnic Albanians but also those with ethnic Serbs—was through political accommodation. Its objective was to move toward integration rather than assimilation as a means of preventing violent challenge to the government from within. Political accommodation was exercised by including ethnic Albanians in the government, by permitting the formation of ethnic Albanian political parties, and by implementing certain cultural and language rights. Of particular concern to the government in those first two years of independence was not only that the ethnic Albanians sought more concessions than it could then grant, but also that it ran the risk of alienating the more nationalist Slavic Macedonians in granting any concessions at all. One of the most influential of the nationalist parties was the VMRO, which spared no occasion to accuse the government of making too many concessions to ethnic minorities.

Accommodating the Ethnic Serbs

Although most ethnic tension in Macedonia has emanated from differences between ethnic Albanians and Slavic Macedonians, the concerns of other minorities also required preventive efforts on the part of the political leadership. This was especially the case with ethnic Serbs, who proved to be a destabilizing factor in the early years of Macedonia's independence. Small in number, a mere 44,000 or 2 percent of Macedonia's population, the ethnic Serbian community in Macedonia was never significant enough to constitute the threat to national survival that ethnic Serbians did in Croatia or Bosnia. Nevertheless, in the first three years of independence, Macedonians took the ethnic Serbs' potential for secession and the possibility of Serbian invasion very seriously. Indeed, Serbia made frequent border incursions into Macedonian territory, and Macedonian leaders expressed anxiety over Serbian intentions (Perry 1992, 1996). Several journalistic accounts spoke of "conditions resembling those of Bosnia-Hercegovina and Croatia prior to the outbreak of war there" ("Zum Aufkeimen" 1993, 7).

Among the most widely discussed scenarios was that Milošević might intervene in Macedonia, using the country's ethnic Serb population as a pretext for military action. Belief in such a scenario was fed by the propaganda tactics of the rump Yugoslavia, which referred to the "300,000 Serbs" living in Macedonia

(Perry 1992, 43), a grossly exaggerated number.[7] Reports that ethnic Serbs in Macedonia were being discriminated against also began to appear in Belgrade newspapers, and some ethnic Serbian activists, following the lead of Serbian Radical Party leader Vojislav Šešelj, openly called for creation of an autonomous Serbian region in northern Macedonia (Bugajski 1994, 121–22; Poulton 1995).

Organized into political parties and associations, among them the Democratic Party of Serbs in Macedonia (DPSM) and the Association of Serbs and Montenegrins in Macedonia (ASMM), ethnic Serbian activists were strongest throughout 1992 and 1993, when in various marches and protests, they voiced their grievances, especially about the "violation of their cultural rights" ("Zum Aufkeimen" 1993). They demanded to be explicitly listed in the preamble of the constitution among the other "nationalities"; to have the same rights and privileges as other ethnic groups, especially because in the former Yugoslavia they had held the status of "nation" (*narod*); to be allowed to practice their religion; to be provided with education in the Serbian language; and to have Serbian-language radio and television programming (ICFY Source 1996).

Although these were not unreasonable demands, what alarmed authorities most were a series of actions perceived by non-Serbian Macedonians as provocative and destabilizing. Following the example of ethnic Albanians in Macedonia, ethnic Serbs also boycotted the referendum on sovereignty. They then proceeded, however, to proclaim their own Serbian republic (ICFY Source 1996), hoisting Serbian flags in the town of Kučevište, during New Year's celebrations on January 1, 1993, which led to a clash with police called in to remove the flags. The situation became even more tense the next day, when 500 Serbian activists held a rally and blocked access to the town, claiming that the police had injured 13 of their citizens. Despite efforts to defuse the crisis, DPSM members used the incident to accuse the government of mistreatment and discrimination, even warning that ethnic Serbs would have to make arrangements for "self-protection" (Bugajski 1994, 122; Geroski 1995; Poulton 1995, 76).

By now, it had became obvious to Macedonia's leadership that the ethnic Serbian problem demanded a long-term settlement. To prevent further outbreaks of extreme Serbian nationalism, the Macedonian government and the DPSM leaders agreed to work out their differences in a trilateral forum under the auspices of the Working Group on Ethnic and National Communities and Minorities of the International Conference on the Former Yugoslavia. Ethnic

7. See, for example, the Montenegrin newspaper *Pobjeda* (Victory), February 22, 1992 (Perry 1992, 43). Following Macedonia's declaration of independence in 1991, a Serbian vice prime minister allegedly declared that there were 300,000 ethnic Serbs in Macedonia who were being suppressed (Meier 1991b, 14).

Serbian leaders also signed an agreement with the Macedonian government granting them constitutional recognition as a minority, more media access, and assistance with Serbian-language education in return for halting their agitation against the Macedonian state (ICFY Source 1996).[8]

Since the signing of that agreement in the summer of 1993, there have been no major confrontations between ethnic Serbians and the authorities in Macedonia. Minor irritations persist largely expressed as strongly worded attacks on Macedonia's foreign policy course and on the government's alleged repression of ethnic Serbs in Macedonia.[9] For example, in 1995, when the Macedonian government refused to consider a DPSM-sponsored plan to provide a refuge for Krajina Serbs in the predominantly ethnic Serbian northern part of Macedonia, DPSM leader Dragisa Miletic accused officials of "operating under the directives from the U.S., Turkey and Germany." In the past, Miletic called Macedonia the "Former Yugoslav Republic of Macedonia" instead of using its constitutional name, the Republic of Macedonia. Moreover, he once accused the government of allowing "the Muslim religion and Fundamentalism to penetrate into the Balkans and Europe" because of its cordial relations with Turkey ("We Do Not Guarantee Safety" 1995, 1–2).

Accommodating the Ethnic Albanians

The ethnic Albanian problem has been much more difficult to manage than any other minority problem in Macedonia. One reason for this is the long-standing discrimination that ethnic Albanians experienced under the Tito regime, which prohibited all forms of Albanian nationalism. Discrimination against ethnic Albanians also flared up again during the 1980s, particularly in Kosovo, where the Serbian government cracked down on Albanians, and then once more in 1990 when it dissolved the Kosovo Assembly. Even in Macedonia during the 1980s, discrimination against Albanians was widespread and many of Macedonia's ethnic Albanian intellectuals moved to Kosovo (Milcin 1996).

8. An ICFY source noted that Serbia's President Milošević was displeased with the ethnic Serb demand to be recognized as a "minority" because ethnic Serbs had traditionally held the status of "nation" (*narod*).

9. There were a few minor outbreaks of anti-NATO, anti-American sentiments by Macedonian Serbs when NATO air strikes began in late March 1999. One occurred on March 25 when Serb Macedonians, accompanied by non-Serb sympathizers threw stones and fire bombs at the U.S. embassy in Skopje and tried to destroy cars belonging to the OSCE and other international agencies. Ethnic Serbs also staged protests and demonstrations, and there were isolated attacks on British and French NATO soldiers. NATO's French contingent was stationed in the Kumanovo area, which has an ethnic Serb majority (Stanley 1999, A8).

Another reason is that ethnic Albanians and Slavic Macedonians have distinctly different cultures, which center primarily around religion and language but also on a distinct way of life. Although these cultural differences are less clearly visible in Skopje, they can be readily seen in the predominantly ethnic Albanian cities, towns, and villages of western Macedonia, most notably in the city of Tetovo, and in the towns of Gostivar and Debar along the border with Albania, where they express themselves in dress, social norms, language, religion, and architecture.

Although relations between ethnic Albanians and Slavic Macedonians remain strained even eight years after independence, and although some observers speak of a growing polarization, it must be emphasized that much of the prevention of violent conflict has come as a result of the willingness of both sides to pursue dialogue, to remain moderate, and to abstain from extreme nationalist rhetoric that could incite violence. Moreover, leaders on both sides have nurtured a careful balance of power. As long as ethnic Albanians voice their demands for "access" to the system (Gurr 1994, 1995), that is, power sharing and political, cultural, and economic rights, rather than secession, the likelihood of violence is reduced.

Even before independence, the Macedonian government opted for a policy of accommodation and political dialogue as far as ethnic Albanians were concerned. In the 1990 elections, it permitted the formation of ethnic Albanian political parties, all of which had specific ethnic agendas, some more outspoken on Albanian territorial autonomy than others. Formed in April 1990 with a platform calling for constitutional changes, educational rights, the use of Albanian in public life, and an end to all discrimination, the Party for Democratic Prosperity (PPD) became the largest ethnic Albanian party. Also constituted in 1990, the National Democratic Party (NPD) entered into a coalition with the PPD in the 1990 elections. Much more openly outspoken and radical on Albanian territorial autonomy and Albanian rights, the NPD went as far as to advocate federalization of Macedonia and creation of a binational state. A few smaller ethnic Albanian parties were also founded, such as the Republican Party (RP), which included Albanian intellectuals and which tried not to be ethnically based, and the Albanian Democratic Union (ADU-LP), which distanced itself from the more radical positions of the NPD and the PPD.

In February 1994, during the second emergency congress of the PPD in Tetovo, the party split into two factions—a moderate and a more radical faction—and for a while there were two PPDs in existence. Although both parties considered themselves to be the legitimate heirs to the old PPD, the more moderate wing of the PPD, under Xheladin Murati, remained as part of the government coalition. Murati was later replaced by Abdurrahman Aliti, who continues as leader of the party. The "new PPD" named itself first the "Party for Democratic Prosperity of Albanians," (PPDsh), and later the "Democratic Party of the Albanians" (PDsh), whose leader, Arbën Xhaferi, a former journalist in Priština, maintains close links with Albanian leaders from Kosovo and Albania (Bugajski 1994; Poulton 1995).

Political dialogue and accommodation have not always come easily, however. A series of incidents made the government question the intentions of ethnic Albanians and their political leaders. Among the most serious was the refusal of ethnic Albanians to participate in the referendum on independence in September 1991. Instead, ethnic Albanians held their own referendum on January 11–12, 1992, called for and organized by the NPD. Interpreting this referendum as the first step toward secession, Macedonian officials declared it illegal. At the time, the Council of Albanian Political Parties, an umbrella organization of ethnic Albanians throughout the former Yugoslavia, responded to the incident by declaring that, if their political and cultural rights could not be obtained through the political process, autonomy was the only option for ethnic Albanians in Macedonia (Schmidt 1995).

Ethnic Albanians were further discredited by their boycott of the 1991 census and the referendum on the new Macedonian constitution in November 1991 and by their contesting the 1994 census, which had been monitored by the United Nations and the Council of Europe. Twenty-three ethnic Albanian parliamentarians walked out of the parliamentary session over their dissatisfaction with the new constitution, which Albanians argued offered them less in terms of group status and collective rights than the 1974 Yugoslav constitution had (Xhaferi 1995). They objected in particular to the preamble, which declared: "Macedonia is established as a national state of the Macedonian people, in which full equality as citizens and permanent co-existence with the Macedonian people is provided for Albanians, Turks, Vlachs, Romanies and other nationalities living in the Republic of Macedonia." The Macedonian government argued at the time that the preamble also spoke of "the guaranteeing of human rights, citizens' freedoms and ethnic equality," and that the constitution was directed, not at the Macedonian nation, but at all "citizens of the Republic," regardless of ethnic background. Nevertheless, because it reflects the broader struggle of ethnic Albanians over achieving the status of "nation" in Macedonia, the debate continues.

Also problematic was the proclamation of the "Republic of Ilrida" in April 1992 in the town of Struga, on Lake Ohrid, only a few kilometers from the Albanian border. Although clearly the action of a handful of ethnic Albanian extremists, it triggered concern among the Macedonian government and the more moderate leaders of the PPD because the "republic" comprised all of western Macedonia (Poulton 1995, 190).

Then, on November 6, 1992, ethnic Albanians clashed with Macedonian police in Skopje's bazaar area, Bit Pazar, which led to a demonstration by thousands of ethnic Albanians in Skopje, then escalated into a riot, in which three ethnic Albanians and one Slavic Macedonian were killed. The Macedonian government claimed the incident had been provoked by Serbian agents—a popular explanation in the early years of independence when Macedonians still feared Serbian intervention (Bugajski 1994, 109; Poulton 1995, 190–91).

On November 17, 1993, tensions between ethnic Albanians and Slavic Macedonians rose again with the discovery of an alleged conspiracy involving two ethnic Albanian government officials, Deputy Minister of Health Imer Imeri and Deputy Minister of Defense Hisen Haskaj. Initial newspaper reports claimed that the two deputy ministers were part of a group of 10 ethnic Albanians who were trying to establish a paramilitary force—referred to as the "All-Albanian Army"—in Macedonia. Moreover, it was alleged that 300 weapons and a recruiting list of 20,000 ethnic Albanians had been found. The government played down the event when it was revealed that the paramilitary force was intended as a defensive unit, to be mobilized in the event of a Serbian attack on Macedonia, rather than as a destabilizing force against the Macedonian state. President Gligorov further defused tensions by contacting the Albanian president to clarify alleged reports that the paramilitary force had the support of Albania (Ackermann 1996, 412; Bugajski 1994, 190; Perry 1994, 84; Schmidt 1995, 26–27). The 10 accused ethnic Albanians were sentenced in June 1994 to 5 to 7 years in prison, but were granted amnesty or released on probation by August 1995 (Human Rights Watch 1996, 44–45). Although Macedonian nationalists have used these incidents to demonstrate that the government's policy of political accommodation is misguided, authorities have resisted pressure to curtail ethnic Albanian rights. Instead, the government has sought to expand these rights gradually, although not to the extent that ethnic Albanians demand.

In addition to permitting the formation of ethnic Albanian political parties and maintaining open dialogue even in times of crises, Macedonia has also opted for power sharing. In the first government, constituted after the 1990 elections, there were 5 ethnic Albanian ministers in the government and ethnic Albanian parliamentarians held 23 seats out of a total of 120 (Perry 1992, 16). Following the 1994 elections, there were 4 ethnic Albanians in the cabinet, including the minister for culture and the minister for labour and social policy. Despite losses at the polls, the Alliance for Macedonia continued its coalition partnership with the PPD. And despite the political crisis of early 1996, 4 ethnic Albanian ministers, 5 ethnic Albanian deputy ministers, and 18 ethnic Albanian members of parliament remained in power (Republic of Macedonia Secretariat of Information 1996). Nevertheless, ethnic Albanian leaders continue to complain that such power sharing does not meet their demands for greater political participation and representation.

The government has also accommodated most of the demands of ethnic Albanians on language and educational issues, such as the right to ethnic newspapers and television programs. For example, in 1996, the state-operated Macedonian television had three-hour daily programs in the Albanian language on the station's second channel, which also broadcasts in the other minority languages—Turkish, Romany, Vlach, and Serbian. Of the 29 municipal radio stations, at least 7 broadcast Albanian-language programs for 6 hours a day (Human Rights Watch 1996, 50). Also, since May 1994, the Albanian newspaper *Flaka e vëllazërimit* (Flame of brotherhood), which previously had been published only three times a week became a daily newspaper, with the financial support of the Macedonian government.

Attempts were also made to remedy some of the grievances ethnic Albanians have regarding professional advancement, as noted in chapter 3. Much of the underrepresentation of ethnic Albanians continues to be in political, legal, and administrative positions, as well as in the police and military forces. Although official numbers are difficult to obtain, and may not necessarily reflect accurately the current situation because each ethnic group manipulates such data to its advantage, underrepresentation continues to plague interethnic relations (Human Rights Watch 1996; Rubin 1996). Whereas the Ministry of Defense has apparently made some progress toward hiring more ethnic Albanians as civilian employees,—ethnic Albanians are said to represent between 16 and 22 percent of its civilian work force—the Ministry of Foreign Affairs and the Ministry of Internal Affairs have yet to correct their ethnic imbalances (Human Rights Watch 1996; Rubin 1996). Some of the underrepresentation in these government positions, however, may be explained in part by the lack of higher education among ethnic Albanians: fewer Albanian than Macedonian students attend secondary schools and universities.

Two serious controversies continue to affect interethnic relations. One is the issue of the Albanian-language university in Tetovo, which has not been resolved despite pressures by the OSCE high commissioner. Here, the Macedonian government has been absolutely unbending because of the wider fear that recognizing such a university would lead to the establishment of parallel institutions in Macedonia. Instead, the government has come up with compromise solutions. One has been to implement a 10 percent quota system for ethnic Albanian students seeking admission into Macedonian universities, which in 1996 was replaced with a separate quota for each minority, the percentages of which are determined by the census data on each minority. According to one source, the proportion of enrolled ethnic Albanian students has more than quadrupled (from 1.3 percent to 9.7 percent) in the last three years (Rubin 1996,

64).[10] A second compromise has been to reopen the Pedagogical Faculty at the St. Cyril and Methodius University in Skopje and to upgrade its Albanian-language program from a two-year to a four-year curriculum. But this is not an acceptable compromise to the de facto rector of the illegal Tetovo University and PPD leader Arbën Xhaferi, who perceive an Albanian-language university not only as the center for Albanian learning but also for Albanian culture. Xhaferi, in particular, pointed out that ethnic Albanians in Macedonia lack their own cultural center, and an Albanian-language university could provide such a cultural base.

The government's compromise solutions have been challenged not only by ethnic Albanian leaders but also by Slavic Macedonians, especially those from a younger generation. After the faculty filed a lawsuit to overturn the 1995 decision by Minister of Education Emilija Simovska that it provide teachers' training in the Albanian and Macedonian languages, Macedonia's National Assembly passed the Law on the Use of the Languages at the Pedagogical Faculty on January 30, 1997, mandating that teacher training could proceed also in the Albanian language (Perry 1997). PPD and PPDsh parliamentarians opposed the law (Foreign Broadcast Information Service 1997e), perhaps because of the still-unresolved Tetovo University issue, whose support by ethnic Albanians might be undermined with an alternative educational option.

Already in early January 1997, Slavic Macedonian university students protested the draft legislation. Demonstrations continued, including the boycott of university seminars, as the National Assembly deliberated on the new legislation. On February 17, the day the law was adopted, more than 3,000 Slavic Macedonian students demonstrated in Skopje, many of whom shouted anti-Albanian slogans. Their ranks were joined by Slavic Macedonian students from secondary schools, who demonstrated in several Macedonian cities and towns, including Skopje, Bitola, and Tetovo. By early March, a group of 15 students went on a hunger strike demanding the resignation of Minister of Education Todorova and the repeal of the law (FBIS 1997f, 1997g; "Law on the Pedagogical Faculty" 1997; Moore 1997; Schmidt 1997). Although the crisis eventually was brought under control by late March—after having caused

10. Rubin notes here the discrepancies in the number of ethnic Albanian students attending university. He quotes the Macedonian prime minister as stating that not even 3 percent of the 10 percent quota have been filled. On the other hand, an issue of the daily newspaper *Nova Makedonija* (New Macedonia) cited the following numbers in February 1997: for 1992–93, 4 percent; for 1994–95, 6.5 percent; for 1995–96, 7.93 percent; for 1996–97, 7.3 percent. Again, these numbers may be inaccurate because they were published at the height of student protests over the language law at the Pedagogical Faculty (Foreign Broadcast Information Service 1997d).

considerable concern among EU member states and the OSCE high commissioner, who visited the country twice in March—it demonstrated that interethnic relations continue to be fragile and can be easily exploited by Slavic Macedonian and ethnic Albanian nationalist groups (FBIS 1997b).

Most ethnic Albanian leaders feel that improvements have not gone far enough or made enough difference in the lives of many ethnic Albanians in Macedonia. Ibrahimi has noted that power sharing in government does not address the more widespread underrepresentation of ethnic Albanians in other professions and in the university system, and that, despite power sharing, ethnic Albanian parliamentarians are always outvoted in the National Assembly. This is the case in other political systems where ethnic parties organize along ethnic issues, that is, single issues, rather than along multiple issue agendas, which attract a wider, more diversified constituency. Ethnic Albanian leaders blame the present government, and especially President Gligorov for the slow progress in meeting some of their demands. Like other ethnic Albanian politicians, Xhaferi insists that the group rights ethnic Albanians seek "are not extreme, nationalist, or chauvinist," but "conform to international conventions," and are inherited from the former Yugoslavia (Ackermann and Chatterjee 1997). Xhaferi has offered his own interpretation as to why the government has not been as forthcoming as it might: it has failed to adopt a new value system and therefore remained essentially communist in its core structure (Xhaferi 1995, 1996b). Gligorov has met these charges by emphasizing that, because Macedonia is a multiethnic democracy and therefore must ensure that all ethnic groups have equal representation and access to the political system, only a gradual approach will lead to the requested changes:

> It's not possible to implement overnight a maximization program because there are other politicial entities in the country that have to accept those solutions. Two-thirds of the population in Macedonia are [Slavic] Macedonians, and one-third consists of all the [other] ethnic groups together. Therefore, if you want to improve some of the ethnic rights, then you have to convince the [Slavic] Macedonian population that that is good, and that it is to the benefit of the country and of the [Slavic] Macedonians as a nation. All this requires time, preparation, argumentation, patience. (Ackermann and Chatterjee 1997)

More liberal observers have agreed that Gligorov walks a fine line between conservative forces, who resist granting ethnic Albanians additional rights, and ethnic Albanian leaders, who remain dissatisfied with the improvements in political and cultural rights.

But despite the grievances, protests, boycotts, and the constant rhetoric that not enough is being done to advance ethnic Albanian rights and status in Macedonia, or that Macedonia still lacks democratic institutions and procedures, ethnic Albanian leaders understand their own role and responsibility in the prevention of violence. They are therefore careful not to upset the delicate communal balance and to maintain the dialogue, even though they continue to complain about the inadequacy of measures. As Ibrahimi puts it:

> I think we have been lucky to establish this country without any conflict at all. And the contributions of [the ethnic] Albanians were a huge part because we know that we can talk to each other. The dialogue is going on in Macedonia. That is our priority. We respect each other, but the promises that are given are not realized. It was always said that things would be realized step by step but unfortunately there's still not a real democracy here. But we have continued to preserve the peace. If we have not learnt the lessons from Bosnia-Hercegovina then we are illiterate. (Ibrahimi 1996b)

Thus far, the delicate political balance between the two groups remains intact despite protests, antigovernment rhetoric, and incidents of sporadic violence. Even ethnic Albanian leaders like Xhaferi do not endorse a violent approach to bring about their demands. Indeed, Xhaferi himself, who does not pass up any opportunity to criticize the Macedonian government, has retreated from his earlier position on territorial autonomy and speaks now in the language of seeking cultural autonomy, or to use his words, "internal self-determination" for ethnic Albanians in Macedonia.

Other ethnic Albanians have pointed to their own responsible behavior, to their understanding that ethnic violence could have triggered a wider Balkan conflict, as the principal reason there was no war in Macedonia. Remaining critical of the government and outspoken about its unfulfilled promises, as most ethnic Albanian leaders are, Ibrahimi expressed a widely held view: "We [the Albanian politicians] followed the policy of Mister Gligorov because dialogue and peaceful politics are much, much better than any other politics with conflicts and wars. We [the Albanians] said that it is much better to use words and the head than to use bullets and remain without a head" (Ibrahimi 1996b).

In a 1997 interview for the Skopje-based ethnic Albanian newspaper *Flaka e vëllazërimit,* Abdurrahman Aliti, the chairman of the PPD, emphasized the heavy responsibility of his party in the power-sharing arrangement, despite "all that has happened to the Albanians lately." Remaining in the coalition was crucial because it "is the only road and there is no other alternative", and that "the participation of the PPD . . . signifies the carrying on of a dialogue" (FBIS 1997a).[11]

Curbing Macedonian nationalism. Slavic Macedonian nationalism also posed a major challenge to the new government, and, as in the case of the ethnic minorities, required a preventive response as well. There were several ways in which the nationalist challenge was met. Efforts were made to reduce the popular appeal of nationalist parties, most of which were anti-Communist, anti-Serbian, anti-Albanian, and pro-independence; to keep extreme nationalist rhetoric out of the political debates; and finally, to downplay national history and popular appeals to myths as much as possible. The objective became to lift Macedonia out of past Balkan history by grounding it firmly in a new image—a Macedonia that was part of a new European structure. President Gligorov and some of the younger members of his Cabinet, such as Prime Minister Branko Crvenkovski and Foreign Minister Ljubomir Frčkovski played a vital role in reshaping the country's self-image.

There was considerable concern that extreme nationalism would not only invite Serbian aggression but also destabilize the country from within. To stem nationalist sentiments that had the potential to escalate into extreme positions—and that had escalated into war in the other republics of Yugoslavia—Macedonia again chose a more balanced approach.

The VMRO. Several nationalist parties surfaced on the scene in 1990 as the Yugoslav republics moved toward their first multiparty elections. In Macedonia, a number of nationalist parties were founded, all of which openly advocated Macedonian independence. These included the Movement for Pan-Macedonian Action (MPMA), created by Macedonian intellectuals in February 1990, under the leadership of Gane Todorovski and Ante Popovski; the Internal Macedonian Revolutionary Organization–Democratic Party for Macedonian National Unity (VMRO), under the leadership of Ljupco Georgievski, formerly a member of the MPMA, who was elected chairman in April 1991; and the Internal Macedonian Revolutionary Organization–Democratic Party (VMRO-DP),

11. Elections in October and November 1998 yielded a victory for a coalition consisting of VMRO, the Democratic Party (DP), and the PPDsh (renamed the PDsh in October 1998). As of November 19, 1998, when the new legislature was constituted, the PPD, along with the SDSM, became an opposition party. The coalition has brought two former nationalist party leaders to the forefront of Macedonian political life, VMRO's leader, Ljubco Georgievski, who became the new Macedonian prime minister, and PPDsh leader Arbën Xhaferi. Kiro Gligorov remains in office as Macedonia's president until the fall 1999 presidential elections.

founded in Ohrid in January 1991, and chaired by its founder, Vladimir Golubovski, who had left VMRO because of political and personal differences (Bugajski 1994).

All these parties were also anti-Albanian in outlook. All indulged in nationalist propaganda at a time when Yugoslavia was beginning to be torn apart by nationalist rhetoric. For example, in November 1990, MPMA advocated banning Albanian parties, which it viewed as a threat to Slavic Macedonians; it made particular reference to the growing Albanianization of the western part of the country. Before the elections in November 1990, MPMA, VMRO, and a number of other smaller nationalist parties formed the so-called Front for Macedonian Unity in an attempt to obtain a bloc of seats in Macedonia's National Assembly, and thus defeat the Reform Communists and the ethnic Albanian parties.

But only the VMRO obtained seats. Established in June 1990, the party had emerged as the last of 17 political parties in Macedonia. Taking its name from a nineteenth-century national liberation movement that fought for independence against Turkish rule, the VMRO claimed to be the party with "the longest tradition in Macedonia."

It was hardly surprising that the VMRO's political agenda took a less conciliatory approach toward the central government in Belgrade. It openly promoted independence for Macedonia and the withdrawal of the Yugoslav National Army (Georgievski 1996a, 1996b). In its first party resolution, the VMRO also called for a united Macedonia, which included parts of other countries but which was to be achieved by political means (Dimovska 1995). Not only did these objectives make more moderate Macedonian politicians nervous; they were viewed by Greece as intolerable irredentist designs on its northern province. Macedonia's adoption of national symbols—such as the Star of Vergina on the Macedonian flag, allegedly made as a concession to the VMRO—set the government on a collision course with Greece (Maleski 1996).

In the 1990 elections, the VMRO won 37 seats out of the 120 available in the National Assembly, the largest number won by any party, but not enough to form a government. Liberal forces were fearful that appointing a nationalist president in Macedonia would dangerously increase tensions between the leaders of the various republics and the Serbian government. In a negotiated agreement, the National Assembly appointed Gligorov as president and Georgievski as vice president. Shortly after the 1990 elections, however, mounting differences between the VMRO's agenda and that of the government caused Georgievski to resign as vice president (he would unsuccessfully run for president in the 1994 elections).

Despite Georgievski's appointment as vice president, the VMRO continued to advance its disruptive agenda, becoming a political liability for the "government of experts" that had been formed in 1992. At its congress in Prilep in April 1991, before Macedonia's independence referendum, the VMRO called for an independent Macedonia and for the creation of a Macedonian national army. These were dangerous statements at a time when Macedonia and Bosnia-Hercegovina were still acting as mediators for a compromise solution to avert armed confrontation between Serbia and Croatia. There was also considerable concern that VMRO might use militant tactics to gain independence from Yugoslavia because of the party's success in invoking the image of Macedonian heroes, such as Goce Delčev, a leader in the Macedonian struggle for liberation against the Turks in the late nineteenth and early twentieth century.

Georgievski later justified his party's more impatient stance toward independence, noting that in 1990 and the early months of 1991, the VMRO believed that the breakup of Yugoslavia would proceed peacefully, on the basis of a negotiated settlement, and that because there was already a growing trend toward independence in Slovenia and Croatia, the time had also come to establish an independent Macedonia. Unlike more moderate forces in Macedonia, Georgievski did not fear an open confrontation with Belgrade, believing that there would not be a war. The answer to the question, whether the VMRO would have used violence to secede from Yugoslavia, as in the case of Croatia, was left deliberately vague by Georgievski in a 1996 interview:

> At the time there was no perception that there would be a war in Yugoslavia. The greatest danger was with the secession of Croatia and Slovenia. There was the possibility then that Macedonia would exist in a mini-federation. That was going to be the worst form of an ex-Yugoslavia. VMRO did not want a mini-federation. At the time we were ready for everything although our energies were all directed towards government and with great pressure we managed to change the attitudes of all parties—the ones who had been previously opposed to independence. (Georgievski 1996a)

Although this statement might indicate the VMRO's readiness to use violence against Serbia if necessary, Georgievski also pointed to the VMRO's and to his own role in having chosen to cooperate with the Macedonian government's preventive course of action:

> It was a fact that all political parties in Macedonia starting from the most radical, which at the time was us, and all the way to the most moderate, insisted upon a peaceful way of leaving the former Yugoslavia; and even more important, not one political party engaged in a radical incident to provoke the former Yugoslav Army. (Georgievski 1996b)

Whatever the VMRO's past rhetoric, the party has reinvented itself as centrist, comparing itself to other European conservative parties. Before the October and November 1998 elections bringing VMRO into office, it was the largest opposition party in Macedonia, running a barrage of attacks on the government for its poor economic performance and corruption, and insisting that the democratic process had come to a halt because communists remained in office and the number of political parties had drastically shrunk (Georgievski 1996a, 1996b; Moore 1998). The VMRO also continued to fly Macedonia's old flag because it regarded the new flag as a forced concession to Greece, made under duress and without a referendum of the Macedonian people (Georgievski 1996b).

That Georgievski has moved the VMRO away from its more nationalist image is the result, according to some observers, of the positive influence of the United States—which Georgievski allegedly has visited several times. There is considerable agreement, however, that the VMRO leaders have acted responsibly to preserve peace despite their nationalist ambitions. As one well-respected Macedonian journalist noted:

> If VMRO nationalists were more militant, they could have raised a war in this country because until 1992, the [YNA], the former Yugoslav army, were still here. There was war in Croatia, and the war started in Bosnia. It was a very tense situation here in Macedonia. I think that nationalists in VMRO were aware of the situation and they were responsible enough not to take any provocative action; and that was the big difference between Macedonia and Croatia, for example. The war in Croatia started with provocative action against the [YNA]. (Geroski 1996)

Forgetting history, moving toward Europe. Most states, whether old or newly emerging, resort to history to legitimize their existence as an independent entity and their right to claim territorial space as a nation. Much of that history is passed down and disseminated through historical myths, which emphasize the role of national heroes, cultural superiority, or other self-glorifying attributes in the making of the nation. Political elites often resort to the use of what are mostly distorted historical myths to stir up nationalist sentiments and obtain broad-based popular support for nationalist causes. Although appeals to a nation's history and myths do not necessarily lead to violence, "chauvinist mythmaking" through "self-glorifying, self-whitewashing, and other-maligning" are the forms of nationalism most likely to cause war (Van Evera 1994).

What can also be regarded as a significant preventive measure in the case of Macedonia is the political leaders' refusal to resort to such excessive mythmaking and glorification of past history. Indeed, in view of Macedonia's bloody history and the persistent Western image of the Balkans as a violent region, deliberate efforts were taken not to appeal to myths and to psychologize history. Macedonia's politicians witnessed the consequences of resorting to chauvinist mythmaking on the part of Croatian and Serbian leaders, especially Milošević. Shrewdly "commandeering the historical language of Serb nationalism from the anticommunists, Milošević found a language to overcome the problem of opposing a state that nationalists in other republics propagandized as Serbia. This language was the Serbian myth of victimization: the defeat of the medieval Serb empire by the Ottomans on the 'field of blackbirds' (Kosovo in 1389)" (Woodward 1995, 92).

Attempts to capitalize on a self-glorifying history of Macedonians as a superior nation could have led to ethnic violence in the multiethnic republic, especially if ethnic Albanians had resorted to the same tactics. Mindful of the need to unify their country, the Macedonian leadership has made every effort to build civic and not ethnic nationalism, with much emphasis placed on using political language reflecting that goal.

Some commentators have pointed out that the Macedonians as a people—rather than as different ethnic groups—have shared the same geographic space for many generations. According to this view, "We lack these myths that the Serbians have. Granted there is Alexander the Great, but that is not a myth [for us], that is, something that the majority has no affiliation with" (Milcin 1996).

That Macedonians do not look upon themselves as "warriors," that Slavic Macedonians and ethnic Albanians have no traumatic history of violent conflict, and that Macedonia has been dominated by outside forces for centuries might also explain why there are so few myths that political elites could have exploited. Slavic Macedonians and ethnic Albanians alike present themselves as peaceful people, although each group also claims to be more peaceful than the other. Indeed, many of those we interviewed believed that the principal reason there was no war in Macedonia was the very peacefulness of the Macedonian character, a belief shared by a keen observer of Macedonian society, Vladimir Milcin:

> I think that Macedonia is not a typical Balkan country in one [respect]. The idea that we are warriors is not so strong here [as] in other Balkan states. Perhaps this comes from history. All the Balkans have some medieval hero and some medieval state. The Macedonians do not have that memory. The idea of [identifying with] Alexander the Great is very new and it is much more popular in Greece than in Macedonia. It is not part of the collective memory. (Milcin 1996)

Forgetting history may well be part of the strategy that the government has chosen to transform Macedonia into a truly European state. "As a matter of fact," noted Milcin, the government does not include people who care for history. For example, when the government made the treaty with Serbia, it asked the Serbian government to only recognize Macedonia from 1944 onward. So they were trying not to push the issue [of history] at all" (Milcin 1996).

President Gligorov has set much of the tone for leaving history out of public discourse and not offering it a place in discussions on the future of the country:

> There is a big danger of history being abused. We know that France, Germany, and Britain and other countries had problems with each other for a couple of centuries. Today they are working together towards improving their neighborly relations. This does not mean that they do not have any problems or crises—but through negotiations the goal of having an European union is being realized step by step. It is the same situation in the Balkans. I don't think a Frenchman or a German or an Englishman need to forget his history but [he has] to see the good things in that history and not dwell only on the negatives. They have to work together. They have to use these good things from history—in the sciences, in schools, in education, and not in everyday politics. (Ackermann and Chatterjee 1997)

Moving toward a more European outlook and identity through association with European institutions has been one way to prevent the emergence of a strong nationalist identity in Macedonia. Gligorov is optimistic that the problem of "renationalization" can only be resolved by associating the Balkan countries with Europe and by integrating them into the European Union. Such a process, he explains, will make interethnic conflicts "a relict of the nineteenth century, a superfluous anachronism" (Reuter 1995, 512).

In conclusion, one can only hope that President Gligorov will be proven correct by future Balkan history. What this chapter has demonstrated however is that political and ethnic leaders have played a critical role in preventing conflicts from becoming violent in Macedonia—be it by accommodative behavior and dialogue, or by abstaining from mythmaking, the misuse of history, or other extreme expressions for the sake of collective mobilization. The next three chapters will explore how third parties have been equally important in keeping Macedonia on a peaceful path.

5

THE PREVENTIVE ROLE OF INTERNATIONAL ORGANIZATIONS

THE FAILURE OF the international community to prevent the war either in Croatia or in Bosnia led to a more concerted engagement of international and regional organizations to avert a spillover of violence into the former Yugoslav Republic of Macedonia. A war in Macedonia and in neighboring Kosovo, it was argued, could easily escalate into a wider regional conflict, involving Serbia, Albania, Greece, Bulgaria, and even Turkey.

Speculation that war would next consume Macedonia was widespread between late 1991 to 1994.[1] Having one significantly large minority group, Macedonia resembled Croatia. And like the ethnic Serbs of Croatia, the ethnic Albanians of Macedonia were largely concentrated in a single geographic region, a circumstance many feared would encourage secession.[2] Moreover, certain factions among ethnic Albanians and ethnic Serbs in Macedonia had proclaimed their own independent "republics," although "republics" served more as rhetorical tools for collective mobilization than as ends in themselves. And finally, Macedonia had a strongly pro-independence and anti-Albanian nationalist movement.

1. Many European and U.S. newspapers predicted the imminent outbreak of violent conflict in Macedonia. See, for example, Borger and Smith 1994, 6; Glenny 1993, A27; Judah 1992, 12; Schleicher 1993, 6; Tanner 1992, 10. As late as 1995, Misha Glenny prophesized that "Macedonia is now heading down the same path as Bosnia" (1995b, 99). The Macedonian government was very disturbed by Glenny's *Foreign Affairs* article (ICFY Source 1999).

2. Although ethnic Albanians live primarily in western Macedonia, many municipalities, cities, and towns in western Macedonia have a mixed population of ethnic Albanians, Slavic Macedonians, and other ethnic groups. According to the 1994 census, Skopje's total population is 541,280, of which there are Slavic Macedonians (354,377); ethnic Albanians (112,914); Turks (12,639); Rom (20,966); Vlachs (2,229); Serbs (19,664); and others (17,431) (Republic of Macedonia Statistical Office 1994a, 3).

However, Macedonia differed from Croatia and Bosnia both in the dynamics of conflict and in the responses to it. As noted in chapters 3 and 4, a moderate, pragmatic government willing to accommodate ethnic minority concerns, to practice a moderate foreign policy toward its neighbors, and to take the initiative in obtaining an international preventive force; political and ethnic leaders willing to engage in dialogue and to exercise restraint; the absence of military and paramilitary forces; and the moderating influence exerted by the leaders both of Albania and of the ethnic Albanians in Kosovo on the ethnic Albanians in Macedonia all contributed to prevent the outbreak of interethnic violence in—and the spread of war to—the Republic of Macedonia. Other significant factors on the side of peace were Serbia's becoming militarily bogged down in Bosnia; the small percentage of ethnic Serbs; having more time to respond to certain developments, on the part of both domestic and international actors; and finally, the curbing of nationalism by the Macedonian people, who feared the consequences of another war in the Balkans.

Far from negating the importance of the preventive role of international organizations in Macedonia, these factors demonstrate how essential the linkage between internally generated conditions and international support for nonviolent resolution of conflict was to the success of preventive diplomacy in the Macedonian case. In addition to the OSCE and its high commissioner on national minorities, the Working Group on Ethnic and National Communities and Minorities of the International Conference on the Former Yugoslavia (hereafter "the Working Group") and the United Nations both performed critical preventive roles, although the Working Group's preventive involvement was largely kept from public view. The success of the United Nation's first ever preventive diplomacy mission was all the more significant because of the organization's perceived inability to intervene effectively in ethnic wars.[3]

This chapter explores the role of the two major international actors—the Working Group and the United Nations—in preventing war in Macedonia. It also discusses how the United Nations and the United States helped Macedonia and Greece de-escalate their conflict and resolve their differences.

THE WORKING GROUP AS "SILENT CONTRIBUTOR"

Little public attention has been given to the role of the Working Group—the first international preventive actors to arrive in the country—in preventing conflict in

3. Rieff (1995, 80) speaks of "the complicity of the United Nations in the Serb genocide," and also contends that "UN peacekeeping was an entirely unsuitable instrument for dealing with an ongoing conflict of the kind taking place in Bosnia."

Macedonia.[4] In October 1991, the Working Group began what would become one of the most extensive preventive diplomatic endeavors, lasting nearly five years. Chaired by the German diplomat Geert Ahrens with a mandate by U.N. Secretary General Boutros-Ghali, it relied on three principal preventive devices: frequent visits to Macedonia, personal shuttle diplomacy, and trilateral forums, which functioned much as problem-solving workshops. Playing a prominent, yet low-profile role, the Working Group was highly successful in facilitating political dialogue through its trilateral forums, in which contending groups could voice their grievances and demands. The Working Group considered the principle threats to ethnic peace to be tensions between Slavic Macedonians and ethnic Albanians, on the one hand, and militant ethnic Serbs supported by Belgrade, on the other. But the Working Group also took up the cause of other minorities such as the Turks, the Vlachs, and the Rom, much as a result of compromises struck by the government in providing education and media in the minority languages and in reducing some of the discriminatory practices that had existed under the old regime.

Intensive negotiations yielded several agreements that struck a balance between ethnic Albanian demands and concessions the Macedonian government was willing to make. Under Ahrens's chairmanship, the Working Group also dissuaded the ethnic Albanian minority from seeking territorial autonomy, an action that would most likely have triggered an armed confrontation. Various other preventive initiatives included organizing a census to mitigate the dispute between Slavic Macedonians and ethnic Albanians over population numbers and averting a possible secession of ethnic Serbs from Macedonia.

Until its dissolution in January 1996, following the Dayton Peace Accords on Bosnia, the Working Group cooperated closely with the U.N. Preventive Deployment Force (UNPREDEP) on humanitarian issues and the promotion of dialogue over human and minority rights, and the OSCE spillover mission.[5] It encouraged the Macedonian authorities to adopt new legislation on education and local self-government, for ethnic Albanians and other minorities, and it helped solve problems over minority language and citizenship issues (United Nations, Secretary-General 1996a, 3).

4. There is almost no literature on the Working Group's role in preventive diplomacy in Macedonia. Information on the Working Group presented in this chapter is based on ICFY documents and on a confidential ICFY source I interviewed in the summer of 1996 and again in May 1999.

5. The Working Group worked especially closely with UNPREDEP after it received a political mandate in 1994 expanding its diplomatic tasks to complement those performed by the Working Group, although cooperation primarily involved the exchange of information. Representatives from the OSCE spillover mission were occasionally participants at the trilateral forums organized by the Working Group in Skopje (ICFY Source 1999).

The Working Group came first into existence in October 1991 as an initiative of the Conference on Yugoslavia, which met on September 7, 1991, under the chairmanship of Lord Peter Carrington. Sponsored by the European Community, it convened in The Hague to mediate a comprehensive peace settlement for Yugoslavia. But frustration over the inability to proceed on such a settlement convinced Carrington to opt instead to draft a constitutional arrangement. Disagreement among EC member states as to what form of intervention should be used in Croatia and France's insistence on a stronger U.N. role, however, led to the collapse of the Hague Conference in August 1992. With it the mandate for the Working Group ended as well.

The Working Group was revived in the same month, when the British government called for the establishment of a second international conference on Yugoslavia, which convened on August 27, 1992, in London. The London Conference adopted a list of principles that were to form the basis for a negotiated settlement in Bosnia, including the maintenance of territorial integrity and the protection of minority and human rights. The London Conference created the Working Group on Ethnic and National Communities and Minorities, which dealt with minority issues in, among others, Macedonia, Croatia, Vojvodina, and Sandjak. The Conference also created a special working group on Kosovo.[6] In September, the London Conference also provided for the establishment of a permanent peace conference, the International Conference on the Former Yugoslavia (ICFY).

With its headquarters in Geneva, the ICFY constituted a collective effort between the United Nations and the European Community, with former Secretary of State Cyrus Vance and former British Foreign Minister Lord David Owen representing the two organizations as cochairmen of the conference's Steering Committee. Both men were also responsible for drafting the Vance-Owen Plan from November 1992 to May 1993, a constitutional proposal calling for the division of Bosnia-Hercegovina into ten regions with a central government in Sarajevo. The ICFY's original mandate was to seek a political settlement for all the Yugoslav conflicts, but it soon became a peace conference for Bosnia, given that the two cochairmen concentrated their energies and resources on Bosnia. Many of the minority rights questions were left to the Working Group (Burg 1995; Gaer 1993; ICFY Source 1996, 1999; Owens 1995; Woodward 1995, 179–180).

From the outset, Ahrens adamantly rejected any territorial demands by eth-

6. Lord Owen dissolved the special working group on Kosovo on July 1, 1993, under opposition from steering group representatives. He also repeatedly marginalized the Working Group (ICFY Source 1999).

nic Albanians—whether in the form of autonomy or as a separate state—arguing that the size of Macedonia did not allow for separate territorial arrangements.[7] Its decision to resist territorial division in Macedonia earned the Working Group the respect of the Macedonian government. In return, the authorities agreed to address various minority group demands, which led to some crucial changes in the constitution and to greater access for ethnic minorities to education and the media. To create a neutral environment where political dialogue could be facilitated, the Working Group set up a trilateral framework, a forum composed of ethnic Albanians, government representatives, and Working Group members. The same arrangement was adopted in the case of ethnic Serbs, who also sought to voice their demands and grievances in an internationally sponsored forum.

Mediating Between Ethnic Albanians and the Macedonian Government

The involvement of Macedonia's ethnic Albanian leaders with international actors did not begin with the arrival of the Working Group in Macedonia. Already in January 1992, ethnic Albanian political leaders such as Nevzet Halili of the PPD had approached the Hague Conference to draw attention to the ethnic Albanian minority problem in Macedonia, and if possible, to solicit international support for their cause. At that time, Halili had demanded territorial autonomy for Albanians, either in form of a separate state or as a regional enclave within Macedonia. The Working Group successfully channeled these demands into a diplomatic forum that allowed for constructive political dialogue between the contending parties.

Most problematic were issues that arose out of the anxiety ethnic Albanians felt over their status in a newly independent Macedonia. Acting from that anxiety, ethnic Albanian leaders strongly opposed a sovereign and internationally recognized Macedonia and used different means to avoid that outcome. Halili

7. Macedonia's ethnic Albanians pursued only temporarily the creation of an independent republic, Ilrida. The main task of the Working Group was to convince them not to insist on territorial autonomy. Important was the June 1992 "Lake Ohrid walk" between Geert Ahrens and Nevzet Halili, in which the ethnic Albanian leader gave up the pursuit of territorial autonomy. Ahrens repeatedly told ethnic Albanians that territorial autonomy would affect the capital, Skopje, leading to the creation of the ethnic division of the city similar to the Bosnian city of Mostar, which was divided between Croats and Bosnian Muslims. His many warnings that ethnic Albanians could take Macedonia down the path of Bosnia were depicted in a popular Albanian caricature, showing Ahrens with a blood-stained map, with an Albanian comment: "Look, folks, here I bring you the latest map of the Bosnian war" (ICFY Source 1999).

first tried to convince the Badinter Commission to withdraw its recognition of Macedonia. In a letter submitted to the commission in January 1992, Halili accused the Macedonian government of not having taken necessary action to obtain recognition. In particular, he pointed out that although the Macedonian government had created a council on interethnic relations, it was merely a consultative body, lacking power to pass mandatory decisions. Moreover, only two representatives were members of the various minority nationalities, whereas three members were Slavic Macedonians, including the council's president.

Halili vehemently criticized the Macedonian government for refusing to implement a special status for Albanians, for turning aside ethnic Albanian demands for political and territorial autonomy, and in particular, for obstructing and declaring illegal the referendum held by ethnic Albanians on January 11–12, 1992. Halili described police interference at 260 voting stations, which included confiscation of ballots, and threats against ethnic Albanians and the leaders of Albanian parties. He made much of the fact that the referendum had revealed that the number of ethnic Albanians was much closer to 800,000 than to the official number of 443,000, or 23 percent, given by the Macedonian authorities. He objected to article 48 of the Macedonian constitution, which guaranteed the free expression of national identity, the protection of cultural and religious identity, and the establishment of institutions and associations, but which at the same time restricted the right to education in the Albanian language on the primary and secondary school levels. Ethnic Albanians were also not free to use Albanian national symbols, hence were denied free expression of their national identity. Moreover, ethnic Albanians lacked representation in municipal and local governments, particularly in ethnic Albanian–dominated population centers such as Tetovo and Gostivar, close to the Albanian border. Concluding, Halili emphasized that the Badinter Commission had failed to consult with ethnic Albanians in Macedonia before granting recognition to the country.

Although several of the grievances raised by Halili and other ethnic Albanian leaders were satisfactorily addressed with the assistance of the Working Group, the OSCE, and its high commissioner, a few issues, such as making Albanian an official language or creating an Albanian-language university, remained unresolved and are contentious to this day.

Ethnic Albanian representatives coming before the Working Group proposed that the wording of article 7 of the Macedonian constitution, which mandates the use of the Macedonian language as the official language but which provides for the official use of other languages in addition to Macedonian if there is a majority of inhabitants belonging to that nationality, be changed to explicitly designate the Albanian language and alphabet as also official in areas of local self-government where ethnic Albanians constituted 10 percent or more of the population. Moreover, ethnic Albanians requested that Albanian also be made an official language in the central governmental organs and in those municipalities populated by Albanians. On the use of national symbols, the Macedonian government agreed in 1994 to allow the Albanian flag to be displayed on Albanian national holidays.

In the summer and fall of 1994, the Working Group intervened in the crisis over the breakup of the PPD and the creation of Tetovo University. After the violent episode during the opening ceremonies of the university, the Working Group conducted a series of eleven three-day negotiation meetings, focusing in particular on working out the law on local self-government, which would also regulate the use of the Albanian language. Much of the discussions with respect to Tetovo University, which continued throughout 1995, were conducted in the trilateral forum and focused on two options: Did ethnic Albanians want a private university, or were they willing to accept an Albanian-language university within the public educational system? Speaking for the government, the Macedonian education minister argued that the distinctiveness of "nations" in Macedonia was not in question, but that there should not be a total separation, which was likely to happen if the entire educational structure was divided into separate instruction in the minority languages. Arbën Xhaferi, representing an ethnic Albanian faction that strongly supported a separate university, replied that the integration of an Albanian-language university was to be preferred over a private one, but that ethnic Albanians were driven into the direction of the latter because the Macedonian government failed to develop a greater understanding of the need ethnic Albanians have for higher education.

Little progress was made toward resolving the dispute over Tetovo University, and the issue remains one of the most confrontational, dividing ethnic Albanians and Slavic Macedonians to this day. Moreover, with the dissolution of the Working Group in early 1996, there has been no neutral forum to work out the existing differences and opinions on the dispute.

Census of 1994

Because population statistics were often "abused" in the political struggle over demands, particularly when it came to territorial autonomy, and because ethnic Albanians had boycotted the 1991 census, Ambassador Ahrens suggested that a new, internationally monitored census be conducted. The new census would obtain accurate numbers on the ethnic Albanian population, some of whose leaders claimed that they represented between 30 and 40 percent of the population, thus were entitled to the status of "nation," and on the ethnic Serbian population, whose leaders also inflated their numbers to justify their pursuit of an independent republic.

To assure that the census would be acceptable to the leaders of all the ethnic groups, Ahrens proposed that it be conducted by an international expert group of the Council of Europe. Under the directorship of Werner Haug from the Swiss Statistical Office, the census was carried out in the summer of 1994 with the financial support of the EU. To assure universal participation in the census, Ahrens relied on his personal diplomatic skills, visiting as many as 24 different counties, including 5 in Skopje, to talk to ethnic Albanians and to convince them to participate in the census. Although the Working Group left the organizing of the census to other international agencies, such as the Council of Europe and the OSCE, it played an influential role in making the new census acceptable to the Macedonian government and the ethnic Albanian leaders.

Mediating Between Ethnic Serbs and the Macedonian Government

The Working Group's other major objective was to defuse the crisis with Macedonia's ethnic Serbian population. Although ethnic Serbs in Macedonia did not constitute a numerically significant minority, the Serbian community was politically organized in the Democratic Party of Serbs in Macedonia (DPSM). The first round of negotiations between representatives of the Working Group, the Serbian party leadership, and the Macedonian government began in 1992. The Working Group's characteristic trilateral forum was also adopted to mediate the ethnic Serbian conflict. Even though the ethnic Serbs in Macedonia seemed less inclined to resort to violence, there was considerable concern over the possibility of internal unrest, especially if Serbia were to provide organizational support.

Indeed, much of the anxiety over ethnic Serbian intentions was driven by allegations that the Democratic Party of Serbs in Macedonia was receiving support from Belgrade. Moreover, that nationalist ethnic Serbs in Macedonia had proclaimed a Serbian republic—with its own constitution—and had engaged in a series of provocative incidents was viewed by Skopje as alarming evidence that ethnic Serbs in Macedonia were stirring up interethnic trouble as a pretext for Belgrade's intervention.[8]

The Working Group set out to defuse this potentially explosive situation. As in its mediation with the Albanians, the group asked ethnic Serb leaders to voice their demands in trilateral meetings with government representatives. In

8. Ethnic Serbs pursued an independent republic only for a short period of time. The Working Group's main task was to convince ethnic Serbs to recognize the Macedonian state and not to hope for their inclusion within Serbia (ICFY Source 1999).

one such meeting in early December 1992, DPSM leader Stamenkovic took great pains to emphasize that ethnic Serbs in Macedonia did not seek to jeopardize ethnic relations, but that they demanded cultural autonomy, particularly in the areas of religion, education, and access to the media, and they sought to change their constitutional status.

Ethnic Serb leaders demanded that Serbian priests be allowed to conduct church services in Serbian and to hold services in all parishes having a Serbian majority. Government representatives readily acceded to these demands, taking the position that separation of church and state in Macedonia did not limit the rights of religious communities. The government also agreed to use its influence to promote dialogue between the Serbian Orthodox and the Macedonian Orthodox Churches, whose relationships had been problematic ever since Macedonia's declaration of independence.[9]

Responding to demands for Serbian-language education at all levels, from preschool to university, and for Serbian-language textbooks, the government argued that it could do little. Schools in Macedonia had their own authority to decide whether separate Serbian-language classes were needed. Thus it was up to the Serbian parents to plead their case with the school authorities. The government also pointed out that because preschools were not compulsory in Macedonia, it could not interfere to force a decision on the issue. Finally, it noted that it in no way opposed the introduction of new textbooks in the Serbian language.

In demanding to have the same access to the media that other ethnic minorities had, ethnic Serbian leaders called on the government to provide financial support for the printing of a Serbian-language newspaper and to authorize a thirty-minute-per-day Serbian-language program on national television and on national and local radio. The government claimed that it lacked the economic resources to provide support for a Serbian-language newspaper and that it lacked the authority to dictate policies to the television and radio stations. Requests for additional broadcasting times should therefore be directly addressed to the editorial boards of these stations. When ethnic Serbian representatives immediately objected, Ambassador Ahrens urged the government to help bring the matter to the attention of the responsible authorities at the television and radio stations.

Finally, much to the surprise of the government, ethnic Serbs demanded to

9. Religious demands were particularly difficult to negotiate because they were linked to broader political issues. In particular, ethnic Serb leaders declared that for the Serb Orthodox Church, Macedonia remained a part of Serbia (ICFY Source 1999).

be constitutionally recognized as a minority, as less important ethnic groups had been. Indeed, the failure of the Macedonian government to do so in the Serbian case was yet another example of what was perceived to be its insensitivity toward Serbs in Macedonia. Moreover, to have greater access to the political system, Serb leaders demanded that electoral laws be changed to allow them to have their own representatives in the National Assembly. The government responded by noting that it had seemed inappropriate to refer to ethnic Serbs in Macedonia as a "minority" because they had always regarded themselves as a "nation" (*narod*), but that the government had no objection to amending the constitution and the electoral laws to accommodate these demands. Ambassador Ahrens lent his support to a constitutional amendment but only if it guaranteed the equal treatment of ethnic Serbs.

These trilateral talks eventually culminated in the "Agreed Minutes," signed on August 27, 1993, by Ambassador Ahrens, Jakov Gerasimov, a member of the CSCE Spillover Monitor Mission to Skopje, Professor Boro Ristic from the Democratic Alliance of Serbs in Macedonia, and the Minister of the Interior Ljubomir Frčkovski. This document listed the ethnic Serbian demands that had been discussed and agreed upon. The government agreed to treat ethnic Serbs equally with other ethnic minorities. It was prepared to recognize ethnic Serbs as a "minority" in the preamble of the constitution and in article 78. In return, the ethnic Serbs committed themselves to "fulfill their aspirations only within the framework of the existing Republic of Macedonia," although they reserved the right to repudiate their obligations to the Macedonian government if it failed to achieve the necessary constitutional changes within eighteen months.

Despite its earlier position, the Macedonian government agreed to provide the same media support for ethnic Serbs that it provided for other minorities. It also made substantial commitments regarding Serbian-language education. Serbian-language instruction would be provided at the elementary school level if the parents of at least 15 children requested it; at the secondary school level, if the parents of at least 25 students requested it.[10] Moreover, the government promised to provide Serbian-language textbooks and other instructional materials needed to conduct classes in Serbian.

Finally, the Macedonian government agreed to protect Serbian historical sites and the cultural inheritance of ethnic Serbs, to support Serbian cultural organizations and institutions, and to guarantee ethnic Serbs in Macedonia the right to choose their own church.

10. As an additional guarantee, the CSCE mission in Skopje agreed, upon the request of either parents or the Macedonian government, to monitor the provision of Serbian-language instruction.

From Mediation to Direct Talks

The Working Group worked incessantly with ethnic Albanian leaders until its dissolution in early 1996. It was able to deal with the most pressing issues early on, in particular, with those pertaining to territorial autonomy, which could have resulted in the division of Macedonia. Ambassador Ahrens and the other representatives of the Working Group convinced ethnic Albanian leaders to participate in direct talks with the Macedonian government over provisions in the constitution, the law on local self-government, and other specific issues concerning educational and language policy, citizenship, national symbols, minority representation, and media access.

The Working Group's strategy was to deal with divisive issues step by step, relying heavily on personal diplomacy. This meant that Ambassador Ahrens, in particular, often met personally with President Gligorov, with high-ranking members of the cabinet, and with ethnic Albanian leaders such as Arbën Xhaferi. The Working Group had many success stories: ethnic Albanians and the Macedonian government agreed to Macedonia's being designated as a "state of citizens"; minority-language media coverage was substantially increased for all minorities in Macedonia; the law of local self-government was finally accepted and adopted; the Pedagogical Institute went into operation with a four-year Albanian-language program; Albanian-language secondary school classes doubled; and the minister of the interior and ethnic Albanian leaders reached a gentlemen's agreement on the display of national symbols. In return for concessions on educational rights, media access, and group status, ethnic Serbs promised to be loyal to the Macedonian state.

Personal diplomacy was also critical in persuading the Macedonian government to appoint ethnic Albanians to the cabinet on the basis of their percentage in the population at large rather than their percentage in the National Assembly; to increase ethnic Albanian representation in the military and the diplomatic corps, and to hold an internationally supervised census to resolve disputes over the population of ethnic groups—particularly ethnic Albanians and ethnic Serbs (ICFY Source 1996).

The Working Group was less successful in mitigating the tension over Tetovo University,[11] where its mediation efforts were cut short by the dissolution of the International Conference on the Former Yugoslavia.[12]

11. During the Tetovo incident, the Working Group was also preoccupied with minority issues in Croatia.

12. Moderate ethnic Albanian leaders, in particular, expressed the fear that Macedonia's ethnic Albanians would become radicalized without the mediating influence of the Working Group

That its members, particularly its chairman, Ambassador Ahrens, enjoyed the trust of the leaders of all contending groups accounts for much of the success of the Working Group. It was a trust built over several years of frequent meetings, and it served as an important ingredient in finding compromise solutions for the divergent positions of the conflicting parties. The Working Group's representatives were able to get even the more nationalist ethnic Albanian leaders to the negotiation table with the Macedonian authorities. Perhaps the involvement of an international actor compelled the government to make concessions they might not otherwise have made. But it is also important to note that international mediation made it also easier for the Macedonian government to justify concessions to ethnic Albanians, even as Slavic Macedonians looked on with increased weariness over meeting the demands of Macedonia's ethnic groups.[13]

THE UNITED NATIONS AND PREVENTIVE DIPLOMACY

Significant changes have occurred in the modus operandi of the United Nations since the ending of the Cold War in the late 1980s. With the disengagement of the Soviet Union and the United States from the Third World, the United Nations was able to assume three new functions. One of these came to be known as "postconflict peacebuilding," which included operations such as the Transition Assistance Group in Namibia, the U.N. Angola Verification Mission, and the U.N. Transitional Authority in Cambodia (Durch 1993; Goulding 1993; Weiss, Forsythe and Coate 1994). The second was the active involvement in humanitarian operations (Iraq, Somalia, Rwanda, Bosnia) and the management of ethnic conflicts (Croatia, Bosnia). U.N. activities in Croatia and Bosnia deserve particular attention because they constitute in the eyes of many, the more serious of the failures of the United Nations to intervene in ethnically rooted conflicts (Ackermann and Pala 1996). The third, new function was pre-

because more radical elements were already using the university issue for their own political purposes. The strongest proponent for the continuation of the Working Group, however, was Arbën Xhaferi, from the more radical Albanian party PPDsh.

13. One of the major handicaps of the Working Group was that the ICFY gave priority to reaching a peace settlement in Bosnia, and that the Working Group's chairman was often required to interrupt his negotiations in Macedonia to shift his attention to Bosnia's minority problems. What supported the Working Group's success in Macedonia, however, was that the mandates of the various international actors—the Working Group, the United Nations, and the CSCE/OSCE—even if overlapping at times, did not generate conflicting relations among its representatives, as was the case in some of the other international organizations that were involved in the mediation of the Yugoslav conflict. Generally, there was good coordination among the Working Group, the United Nations, and the CSCE/OSCE in Macedonia (ICFY Source 1999).

ventive diplomacy, whose key component, preventive deployment, was inaugurated with the dispatch of preventive peacekeepers to the Republic of Macedonia (Ackermann and Pala 1996; Kaufman 1996; Moeller 1997). Although this mission has been relatively successful, it is still the only U.N. preventive deployment activity. Indeed, the United Nations' new commitment to preventive diplomacy remains effectively confined to the rhetorical level because of financial constraints, the impediments of collective decision making, and the lack of political will and support from member states.

Deliberating on the future of collective security action in the post–Cold War era, the Security Council agreed in January 1992 to make the United Nations more efficient in three tasks: preventive diplomacy, peacekeeping, and peacemaking. Secretary-General Boutros-Ghali added also the concept of postconflict peacebuilding, elaborated in his report *An Agenda for Peace,* which he introduced publicly on June 17, 1992.

As mentioned in chapter 1, U.N. Secretary-General Hammarskjöld was the first to coin the term *preventive diplomacy.* At the time, the concept was much different in its operational scope. Boutros-Ghali (1992) not only underlined the new role of the Security Council "as a central instrument for the prevention and resolution of conflicts and for the preservation of peace," but also described the essence of conflict prevention: "to seek to identify at the earliest possible stage situations that could produce conflict, and to try through diplomacy to remove the sources of danger before violence results." Boutros-Ghali clearly intended for preventive diplomacy to be closely integrated with peacemaking and peacekeeping, and ultimately postconflict peacebuilding. He reasoned that preventive diplomacy could—like peacemaking and peacekeeping—"strengthen the opportunity for postconflict peacebuilding, which can prevent the occurrence of violence among nations and people" (Boutros-Ghali 1992).

The United Nations widely publicized *An Agenda for Peace.* Thus it was not surprising to find it published in the well-known and influential foreign policy journal *Foreign Affairs.* Pessimistic observers shrugged the report off as yet another attempt by the United Nations to safeguard its existence into the twenty-first century. Much of this ambitious and forward-looking agenda did not receive sufficient attention. Coming shortly after the outbreak of war in Bosnia, the report fell victim to a strong public perception that the United Nations was failing in its peacekeeping operations in Yugoslavia and indeed was at least partly to blame for that failure. Thus, too, the more successful preventive action of the United Nations in neighboring Macedonia went largely undetected. What was significant about *An Agenda for Peace,* however, was that it extended for the first time the scope of U.N. activities to a "previolent conflict phase" or a stage of nonescalated conflict rather than limiting itself to a cease-fire environment.

Genesis of UNPREDEP

The United Nations Preventive Deployment Mission (UNPREDEP) in Macedonia is the "first and only preventive diplomacy mission" of all of the United Nation's seventeen global operations (Lewis 1997, A4). According to UNPREDEP's Chief of Mission Henryk Sokalski (1996b), UNPREDEP is unique also because "in most peacekeeping operations in the history of the United Nations, the U.N. would join the country in question either after a war or during war operations." In the case of Macedonia, the U.N. peacekeepers came "in conditions of peace but to prevent any outbreak of war."

The earliest involvement of the United Nations in the former Yugoslavia began with Security Council Resolutions 713, 743, and 776. Although many more resolutions were to follow, these three resolutions laid the groundwork for the future U.N. engagement in the region. The United Nations' relatively late emergence on the stage of third parties attempting to resolve the conflict in Croatia came largely as the result of what was perceived as a failure of the European Community to prevent further escalation of hostilities. Stepping into a situation where European actors had already failed, the Security Council called on U.N. member states to implement a weapons embargo in September 1991.[14] Appointed U.N. special envoy for Yugoslavia in October 1991, Cyrus Vance then became the cochair of the International Conference on the Former Yugoslavia (ICFY), sponsored by the European Community and the United Nations. In 1992, the Security Council approved the Vance-Owen Peace Plan, and established the U.N. Protection Force (UNPROFOR) to oversee the cease-fire and the demobilization of troops in Croatia.[15] In September 1992, after the war in Bosnia had erupted, the Security Council established UNPROFOR II to protect humanitarian aid and to secure U.N. designated safe areas.[16]

On December 11, 1992, Security Council Resolution 795, approved unanimously, authorized the immediate preventive deployment of U.N. peacekeepers to Macedonia's borders with Albania and the Federal Republic of Yugoslavia with an explicit preventive mandate—the first ever such action taken by the United Nations.[17] An UNPROFOR preventive deployment was officially justi-

14. "Resolution 713, Adopted by the Security Council at Its 3008th Meeting on 25 September 1991," S/RES/713.

15. "Resolution 743, Adopted by the Security Council at Its 3055th Meeting on 21 February 1992, " S/RES/743.

16. "Resolution 776, Adopted by the Security Council at Its 3115th Meeting on 14 September 1992, " S/RES/776.

17. Responding to President Gligorov's request for U.N. peacekeepers, Secretary-General Boutros-Ghali had, on November 28, 1992, dispatched an exploratory mission from the UNPROFOR headquarters in Zagreb to Macedonia, where it had remained until December 3. On the basis

fied on two grounds: (1) concerns over "possible developments which could undermine confidence and stability in the former Yugoslav Republic of Macedonia or threaten its territory"; and (2) "the request by the Government in the former Yugoslav Republic of Macedonia for a United Nations presence." Resolution 795 also emphasized the United Nations' willingness to coordinate preventive actions with the CSCE Spillover Monitor Mission to Skopje, which had already been set up in September 1992 (U.N. Security Council 1992).

Resolution 795 authorized Boutros-Ghali to deploy military, civilian, and administrative staff as well as police monitors immediately "upon receiving the consent of the Government in the former Yugoslav Republic of Macedonia." Authorities in Albania and the Federal Republic of Yugoslavia were to be informed of the action as well. The mandate of the UNPROFOR "Macedonian Command," as the preventive force came to be called, came to include the following: (1) monitoring parts of the border areas with Albania and the Federal Republic of Yugoslavia (i.e., Serbia and Montenegro); (2) strengthening the country's stability by providing preventive forces; and (3) reporting on developments that would constitute a threat to the country (U.N. Division of Information 1995; Engström 1995). The U.N. preventive deployment mission was thus to provide early warning by monitoring and reporting on events and, more important, to serve as a deterrent by increasing the costs of Serbian aggression (Sokalski 1996a).

That the situation in Macedonia was judged to be critical is evident in the swiftness with which the deployment was executed. Within twenty-four hours of the passing of Resolution 795, two civil affairs officers arrived in the Republic of Macedonia. They were followed by a senior U.N. military observer (UNMO) on December 17, and U.N. civilian police officers (UNCIVPOL) on December 28. On January 6, 1993, the first UNPROFOR unit, consisting of 500 Canadians, was dispatched, and on January 25, Brigadier-General F. Saermark-Thomsen took over the UNPROFOR Command in Macedonia. The Canadian soldiers were replaced in February 1993 by 700 soldiers from the Scandinavian countries—the "Nordic Battalion" (NORDBAT), which was supplemented by U.S. soldiers that very summer. That the preventive force was deployed to Macedonia in such a timely manner attests not only to the importance the United Nations was placing on preventive measures, but also to its urgent desire to get a preventive mission in place as soon as possible (Ackermann and Pala 1996, 416).

---

of the mission's assessment, Boutros-Ghali had requested that the Security Council authorize deployment of an enlarged UNPROFOR preventive force to Macedonia to monitor and report on developments threatening the stability of the country (Archer 1994; United Nations 1995).

After General Baril, the military advisor to the U.N. secretary-general, made an informal request to the Swedish government, the decision to deploy Scandinavian troops was made at the Stockholm meeting of foreign ministers from the Scandinavian countries on December 14–15, 1992. Finland, Norway, and Sweden agreed to form a joint Nordic battalion, whereas Denmark offered to send only staff personnel because of its already considerable UNPROFOR military commitments in other parts of the former Yugoslavia. Boutros-Ghali issued a formal request for a Nordic Battalion on December 23, 1992.

By February 13–14, 1993, a major segment of the Nordic Battalion had arrived in the Republic of Macedonia. The battalion, which was put together from troops of four countries under a joint command structure became fully operational on February 19. Because it was the only U.N. presence at the time, NORDBAT was deployed along the whole area of operation, that is, the northern border with Serbia and most of the western border with Albania, a large region for so few troops. However, by the summer of 1993, U.S. troops were able to join NORDBAT soldiers, and were dispatched into the northeast sector of the country (Archer 1994; NORDBAT-UNPREDEP 1996). The addition of U.S. troops was another important component in the early warning and deterrence function of the U.N. preventive force. Furthermore, it provided assurance to Macedonia's leadership that the United States was seriously committed to preventing the spillover of war from Bosnian-Hercegovina.

U.S. participation in the preventive force had been announced on June 11, 1993, when U.S. Secretary of State Warren Christopher took up the matter during a meeting of the North Atlantic Cooperation Council in Athens. At the meeting, concern over the war in Yugoslavia and its spillover potential dominated much of the discussions. In a statement issued in Athens, the NATO foreign ministers expressed grave concern over the widening of the war into other Balkan countries but lauded the preventive measures initiated by the United Nations and the CSCE. The foreign ministers also "welcome[d] the US offer of troops to augment the UN contingent already in the Former Yugoslav Republic of Macedonia" ("Statement Issued" 1993, 24).

Three important concerns propelled the Clinton administration to be part of this mission. First, it was Secretary Christopher's opinion that the United States, in its foreign policy approach, should move more in the direction of preventing rather than reacting to conflict. Already in his confirmation hearings, Christopher had stated that most explicitly:

> We can't afford to careen from crisis to crisis. We must have a new diplomacy that can anticipate and prevent crisis. . . . We cannot forsee every crisis in the world, but I strongly believe that preventive diplomacy can free us to devote more time and effort to facing problems

here at home. I would very much like to be known as someone who is involved in preventive diplomacy. Crisis management, of course, is important, and I'm sure there will have to be a lot of crisis management. But I'd very much like to be a crisis preventer. (Cited in Lowenthal 1993, 3)

Second, the Clinton administration was aware that the deterrent potential of the U.N. preventive force would be substantially upgraded if U.S. troops became an integral part of it. In his statement to the NATO summit participants, Secretary Christopher emphasized the deterrent and symbolic function that U.S. troops would fulfill. Meanwhile in Washington, President Clinton was busy allaying voters' concerns by emphasizing that the American commitment would be a limited one and would not involve combat. By doing so, he also gave a clear signal that the United States would not fight a war in Macedonia. He justified U.S. participation by stressing that although the United States had made a commitment to support the United Nations in Macedonia "it's a very limited thing—no combat—but a chance to limit the conflict" (Cited in Sciolino 1994). A third concern motivating U.S. troops in the U.N. preventive force deployed to Macedonia was the need "to limit the conflict [in Yugoslavia] to its present parameters . . . to make sure that we don't have a Balkan-wide conflict" (Clinton 1996, 804).

On June 18, 1993, the Security Council specifically authorized the deployment of U.S. troops to expand the UNPROFOR contingent in Macedonia, welcoming "the offer made by [the United States] to contribute additional personnel to the UNPROFOR presence in the former Yugoslav Republic of Macedonia" (U.N. Security Council 1993c).[18] The first U.S. contingent, the 502d Infantry Regiment, arrived from Berlin on July 12 to assume duties shortly thereafter. The U.S. force was increased from 300 to 550 soldiers in April 1994, to replace peacekeepers from the Nordic Battalion, who were being redeployed to Bosnia-Hercegovina. More than a year later, on December 23, 1994, in his fourth report to Congress on the deployment of U.S. forces to Macedonia, President Clinton evaluated the critical importance of U.S. participation as "part of our continuing commitment toward resolving the extremely difficult situation in the former Yugoslavia" (Macedonian Information Center 1994, 101). The preventive U.N. mission in Macedonia was unique not only because it is the first and only preventive diplomacy operation, but because, also for the first

18. "Resolution 842, Adopted by the Security Council at Its 3239th Meeting on 18 June 1993," S/RES/842.

time in the organization's history, a U.N. peacekeeping force included a major contingent of U.S. soldiers.

From January 1993 to March 1995, the preventive peacekeeping mission in the Republic of Macedonia formed a part of UNPROFOR, as did the other two U.N. operations in Croatia and Bosnia. The preventive force was however referred to as the "UNPROFOR Command in Macedonia." But on March 31, 1995, following requests from the governments of Croatia and the Republic of Macedonia for U.N. forces separate from UNPROFOR, the Security Council reorganized U.N. operations in the former Yugoslavia.[19] Three distinct commands were created: the command in Macedonia was renamed the "United Nations Preventive Deployment Force" or UNPREDEP (U.N. Security Council 1995);[20] the command in Croatia came to be known as "the United Nations Confidence Restoration Operation" or UNCRO; and the acronym UNPROFOR became entirely reserved for the command in Bosnia-Hercegovina. At the time, all three commands remained linked though under the overall command of the U.N. Peace Forces (UNPF) with headquarters in Zagreb, although UNPREDEP eventually became an independent mission on February 1, 1996, reporting directly to the United Nations' New York headquarters.[21] The reorganization of U.N. forces in the former Yugoslavia acknowledged the unique nature of the mission to Macedonia, separating the only U.N. preventive operation from the peace enforcement and humanitarian missions of Croatia and Bosnia.

The United Nations' preventive involvement in Macedonia was based on three mandates: military, political, and humanitarian-developmental. Spelled out in the secretary-general's report on December 9, 1992, the military mandate was limited to monitoring and reporting any developments considered destabilizing or threatening to Macedonia along its borders with Serbia and Albania. But as the United Nations' presence in Macedonia grew, it also found itself playing more and more a political role, partially because of the waning threat to Macedonia's territorial integrity and the increasing necessity to address internal conflicts. In the words of Assistant Secretary-General Henryk Sokalski:

19. "Resolution 981, Adopted by the Security Council at Its 3512th Meeting on 30 March 1995," S/RES/981; "Resolution 982, Adopted by the Security Council at Its 3512th Meeting on 30 March 1995," S/RES/982; "Resolution 983, Adopted by the Security Council at Its 3512th Meeting on 30 March 1995," S/RES/983.

20. See also *Report of the Secretary-General Pursuant to Security Council Resolution 947 (1994)*, 22 March 1995, which advises the Security Council with respect to the extension on UNPROFOR for an additional six months as stipulated in Security Council Resolution 947 (1994). Boutros-Ghali, in his report, suggests the creation of separate but interlinked U.N. operations in Croatia, Bosnia, and Macedonia.

21. UNPREDEP became an independent mission as a result of the termination of mandates of UNCRO, UNPROFOR, and the UNPF Headquarters.

> Originally this operation mainly concentrated on military deployment. A war was raging in the North. The situation was extremely tense. You needed, first of all, some kind of a barrier in terms of military involvement, military deployment. And this happened very quickly. But as the time passed, the Security Council also decided to strengthen its political component. (Ackermann and Chatterjee 1997)

A political mandate was added on March 31, 1994, with the passage of Security Council Resolution 908, which "encourage[d] the Special Representative of the Secretary-General of the former Yugoslav Republic of Macedonia, to use his good offices as appropriate to contribute to the maintenance of peace and stability in the Republic" (U.N. Security Council 1994).[22] Adding the political mandate complemented the military mandate by including preventive actions directed toward internal conflicts, through mediation efforts and the facilitation of political dialogue.

Then in the spring of 1995, a humanitarian-developmental mandate was added to U.N. preventive operations in Macedonia. This mandate was "based on the profound conviction that many potential conflicts have economic and social roots" (Sokalski 1996b). In his report in May 1996, Boutros-Ghali listed all the varied tasks for which UNPREDEP has assumed responsibility over time, including "preventive deployment, good offices, measures to build confidence, early warning, fact-finding, monitoring and reporting, as well as selected social and developmental projects" (U.N. Secretary-General 1996b, 3).

UNPREDEP in Practice

The military mandate, which was renewed every six months—usually at the end of May and the end of November—was carried out through fixed and temporary observation posts along Macedonia's border with Serbia and Albania, and air and ground patrols.[23] Most of the observation posts were spread along Macedonia's northern and western borders, with Serbia and Albania, respectively. In 1996, the number of observation posts, was reduced from 29 to 24. U.N. military observers (UNMOs) and U.N. civilian police (UNCIVPOL), primarily deployed along the Albanian borders, assisted in preventive activities by patrolling border crossings, custom stations, and villages. Contact with local

22. "Resolution 908, Adopted by the Security Council at Its 3346th Meeting on 31 March 1994," S/RES/908.

23. In December 1997, UNPREDEP's mandate was extended until August 31, 1998, and then again until February 1999.

people was particularly important in the detection of unusual developments. U.N. civilian police also played a crucial role by maintaining contacts with the local Macedonian police and by monitoring the treatment of individuals in custody. In 1996, when I visited UNPREDEP, the total number of UNPREDEP peacekeepers was approximately 1,050, with two mechanized infantry battalions: NORDBAT-1 (Denmark, Sweden, Finland, Norway) and USBAT (United States). During that time, there were also 35 U.N. military observers, 26 members of the U.N. civilian police, and 168 civilian U.N. personnel—a combined civilian and military staff coming from 40 different countries (U.N. Secretary-General 1996b, 2).[24]

U.N. peacekeepers dealt with a number of different monitoring tasks. One of the most frequently exercised activity was to monitor the administrative line drawn by the United Nations between Serbia and Macedonia. In the absence of physical markers clearly identifying the border between the two countries, the incidents UNPREDEP soldiers had to deal with most often were border encroachments; this was especially so in the early years of independence. For example, in the summer 1994, Serbian soldiers took positions on the Macedonian side and had to be persuaded by U.N. soldiers to leave the area. In April 1995, when Macedonian soldiers accidentally strayed into Serbian territory and were taken hostage, the U.N. commander in Macedonia intervened personally by making contact with Serbian authorities. The result of human error because of the similarity of terrain on both sides, rather than provocative acts, minor incursions into Macedonia were simply handled by approaching Serbian soldiers and informing them of their presence on Macedonian territory. Thus an essential task of UNPREDEP was to monitor the U.N. administrative line.

At crucial border crossings, such as into Albania, UNPREDEP soldiers also monitored smuggling activities, which only occasionally involved weapons, and border traffic as well as illegal border crossings. Although some Macedonian villages live entirely from smuggling, U.N. peacekeepers could only monitor and report on such activities, but were prohibited from inspecting cars. At a U.S. observation post in 1996, UNPREDEP soldiers observed the creation of a new Serbian mortar position and a new trench over several days, keeping close watch to determine whether this border fortification constituted a hostile intention.

The monitoring of political, economic, and social conditions was mostly

24. The total authorized force remained relatively constant in terms of its troops. In 1995, there were 1,096 peacekeepers, with 556 soldiers in NORDBAT-1 and 540 in USBAT. See (U.N. Secretary-General 1995, Annex I, 16). In 1997, UNPREDEP began with a phased reduction in anticipation of the termination of its mandate by the end of that year. UNPREDEP's mandate was extended to February 28, 1999, and an increase of peacekeepers to 1,050 was also authorized.

the responsibility of UNPREDEP's chief of mission, who engaged the Macedonian authorities and political and ethnic leaders in political dialogue in times of crisis, often in coordination with the OSCE Spillover Monitor Mission to Skopje. Among the more concrete political tasks performed by UNPREDEP in earlier years was the monitoring of presidential and parliamentary elections, such as those in October 1994, monitored in cooperation with the CSCE, the European Union, the Council of Europe, and several NGOs. On the eve of these national elections, UNPREDEP Chief of Mission Hugo Anson convinced the contending political parties to commit themselves to avoid interethnic strife by adhering to democratic norms and by abstaining from extreme nationalist language during the election campaign (Williams 1995).[25]

UNPREDEP was less successful in the economic realm. UNPREDEP's Civil Affairs branch initiated studies on how to coordinate bilateral and multilateral assistance and to direct international funding to those sectors in need of support, yet there was never much progress in terms of assisting Macedonia to stabilize economically, in part because of the limits set by UNPREDEP's mandate. More often, though, there was little support in the international community for a massive economic stabilization program, however much it was needed during Macedonia's early years of independence to offset the negative effects of political and ethnic tensions, the Greek embargo, and international sanctions against Yugoslavia, all of which weakened an already fragile economy. Although Boutros-Ghali requested compensation in March 1995 for Macedonia's support of the sanctions against the rump Yugoslavia, such compensation was never forthcoming, and Macedonia continued to muddle through as best as it could.

The third mandate, added to what already was a successful mission, concerned itself with more long-term social developmental problems experienced in the country. Released following *An Agenda for Peace,* Boutros-Ghali's *An Agenda for Development* (1995, 99) outlined this mandate, stressing the need for preventive development as a "necessary complement to preventive diplomacy . . . anticipating and responding to crises, natural and man-made, before they occur."

Many of Macedonia's social development problems were addressed through specific projects sponsored by the United Nations, such as the one I witnessed in the early summer 1996 in the village of Saraj, some 20 kilometers outside of Skopje. In this Bosnian refugee camp, which housed families most of whom had fled to Macedonia at the end of 1992, a U.S. soldier from the UNPREDEP force was holding a land mine detection training workshop for Bosnian children returning to Bosnia. The project had been financed by UNICEF, and UNPRE-

25. The request had been made by Mr. Stojan Andov, who was then president of Macedonia's National Assembly.

DEP conducted it in cooperation with the U.N. high commissioner for refugees. There were several other developmental projects in which international organizations cooperated, many of which undertaken according to emerging needs, such as the delivery of water pipes to remote villages using U.N. helicopters. Although social developmental projects were generally the domain of the U.N. Developmental Agency in Macedonia, much of UNPREDEP's involvement in such activities was generated by the UNPREDEP Chief of Mission Sokalski, who took a strong professional and personal interest in promoting developmental and humanitarian issues. Sokalski believed that such small-scale activities, though only a drop in the bucket, nevertheless helped mitigate ethnic and social tensions (Sokalski 1996a).

UNITED NATIONS–SPONSORED NEGOTIATIONS BETWEEN MACEDONIA AND GREECE

The United Nations' involvement in Macedonia was not been limited to preventive deployment. It assumed a different preventive role, that of mediator in the Greek-Macedonian negotiations that followed imposition of a Greek embargo in February 1994. In this preventive effort to avert the further economic isolation and destabilization of Macedonia, the United Nations received critical backing from the United States. Little is publicly known about the extent of U.S. intervention in restarting negotiations between Greece and Macedonia after the 1994 embargo. Washington was eager to let the United Nations assume a broader role in conflict resolution; moreover, the United Nations was widely recognized as an impartial body, which was not the case for the United States with its well-established links to the Greek government through NATO. However, the United Nations and the United States share credit for the successful completion of an interim agreement in September 1995, which led to the normalization of relations between Greece and Macedonia.

The United Nations' role in addressing the Greek-Macedonian dispute did not begin with the Greek embargo. Already on April 7, 1993 the Security Council called on Greece and the Former Yugoslav Republic of Macedonia to cooperate with the cochairmen of the Steering Committee of the International Conference on the Former Yugoslavia to settle their differences (U.N. Security Council 1993b).[26] The Greek-Macedonian conflict, dating back to Macedonia's independence, shifted to the United Nations with Macedonia's application for

26. "Resolution 817, Adopted by the Security Council at Its 3196th Meeting on 7 April 1993," S/RES/817.

membership there, made public on January 7, 1993 (Perry 1993b, 3). Greece's objections to Macedonia's membership focused on several issues: Macedonia's insistence on the name "Republic of Macedonia," its use of Greek national symbols, and its hostile propaganda.[27] As President Gligorov stated on July 30, 1992, in his official request to the secretary-general, U.N. membership "would be a very significant step towards the peaceful situation of the crisis in the territory of the former Yugoslavia" (Cited in "Controversy over Macedonia" 1993, 12). Gligorov's request, circulated as an official U.N. document on January 22, 1993, met with an immediate Greek response. Foreign Minister Michael Papaconstantinou strongly objected to the Macedonian application and the use of the country's name as "the Republic of Macedonia." Citing further destabilization of the southern Balkans as reason for Greek objections, the foreign minister emphasized the expansionist claims of Macedonian nationalists. He pointed out that the government in Skopje had adopted for its country the name of a geographic area stretching across four different countries. Papaconstantinou then asked the Security Council to assist in resolving the dispute: "This is a clear case where preventive diplomacy is urgently needed" ("Controversy over Macedonia" 1993).

After Security Council consultations, on April 8, 1993, Macedonia was admitted to the United Nations as the 181st member under the name "Former Yugoslav Republic of Macedonia" (FYROM). But the dispute between Greece and Macedonia continued over the unaddressed issue of the name, over the use of national symbols such as the flag, which proved a problem even at U.N. headquarters in New York, and over what Greek authorities perceived as hostile, nationalist propaganda, including the alleged release of geographic maps showing a "Greater Macedonia."

That the United Nations, rather than a European organization, such as the CSCE or the European Community, came to take the leading role as mediator was mainly the result of the inability of regional organizations to induce Greece to adopt a more conciliatory approach.[28] Having imposed a limited embargo in 1993, after Macedonia was admitted to the United Nations, Greece then imposed a total embargo on February 16, 1994, under its new prime minister, Andreas Papandreou: the Greek-Macedonian conflict was on the verge of becoming intractable. The embargo was intended to coerce Macedonia to change its name

27. The Greeks, for example, claimed that Skopje published maps which showed Greek Macedonia as part of a Greater Macedonia ("Streit um den Sonnenstern" 1993, 7).

28. There were several attempts led by Germany and France to convince Greece to change its obstructive foreign policy vis-à-vis Macedonia (e.g., "Athen erweitert Blockade" 1994, 2). Also, other European institutions such as the Western European Union criticized Greece's foreign policy (e.g., Perry 1993a, 3).

and to make a number of other concessions with regard to its flag and the wording of sections of article 49 of its constitution. Moreover, the Papandreou government adopted an increasingly intransigent nationalist position toward Macedonia.

The United Nations' intermediary role began officially with the appointment of Cyrus Vance as U.N. special envoy in October 1991. On May 14, 1993, Vance introduced a draft paper for mediation, which he had developed with Lord Owen—both of whom served as ICFY cochairs.[29] At the time, the two contending parties agreed to the general provisions of the draft, including economic and cultural cooperation and confidence-building measures. But no agreement could be reached on Macedonia's name. To ease some of the tensions over the name, Vance and Owen offered several possible alternatives, such as the name "New Macedonia" (Nova Makedonija). Both sides rejected them ("Neue Vermittlungsmission" 1994, 4; "Die UNO-Vermittlung" 1994, 5).

On May 27, the Greek government and, on May 29, the Macedonian government submitted letters to the Security Council in which each party basically agreed to negotiations but objected to specific provisions of the Vance-Owen draft proposal.[30] In response, the Security Council, on June 18, 1993, urged the ICFY to continue its mediation efforts (U.N. Security Council 1993d).[31] However, the dispute remained unsettled because Greece's new Socialist government, which took office in October 1993, decided to break off direct negotiations.

In December 1993, Foreign Minister Stevo Crvenkovski, appealed to Secretary-General Boutros-Ghali for assistance in reopening negotiations with the Greek government (Perry 1993a, 3).[32] Prime Minister Papandreou spelled out the conditions for the resumption of talks—the removal of the Star of Vergina from the Macedonian flag and the amendment of the Macedonian constitution with regard to Macedonians living outside the country (Engelbrekt 1994, 4).

Following the total embargo in 1994, U.N. Special Envoy Vance once more was called on to use his mediation skills, assisted by Matthew Nimetz, President Clinton's special emissary. By now, the United States actively sought to assist the United Nations, fearing that further destabilization threatened Macedonia's exis-

29. The Vance-Owen draft is included in Annex V: "Draft Proposed by Cyrus Vance and Lord Owen, 14 May 1993," in (U.N. Security Council 1993a). See here also Annex I: "Report of the Secretary General Submitted Pursuant to Resolution 817 (1993)."

30. The letters are part of the Addendum of S/25855 (1993), 3 June 1993. See Addendum 1: "Letter Dated 28 May 1993 From the Secretary-General Addressed to the President of the Security Council"; and Addendum 2: "Letter Dated 3 June 1993 from the Secretary-General Addressed to the President of the Security Council."

31. "Resolution 845, Adopted by the Security Council at Its 3243rd Meeting on 18 June 1993," S/RES/845.

32. The letter was published in the Macedonian daily newspaper *Nova Makedonija* on December 2, 1993.

tence. After all, the United States could not, on the one hand, contribute peacekeepers whose explicit mandate was to guarantee the stability of the country, and, on the other, turn a blind eye to Greece's obstructive policy toward Macedonia.

Vance and Nimetz drafted a revised document which served as the cornerstone for new negotiations. In it, Greece was asked to lift the embargo as a first step in return for concessions on the Macedonian side, such as changes in the constitution, the removal of the Star of Vergina from the flag, and abstention from propagandistic campaigns ("Die UNO-Vermittlung" 1994). The U.N. strategy was to create a compromise solution whereby each of the contending parties would make concessions in order for negotiations to move forward. All other details were to be worked out once the talks progressed.

Negotiations deadlocked over Macedonia's name. Vance and Nimetz shuttled incessantly between the two parties to create a climate in which a compromise could be reached. In June 1994, Nimetz traveled to Skopje and Athens to set up a preliminary negotiation framework for a meeting one week later between Vance and the Greek and Macedonian foreign ministers in New York ("Neue Vermittlungsmission" 1994). Talks were interrupted at Gligorov's request, who cited the upcoming October elections as a reason.

Nimetz resumed talks with Athens and Skopje in December 1994, after consultations between President Gligorov, Secretary-General Boutros-Ghali, and U.N. Special Envoy Vance in Geneva in November failed to yield any definite results. Hopes ran high that an agreement could be reached soon because Gligorov was reelected and would be able to obtain the two-thirds majority to initiate the necessary changes in the constitution. In its next step, the United Nations proposed that three names be used in reference to Macedonia—within the country, the name "Macedonia" would be permitted; within the international community, Macedonia would refer to itself as the "Former Yugoslav Republic of Macedonia"; and in bilateral relations with Greece, Macedonia would use the name of the "Republic of Skopje." Although it sought to obtain Greek cooperation for a dialogue by providing an alternative to the controversial issue of the name "Macedonia," the U.N. proposal was not well received by the Macedonian government. Following this diplomatic failure, Nimetz decided to adopt a different formula: the United Nations would get an agreement on the constitution and the flag first; but the more contentious issue of the name would be reserved for last ("Neuer Vermittlungsanlauf der USA" 1994, 4; "Neuer Vermittlungsanlauf im Mazedonienzwist" 1994, 5). There was only one other problem. How to get the conflicting parties to meet face-to-face?

Until this point, the two parties had never met at one table. Instead U.N. mediators conducted parallel meetings with the representatives from each country. These parallel meetings resumed on February 6, 1995. During a meeting between Gligorov and Boutros-Ghali in Copenhagen on March 10, the United

Nations secretary-general urged the Macedonian president to agree to direct meetings with Greek officials. Between March and June, the U.N./U.S. mediation team continued to conduct talks with the two parties. But a breakthrough was still not in sight. Although Gligorov, in a radio address commemorating the second anniversary of the country's admission to the United Nations, indicated that Macedonia was willing to resolve the conflict with Greece, Macedonian representatives, citing domestic difficulties, did not accept the invitation of Vance to meet in New York on April 6. Instead, Macedonia asked for a rescheduling. During his visit to Greece in July, Boutros-Ghali once more took the opportunity to ask Greek authorities to consider the U.N. proposal favorably ("Mazedonien zu Grenzvertrag" 1995, 4).

Although many of the details had been worked out, two critical factors complicated an earlier settlement. One was to persuade President Gligorov to accept the "small package"; the other was to stop the flow of side letters, which both parties were submitting. The "small package" reflected the U.N. strategy to leave the name issue to subsequent negotiations, and instead seek changes in Macedonia's constitution and national symbols. In return, Greece would lift its embargo. By early August, during a meeting between Nimetz and Gligorov, the Macedonian President made acceptance of the "small package" contingent on the prior removal of the embargo. By that time, Greece had already agreed to the "small package" but was not willing to give in on the lifting of the embargo before the implementation of the demanded changes. Also, critical voices within the Greek opposition party continued to favor a "large package," which entailed the resolution of the name issue simultaneously with the other issues ("Amerikanische Initiative" 1995, 7).

The side letters—which interpreted the meaning of agreements—were equally problematic. For example, there was considerable controversy over what to call the symbol in the Macedonian flag that the Greeks referred to as the "Star of Vergina," a designation rejected by the Macedonian delegation. By early September 1995, after a change in the Greek government, an agreement seemed imminent. When, however, negotiations once more threatened to break down, Assistant Secretary of State Richard Holbrooke stepped in at the last minute (State Department Source 1995). Holbrooke shuttled between Athens and Skopje for talks with Greek Prime Minister Papandreou and Macedonian President Gligorov (Goodman 1995, 13). Holbrooke had already picked up the issue in early April, when he visited Athens to speak with Foreign Minister Papoulias and Prime Minister Papandreou ("Mazedonien zu Grenzvertrag" 1995). Holbrooke was successful in getting Skopje and Athens to send their foreign ministers to New York to conclude a basic agreement, leaving divisive matters, such as the changing of the flag or the name to later negotiations, which would deal with the more practical implementations of the accord. Holbrooke viewed an agreement as a crucial step toward regional stability and as an example to be used in negotiations with the warring factions in Bosnia, Croatia, and Serbia that a wider Balkan settlement was attainable (U.S. State Department Source 1995; Robinson and Hope 1995, 2).

On September 13, 1995, an interim agreement was signed in New York in which the Republic of Macedonia agreed to remove the Star of Vergina from its flag and to disavow any claims to Greek territory. Greece, in return, agreed to lift the embargo and to halt its opposition to Macedonia's membership in multilateral organizations. Both governments also agreed to respect each other's territorial integrity and to establish diplomatic relations. Moreover, the two parties promised to work out all practical matters in subsequent bilateral meetings, including the issue of the name which was to be decided in a conference sponsored by the United Nations (U.S. State Department Source 1995; U.S. Department of State 1995).[33] On October 9, Macedonia's National Assembly ratified the interim agreement with only two abstentions. On December 16, the Greek and Macedonian ambassadors met in New York for talks on the name issue, followed by further discussions, none of which have resulted in an acceptable solution (Krause 1995, 6).

The United Nations' mediation role in obtaining a settlement to the Greek-Macedonian dispute proved to be a significant step toward conflict prevention. By drawing on the assistance of the United States, particularly that of Nimetz, a close friend of Vance, the United Nations demonstrated it was willing to work within a cooperative framework, allowing it to achieve a positive outcome for its mediation efforts. Although the United Nations had taken the lead in the mediation, U.S. pressures at the end were crucial to the success of the talks. Washington was driven by two objectives: to achieve a more comprehensive settlement for the former Yugoslavia; and to prevent the further destabilization of Macedonia. The interim agreement opened the way for Macedonia to become a participating member of the OSCE—it only had observer status in the organization since April 1993—to be admitted to the Council of Europe and to join NATO's Partnership for Peace Program. Since then, Greece and Macedonia have moved toward normalization of relations and have pledged to hold bilateral meetings twice a year to facilitate good neighborly relations.

33. There are a variety of press coverage such as ("Skopje's Generous Gesture" 1995, 6; Rüb 1995; Wren 1995, A6; "Griechisch-mazedonische Normalisierung" 1995, 1).

TERMINATING UNPREDEP'S MISSION

In mid-1997, the United Nations was preparing itself for a gradual reduction of UNPREDEP forces and termination of its mandate. When on May 28, 1997, the Security Council renewed UNPREDEP's mandate until November 30, 1997, "in the light of the situation in Albania," it had also decided to reduce U.N. peacekeepers by 300 over two months, beginning October 1, 1997 (U.N. Security Council 1997a; U.N. Security Council 1997d).[34] On December 4, 1997, the Security Council reversed its decision to terminate UNPREDEP, instead extending its mandate until August 31, 1998, at which time peacekeeping troops were to be withdrawn.[35] The Security Council also requested that the secretary-general submit a plan for a follow-up mission, with NATO or OSCE personnel (U.N. Security Council 1997e). UNPREDEP's mandate was further extended to February 28, 1999, for fear the violence in Kosovo might spill over into Macedonia and UNPREDEP's strength was increased to more than 1,000, after having been reduced to 750 (U.N. Security Council 1998b).[36]

Following China's veto at the Security Council on February 26, 1999, UNPREDEP's mission was terminated on March 1, 1999, after Beijing objected to Macedonia's establishing diplomatic relations with Taiwan. Although thirteen out of the fifteen council members voted for UNPREDEP's continued deployment, China argued that the force was no longer necessary, denying that its decision was linked to Macedonia's recognition of Taiwan ("China Vetoes Extension" 1999, 6). It came at an unfortunate time because of the growing escalation of the Kosovo conflict and the first refugee flows from Kosovo—3,000 Kosovars were trying to flee to Macedonia on February 28 ("Kosovars Flee to Macedonia" 1999, 5). Responding to the veto, President Giligorov, who had first initiated the request for a preventive mission, regretted that United Nations peacekeepers were leaving "at a time when the Republic of Macedonia and the region at large, due to the situation in Kosovo, perhaps need their presence here the most" (Foreign Broadcast Information Service 1999a).

What can be said is that the success of UNPREDEP is beyond doubt and was conducted much in the way envisioned by Boutros-Ghali's *An Agenda for Peace*. Commenting in 1996 on what has made UNPREDEP successful,

34. "Resolution 1140, Adopted by the Security Council at Its 3836th Meeting on 28 November 1997," S/RES/1140.

35. "Resolution 1142, Adopted by the Security Council at Its 3839th Meeting on 4 December 1997," S/RES/1142.

36. "Resolution 1186, Adopted by the Security Council at Its 3911th Meeting on 21 July 1998," S/RES/ 1186.

Boutros-Ghali emphasized that although it should never be a static concept, "preventive deployment can work where there is political will, a clear mandate and purpose, and the necessary commitment on the part of all parties concerned" (U.N. Secretary-General 1996a, 6).

UNPREDEP's efforts to address some of the social and economic tensions in the country—even though less visible than its preventive peacekeeping—made a small contribution not only to democratization but also to long-term conflict prevention, much in the spirit of *An Agenda for Development,* in which former Secretary-General Boutros-Ghali emphasized that "only sustained efforts to resolve the underlying socio-economic, cultural and humanitarian problems can place an achieved peace on a durable foundation."

UNPREDEP was significantly hindered in pursuing a more active program of economic and social development by a shortage of both financial resources and trained personnel. Indeed, if one lesson is to be learned with regard to UNPREDEP, it is that preventive diplomacy and preventive deployment must be supplemented with economic assistance. In all countries of Central and Eastern Europe, even if economic discrimination is not a major source of ethnic conflict, economic transitions have caused socioeconomic dislocations severe enough to threaten interethnic relations. Thus, UNPREDEP's efforts toward social and economic development remained on a small scale, such as organizing humanitarian campaigns, using U.N. helicopters to deliver water pipes to inaccessible mountainous areas, making scholarships available for study abroad, or simply maintaining close contacts with the many social and humanitarian organizations that exist in Macedonia, such as the Macedonian Red Cross. One can only agree with Chief of Mission Sokalski that UNPREDEP succeeded in its most important role—to prevent violent conflict, although Sokalski was quick to point out that it had done so only with the help of others. It is with this in mind that the role of the other preventive actors is explored in the next two chapters.

6

THE CSCE/OSCE IN MACEDONIA

SINCE 1990, THE CSCE/OSCE has been increasingly engaged in the prevention and management of conflicts in Europe. Initially directed to respond to the management of interstate rather than intrastate conflicts, the OSCE has emerged as a prominent actor for preventive engagements in ethnic and communal tensions. In the last few years, there has been a proliferation of OSCE long-term missions to different countries and regions in Central and Eastern Europe and in the former Soviet Union, including Bosnia, Croatia, Estonia, Georgia, Latvia, Macedonia, Moldova, Tajikistan, Vojvodina, Sandjak, and Kosovo. But Macedonia stands out as one of the CSCE/OSCE's most successful missions since 1992.

The CSCE/OSCE-Macedonian relationship has been both unique and frustrating. Although Macedonia was not officially admitted as a fully participating OSCE state until October 1995 because of objections by Greece, the CSCE/OSCE was among the first international organizations to arrive in the country on a preventive mission. The CSCE/OSCE was also one of the first European organizations to which the newly independent country applied for membership at a time when it was crucial for Macedonia's stability to be associated with a European security structure. But the road to full membership was strewn with many obstacles. Beginning in January 1992, nearly four months after gaining independence, Macedonia filed its first application for membership. Several others followed—perhaps as many as twenty. Each time, however, the application process was blocked by the European Community, where Greece used its influence to prevent Macedonia from becoming a CSCE member. When a compromise was reached in early 1993 on the name issue, and Macedonia was admitted to the United Nations as the "Former Yugoslav Republic of Macedonia" (FYROM) it was also granted CSCE "silent" observer status, under which the Macedonian delegation was prohibited from making comments, even in deliberations over their own country. In June 1994, Macedonia was given the status of regular observer, and in the fall of 1995, it became a fully participating member, increasing the number of OSCE member states to 54, compared to the 35 states that signed the Helsinki Final Act in 1975 (Ackermann 1997, 1998b; OSCE Source 1997).

THE CSCE/OSCE IN THE POST–COLD WAR ERA

The history of the Organization for Security and Cooperation in Europe (OSCE), formerly known as the Conference on Security and Cooperation in Europe (CSCE), is well documented (e.g., Bloed 1993; Heraclides 1993; OSCE Secretariat 1995; Rotfeld 1996). Founded in 1975 in Helsinki as a forum to facilitate East-West dialogue and to address political, military, economic, cultural, and human rights issues, the CSCE underwent profound changes in the mid-1980s, as the Soviet Union under Mikhail Gorbachev was restructuring itself and its relations with the West.

These changes culminated in the signing of the Charter of Paris for a New Europe at the Paris summit in November 1990, which formally ended the Cold War and which transformed the CSCE from an international regime to a regional organization. The charter created permanent bodies and institutions such as the Council of Foreign Ministers (renamed the "Ministerial Council" in 1994); the Committee of Senior Officials (CSO; later renamed the "Senior Council"); the CSCE Secretariat, first located in Prague, then transferred to Vienna; the Office for Free Elections in Warsaw (now known as the "Office for Democratic Institutions and Human Rights"), and the Conflict Prevention Center in Vienna, specifically designed to assist the Council of Foreign Ministers in reducing conflicts; and it called for regular summit meetings of heads of state and government (OSCE Secretariat 1996a, 8–9).

To expand the organization's ability to undertake political consultation and dialogue and to make decisions, the post of Secretary-General was created in December 1992, and the Permanent Committee (now the "Permanent Council") in December 1993.

Reflecting its new operational role in security issues in Europe, the CSCE dispatched conflict prevention missions to the Republic of Macedonia, to the Federal Republic of Yugoslavia (Serbia-Montenegro), and to Kosovo, Vojvodina and Sandjak, all in September 1992, to Estonia in February 1993, to Latvia in November 1993, and to Ukraine in November 1994; it sent crisis management missions to countries where violence had already erupted—to Georgia in December 1992, to Moldova in April 1993, and to Tajikistan in February 1994 (Bothe, Ronzitti and Rosas 1997; OSCE Secretariat 1996a, 17–35; Höynck 1994, 72). In coordination with the European Community's sanctions assistance missions (SAMs), the CSCE monitored the sanctions against the Federal Republic of Yugoslavia (Serbia and Montenegro) and the Serbian Republic (Republika Srpska), the "independent" republic created by ethnic Serbs in Bosnia (OSCE Secretariat 1996d, 4).[1]

When war broke out in Yugoslavia in 1991, however, the CSCE found itself blocked from taking collective action by the consensus principle, which had governed its decision making since its inception, because of the Yugoslav government's veto; moreover, the CSCE lacked the institutional capacity to deploy fact-finding and monitoring missions (OSCE Secretariat 1996d, 4).[2] Although it issued a common declaration on Yugoslavia at the first meeting of its Council of Ministers in Berlin in June 19–20, 1991, and agreed on a mechanism for consultation and cooperation in situations that demanded immediate action, the CSCE was soon relegated to the back benches, and the European Community stepped in as principal mediator.

Over the next few years, the CSCE/OSCE set as its top three priorities conflict prevention and crisis management; human rights, to include building democracy and the rule of law; and further institutionalization of its structures and cooperation with the United Nations, NATO, the WEU, and the Council of Europe. Apart from its missions, the CSCE also created the Office of the High Commissioner on National Minorities in The Hague with the specific mandate for early warning and early action so as to prevent conflicts in their earliest possible stage.

Conflict prevention, early warning, and crisis management were mentioned specifically in the 1992 Helsinki Summit Declaration to which the CSCE participating states were signatories. The document named two principal instruments of conflict prevention and crisis management: (1) fact-finding and rapporteur missions, organized on the basis of decisions made by the CSO or the Consultative Committee of the Conflict Prevention Center and requiring a "clear mandate" and the consent of the state on whose territory the mission was to be conducted; and (2) peacekeeping missions—to be dispatched in

1. Sanctions assistance missions were created by the London Conference on the Former Yugoslavia in August 1992 as part of sanctions against the Federal Republic of Yugoslavia (Serbia and Montenegro) and the Serbian Republic (Republica Srpska). The missions' costs were shared by the EC/EU, which funded the Sanctions Committee (SAMCOMM), and the CSCE, which financed the missions' operations. Operating from all countries neighboring the Federal Republic of Yugoslavia, including Hungary, Romania, and the Republic of Macedonia (set up in 1992), and Albania, Bulgaria, Croatia, and Ukraine in 1993, the SAMs were terminated by Security Council Resolution 1074 on October 1, 1994 (OSCE Secretariat 1996d, 4).

2. Starting in 1991, the CSCE sent rapporteur missions to CSCE states that were newly admitted.

interethnic as well as interstate conflicts. The heads of state and government attending the Helsinki summit intended to use peacekeeping missions for a variety of purposes: to observe cease-fires, to monitor troop withdrawals, to assist refugees, and to deliver humanitarian and medical assistance. Although the peacekeeping missions were explicitly not to enforce the peace, they were to function in a preventive capacity (CSCE 1992a, 25–31).

The Budapest summit held on December 5–6, 1994, in the midst of the war in Bosnia-Hercegovina, renamed the CSCE the "Organization for Security and Cooperation in Europe" or OSCE and mandated strengthening the Chairman-in-Office, the Secretary-General, the High Commissioner on National Minorities (HCNM), and the Office of Democratic Institutions and Human Rights (ODIHR). More important, however, the Budapest summit reaffirmed the organization's primary commitment to early warning, conflict prevention, and conflict management. Crucial responsibility to fulfill these tasks was assigned to the High Commissioner on National Minorities (HCNM).

Through the HCNM, as envisioned by the Helsinki summit, the CSCE was to play a more proactive role in the prevention of conflict. Originally a Dutch initiative, the HCNM was to be responsible for early warning and early mediation, and thus to function in a preventive capacity at the emerging stage of conflict.

Early warning was to be carried out by collecting information on national minorities, by exploring the role of all contending parties, and, most important, by visiting those states where conflict seemed imminent or where ethnic tensions continued to disrupt the political and social order. To this day, these visits are a particularly important element in the ability of the HCNM to issue early warnings of potential conflicts to the Chairman-in-Office (CSCE 1992a, 20). Furthermore, the Helsinki summit spelled out the nature and scope of the HCNM, and it named the sources from which information was to be obtained: the media, nongovernmental organizations, and the contending parties, themselves, including government officials and representatives of ethnic groups, trade unions, political parties, and religious or other groups.

The first and current high commissioner is former Dutch foreign minister Max van der Stoel, who was nominated for the post at the Stockholm CSCE foreign ministers' meeting in December 1992. The foreign ministers "encouraged the High Commissioner to carefully analyze potential areas of tension, to visit such member states and to hold broad-based meetings on all levels with those parties directly involved with the problem" (CSCE 1992b, 15).

To achieve its dual objective of early warning and conflict prevention in Macedonia, the CSCE/OSCE has applied two principal mechanisms: the Spillover Monitor Mission to Skopje; and periodic fact-finding missions by the HCNM.

SPILLOVER MONITOR MISSION TO SKOPJE

The establishment of the Spillover Mission proceeded in three phases: (1) the dispatch of an exploratory mission in mid-September 1992 to study the conditions for a CSCE observer mission; (2) the arrival of the first chief of mission; and (3) the implementation of the mission's monitoring and mediation tasks.

It was the Bush administration that gave the initiative for the creation of the CSCE Spillover Monitor Mission to Skopje.[3] Established in the fall 1992, the mission had the explicit mandate to prevent a possible spillover of the Bosnian war by monitoring Macedonia's borders with Serbia and Albania as well as its political, economic, and social conditions. That the first three heads of the Spillover Mission were Americans was no accident; it signaled U.S. commitment to a policy of prevention and the maintenance of regional stability.

Meeting after the European Community refused to send observers to Skopje in the summer 1992, the CSCE's Council of Senior Officials (CSO) decided to dispatch an exploratory delegation in mid-September to investigate the conditions in Macedonia and to probe the willingness of the Macedonian government to accept a CSCE mission.

The CSCE delegation met with President Gligorov and other government officials, and with representatives of the ethnic Albanian parties, including Nevzat Halili, then the leader of the PPD.[4] To obtain a better understanding of the potential threats facing Macedonia and to evaluate the destabilizing impact of the war in Bosnia on the country's economic conditions, the delegation visited various checkpoints along Macedonia's border with Serbia, Albania, and Bulgaria (CSCE Secretariat 1992).

Upon its return, the delegation reported to the Chairman-in-Office that "leaders of the [Macedonian] government were eager to receive the CSCE Monitor Mission and to cooperate unreservedly in starting up spillover monitoring operations as expeditiously as possible" (CSCE Secretariat 1992). Furthermore, their report reiterated the fear expressed by Macedonian political leaders of a wider Balkan war and cited potential triggers for violent conflict: Macedonia's cutoff from oil supplies under the Greek embargo, which was destabilizing the country politically and economically; an influx of refugees from Bosnia; the growing likelihood of ethnic violence in Kosovo, which threatened

3. There are conflicting claims as to who initiated the mission. Another observer claimed it was President Gligorov who first requested the Spillover Mission.

4. The CSCE exploratory delegation visited the Republic of Macedonia on September 10–14, 1992. Its visits to Macedonia's border checkpoints included Tabanovce and Sopot, on the border with Serbia; Blace, on the border with Kosovo; Cafa San, on the border with Albania; and Gjiusevo, on the border with Bulgaria.

to add to Macedonia's refugee problem and possibly also to involve its ethnic Albanian population; the lack of a viable defense capability, making it impossible to monitor Macedonia's 240-kilometer border with Serbia; and finally, mounting unrest over ethnic Albanian demands. The delegation recommended establishing a long-term mission because of "a genuine risk of spillover of the Yugoslav conflict," which could be caused by a worsening of the situation in Kosovo or of internal tensions between ethnic Albanians and Slavic Macedonians. The delegation also called for monitoring Macedonia's border with Serbia, and especially with neighboring Kosovo (CSCE Secretariat 1992).

Already on September 8, 1992, the CSCE had deployed missions to Kosovo, Sandjak, and Vojvodina, with an integrated office in Belgrade to monitor the human rights situation and to promote dialogue between authorities and the various ethnic groups.[5] In September 1992, it established a long-term monitor mission in Macedonia, with headquarters in Skopje and with additional posts in Tetovo, close to the Kosovo border, and Kumanovo, a town near the Serbian border.

To avoid the use of the controversial name "Macedonia," the CSCE came up with its own compromise, calling its mission the "Spillover Monitor Mission to Skopje" (Blais 1994, 302; 1995). The mission had a broad mandate: "to monitor developments along the borders of the Host Country with Serbia and in other areas of the Host Country which may suffer from spillover of the conflict in the former Yugoslavia in order to promote respect for territorial integrity and the maintenance of peace, stability and security; and to help prevent possible conflicts in the region" ("Statement of the Head of the CSCE Spillover Monitor Mission" 1992; OSCE Secretariat 1997g; Blais 1994, 302). The mandate was renewable every six months, with the continued support of the Macedonian leadership.

U.S. Ambassador Robert Frowick, later in charge of the OSCE mission in Bosnia, was appointed the first head of mission. Arriving in Skopje in late September 1992, he negotiated the "Articles of Understanding" with the Macedonian authorities. Signed on November 5, 1992, the Articles of Understanding explicitly noted the preventive nature of the Spillover Mission to Macedonia, which was to monitor developments along Macedonia's border, especially with Serbia, and to protect the country's territorial integrity. The articles also committed the Macedonian government to cooperate fully with the

5. In 1993, the missions' staff was increased from 14 to 20. The Kosovo mission was based in Priština; the Sandjak mission in Novi Pazar, and the Vojvodina mission in Subotica. The missions remained until June 28, 1993, when Yugoslavia refused to extend the memorandum of understanding, after its member status in the CSCE had been revoked (OSCE Secretariat 1996a, 19–20).

mission and to provide all information needed to carry out the mission's mandate ("Statement of the Head of the CSCE Spillover Monitor Mission" 1992; Troebst 1994, 125–56; 1997a, 77–103).

With a relatively small staff, fluctuating between 6 and 8 monitors, the OSCE mission operates both on a formal, official level, maintaining frequent contacts with the political elites, party and religious leaders, and various political organizations; and on an unofficial level, meeting with journalists, trade union leaders, and the local population. Indeed, the Spillover Mission depends as much on informal as on formal channels for its early warning capability.

Implementing the Mandate

Under its mandate, the Spillover Mission engages primarily in monitoring and mediating. As part of their monitoring responsibilities, CSCE/OSCE staff members have attended to many different tasks over time, including the situation in Kosovo, all incidents involving ethnic relations, the impact of refugees, border security, and the degree of political and economic stability in Macedonia. But monitoring interethnic tensions has absorbed much of the mission's attention since its arrival in 1992.

OSCE mission members conduct regular trips throughout the country to investigate and to assess potential sources of unrest. Monitors are assigned certain geographic regions, where they visit towns and villages and record indications of interethnic tensions, human rights violations, and border incidents. As independent observers, they also investigate individual incidents involving various ethnic groups. For example, in the spring 1995, the mission investigated the death of an ethnic Albanian killed in Tetovo during the opening ceremonies for Tetovo University. When asked by specific groups, mission members have also engaged in mediation, although their mediation efforts remain minimal, with primary attention given to monitoring political, economic, and social developments in the country.

Reports filed by heads of mission to the CSO offer insights into the preventive efforts of the Spillover Mission. Most of these reports refer to specific incidents involving ethnic minorities in Macedonia. For example, on October 8, 1992, in Kumanovo, a city near the Serbian border with a 10 percent Serbian population, ethnic Serbs had allegedly shot and injured two Slavic Macedonians. By sending two monitors to the site to investigate the allegation the next day, the CSCE helped clarify the circumstances of the shooting, which could have led to a worsening of relations with Serbia. As it turned out, an ethnic Albanian from Macedonia had been slightly injured by a Serbian border patrol while he was stealing firewood when he crossed accidentally into Serbian territory (Troebst 1994, 136).

Another incident investigated by the CSCE mission occurred on New Year's 1992–93. Ambassador William B. Whitman, then the head of the Spillover Mission, described the details of this incident involving ethnic Serbs in his report submitted to the CSO on February 2, 1993:

> Probably fuelled by a combination of local brandies and Serbian nationalism, a group of youths stoned local police, shouted Serbian slogans and hoisted pictures of Milošević, Arkan, and Šešelj. The police reacted in force, arresting three. On January 2, Mission members visited Kučeviste at police invitation and were themselves confronted by an angry mob. On January 3 leaders of a Serb political party visited the Mission, expounding at length on the grievances of the Serb community against the FYR Macedonia's policies. On January 16 the [head of mission] and several members re-visited Kučeviste unannounced to investigate the situation; they found both the village and the local police authorities relaxed and back to normal. ("Report of Ambassador William B. Whitman" 1993)

Whitman's CSO report concluded that while the Macedonian government considered the possibility that the incident "may have been contrived by [ethnic] Serbian nationalists to create a pretext for aggression," and that "the Mission believes that FYR Macedonia's suspicions could easily be well-founded," it was more likely an isolated incident and not evidence of an organized mobilization of ethnic Serbs in Macedonia ("Report of Ambassador William B. Whitman" 1993).

Reports filed by the heads of mission and by the HCNM perform an early warning function by (1) identifying sources of potential conflict in its early stages; and (2) providing reliable, immediate information on the destabilizing conditions directly to the representatives of OSCE member states.

Much of the focus of CSCE monitoring in 1992–94 was on Serbia. For example, Ambassador Norman Anderson, in a report to the CSO meeting at Rome on November 27–28, 1993, described Serbian activities the mission interpreted as signs of intimidation at the very least, as well as a Serbian attempt at destabilizing Macedonia. During a press conference on November 8 with Greek Foreign Minister Papoulias, Serbian President Milošević had claimed he knew something of the existence of an ethnic Albanian separatist movement whose objective was a two-nation state, which would soon lead to separation. Turning toward the Greek foreign minister, he had noted that Greece might soon "have nobody to recognize." Although doubtless made for domestic purposes as much as for displaying Serbia's solidarity with Greece over their aversion to the Republic of Macedonia, such statements were often interpreted in Macedonia as evidence of the aggressive intentions of Serbia ("Report of Ambassador G. Norman Anderson" 1993).

More provocative were several border incidents that required the attention of the mission. Ambassador Anderson described one of these incidents which occurred in mid-November 1993, which had all the potential for provoking a violent reaction:

> Hostile activities of Serbian border guards in recent weeks have included a November 17 "ambush" in which armed Serbs crossed into FYR Macedonia and abducted two Macedonian policemen and a soldier into Serbia. Following a stiff protest by Skopje to Belgrade, the captives were returned the same day, but only after severe beatings. Earlier this month, a Serbian patrol occupied part of a border village claimed by FYR Macedonia. In another incident, Serbian border guards told UNPROFOR soldiers to stay out of a sizeable border area the UN believed to be within FYR Macedonia. The Serbs in a further provocative move warned that they would shoot down UN helicopters overflying Serbian-claimed areas. ("Report of Ambassador G. Norman Anderson" 1993, 2)

Anderson's report concluded that these incidents might be provocative acts directed at UNPREDEP or at the Macedonian government for its support of U.N. sanctions against Yugoslavia.

The Spillover Mission does not operate on its own in Macedonia. Cooperative ties were formed with the United Nations in early 1993, shortly after the arrival of its preventive force.[6] There was a daily exchange of reports between mission and U.N. personnel, and regular meetings between the OSCE head of mission and the UNPREDEP chief of mission. Other close contacts are maintained with personnel from the European Union's PHARE and ECHO programs, the representatives of the U.N. High Commissioner for Refugees (UNHCR), UNICEF, and the World Bank, as well as of the European Union's Sanctions Assistance Mission to Yugoslavia before its termination in October 1994. Cooperation with the EU has involved inclusion of two European Community Monitor Mission (ECMM) members since 1993. The Spillover Mission also forms part of the Crisis Management Committee with Macedonia's

6. The Helsinki Summit Declaration was the first document to note the cooperation between the United Nations and the CSCE, designating the CSCE a "regional organization" under chapter 8 of the U.N. Charter. A framework agreement on cooperation between the two organizations was concluded in 1992. Most OSCE missions negotiate protocols of cooperation locally with the United Nations (Höyck 1994, 70). OSCE-UNPREDEP cooperation was based on an agreement of April 15, 1993.

deputy ministers of defense, foreign affairs, and the interior, the UNHCR, and, formerly, representatives of UNPREDEP (Bøgh 1996; Yates 1996). Some cooperative ties are also kept with several larger NGOs such as Search for Common Ground in Macedonia (SCGM) or the Open Society Institute.

During the census, conducted from June 21 to July 5, 1994, the Spillover Mission and the ODIHR cooperated with teams from the European Union and the Council of Europe (OSCE Secretary-General 1994), which financed the census, providing 1.6 million ECU and 300,000 ECU, respectively, and which helped organize the activities of the Expert Group and the International Census Observation Mission (ICOM) under a memorandum of understanding signed with the Macedonian government (Republic of Macedonia State Census Commission 1995).

The Spillover Mission also played a crucial role in monitoring the parliamentary and presidential elections of October and November 1994, coordinating the activities of international observers from fifteen participating CSCE member states and international organizations. Despite some irregularities in the voting lists and some confusion over voters' eligibility, the mission and international observers from the ODIHR, the CSCE Parliamentary Assembly, the United Nations, the Council of Europe, and nongovernmental organizations confirmed that electoral procedures were democratic.

The Spillover Mission and UNPREDEP

The two organizations have always had similar mandates in Macedonia. Both were entrusted to monitor border incidents, preserve Macedonia's territorial integrity, and prevent a possible outbreak of violent conflict. There were also some similarities in the way the mandates were carried out. As part of their early warning activities, both UNPREDEP and Spillover Mission personnel frequently visited villages and border crossings to inquire whether there had been any incidents or hostile developments.

Although their preventive tasks and responsibilities overlapped, the two organizations complemented each other. UNPREDEP, with its military capability, served a two-pronged function: monitoring and deterrence, whereas the Spillover Mission has never been in a position to act as an agent of deterrence, having neither a military component nor the requisite size. Because UNPREDEP provided a preventive force to monitor and guard Macedonia's borders, the Spillover Mission, although also monitoring the border areas, has been able to devote more attention to internal affairs, such as investigating the arbitrary use of police force (often against ethnic Albanians) or other human rights and interethnic issues, including Tetovo University and the subsequent trials of its admininstrators.

The complementarity of the two organizations was most apparent when one followed Spillover Mission and UNPREDEP staff members along on monitoring assignments, as I did in the summer of 1996. My visit to Malina Maala, a small village populated entirely by ethnic Albanians, on the border with Kosovo, provides one of the many examples on how the Spillover Mission and UNPREDEP cooperated with one another in Macedonia, not only in conflict prevention but also in promoting goodwill and in providing modest support for developmental and humanitarian projects.[7]

A village of 640 ethnic Albanians, Malina Maala is located on a mountainous plateau approximately 1,400 meters high. On our way there, we passed two UNPREDEP observation posts—one with about 16 soldiers, the other with 8. The observation posts were established in 1993 in response to a request from the village mayor. When sheep farmers from his village accidentally crossed into Serbian territory, as they often did, they would be seized by Serbian soldiers—and released only after a handsome sum of money had been collected from the villagers. While in the village, the OSCE mission member asked a local carpenter whether there had been any recent incidents of accidental crossings and payment of ransom. On the way to the village, members of the U.N. civil engineering corp were smoothing out a dirt road, to make it accessable to UNPREDEP and OSCE trucks. Later, the mayor of the village showed the OSCE mission member a huge rock blocking one of the roads to a neighboring village. Without technical support, OSCE mission members often appealed to UNPREDEP for assistance, as was the case here. Several weeks later, U.N. civil engineers removed the rock so that villagers could again use the road. This example represents only one of many instances of complementary cooperation between the Spillover Mission and UNPREDEP (see also Burci 1997, 289–314).

HIGH COMMISSIONER ON NATIONAL MINORITIES

The HCNM performs one of the most important tasks of early warning and preventive diplomacy (see, for example, Estébanez 1997, 123–66; Huber 1993, 285–310; Leatherman 1994, 35–54; Van der Stoel 1994a, 43–51; Zaagman 1994, 113–75; Foundation on Inter-Ethnic Relations 1997a, 1997b). The

7. Malina Maala is representative of the many small and isolated villages in Macedonia. Populated entirely by ethnic Albanians, few Slavic Macedonians have ever set foot here. The village often lacks electricity because the Macedonian authorities are still in the process of building new lines to provide power, formerly supplied by Serbia. There are no doctors, no medical facilities, no paved roads, and no regular jobs for the villagers. Schooling is only provided through the eighth grade. After that, students must attend school in Skopje. Only two students did so in 1995. None did in 1996, when I visited the village on graduation day, June 5, 1996.

Concluding Document of the Helsinki Summit, in authorizing creation of the HCNM as an instrument for conflict prevention, in 1992, kept its mandate deliberately vague. It has been up to High Commissioner van der Stoel to define and carry out the mandate as appropriate to the different aspects and circumstances of ethnic conflict. Van der Stoel has pointed out at various occasions how he interprets his mandate:

> Neither the High Commissioner's mandate nor other CSCE texts define what is meant by early warning or preventive diplomacy, but we can make some assumptions. As a working definition I would say that early warning should provide the relevant CSCE bodies with information about escalatory developments, be they slow and gradual or quick and sudden, far enough in advance . . . for them to react timely and effectively, if possible still leaving them time to employ preventive diplomacy and other non-coercive and non-military measures. ("Keynote Speech" 1994, 7)

Regular fact-finding missions are among the most important preventive measures of the HCNM in Macedonia. Between 1993 and 1995 alone, one of the most critical periods for Macedonia, van der Stoel conducted twelve visits to the Republic of Macedonia, meeting with government officials and with leaders of the various ethnic groups and parties. In 1993, van der Stoel visited Skopje and other parts of Macedonia twice; in 1994, he made four visits to Macedonia; and in 1995, six (OSCE HCNM 1995a). Indeed, between 1993 and 1997, the HCNM was in Macedonia thirty times, and from February to July 1998, five times.

Typically, van der Stoel follows up each visit with a report to the CSO and recommendations addressed to the Macedonian authorities. Among the many ethnically divisive issues van der Stoel has investigated are citizenship requirements, television and radio programs for minority groups, the professional representation of ethnic Albanians, and educational and language rights for minorities.

Since he began his visits to Macedonia in 1993, Ambassador van der Stoel has concerned himself primarily with differences between Slavic Macedonians and ethnic Albanians. Many of his recommendations to the Macedonian government have addressed the grievances and demands of ethnic Albanians and possible ways to resolve contentious issues. For example, in his letter on November 1, 1993, van der Stoel expressed concern over the educational rights of ethnic Albanians in Macedonia, and he recommended that the government pass the law on local self-government which regulated the use of the Albanian language in areas where ethnic Albanians constituted a majority, as quickly as possible. Van der Stoel's recommendations on the issue of training Albanian-language teachers eventually resulted in the establishment of a four-year curriculum at the Pedagogical Institute in Skopje (CSCE Secretariat 1993).

During his mission on November 8–11, 1994, van der Stoel devoted considerable attention to two other major grievances: job discrimination against ethnic Albanians, particularly in the police, the army, and in public administration; and the limited TV and radio programming available in Albanian. As to job discrimination, van der Stoel explained that

> I am not advocating that persons should be appointed regardless of their qualifications, or that the desirable percentage for each population group would have to be in strict conformity with their precentage of the total population. However, corrective measures are in my view required when there is a big discrepancy between the percentage of members of a certain nationality in a branch of the public service and the percentage of the total population of that nationality. (OSCE Secretariat 1995c)

Although in his reply to van der Stoel the Macedonian foreign minister did not mention the problem of discrimination, he attached a comprehensive list of television and radio programming for all ethnic minorities to demonstrate that Albanian-language programs exceeded the one-hour-a-day limit van der Stoel had implied in his letter.

Following his visit on March 28–29, 1995, van der Stoel once more suggested a compromise to resolve the educational demands of ethnic Albanians, particularly with respect to Tetovo University, which in 1995 became the most contentious dispute among ethnic Albanians, their political leaders, and the Macedonian government. Viewing it as an attempt to create parallel institutions like those in Kosovo, the Macedonian government met the opening of Tetovo University, as an Albanian-language institution of higher learning, with police force. Van der Stoel, stated that, according to article 45 of the Macedonian constitution, citizens have the right to establish private schools at all levels. He also drew attention to the inconsistencies between the Macedonian constitution and the 1990 CSCE Copenhagen Document, which stipulates that national minorities have the right to their own educational institutions if they are established within the existing framework of national legislation.

Although noting with approval the Macedonian government's new policy of a minority quota for university admissions, the high commissioner questioned whether the quota of 10 percent for students of all national minorities was sufficiently high to make a substantial difference in the admission of ethnic Albanian students (OSCE HCNM 1995b). Arguing that Macedonia would have a need for qualified experts from all ethnic backgrounds, van der Stoel proposed a "compromise formula"—the establishment of a Higher Education Center for Public Administration and Business, a private institution, that would cooperate with the universities in Skopje and Bitola, that would offer courses taught in Macedonian, Albanian, and English, and that would also serve as a major language training facility—all at a cost of 1.8 million dollars annually, guaranteed by international financial assistance (OSCE HCNM 1995b). Although a well-meaning proposal, the Macedonian government rejected it.

In March 1997, the Macedonian government's decision to allow the use of Albanian as a language of instruction at the Pedagogical Institute in Skopje sparked student protests by Slavic Macedonian university and high school students. In his visits of March 6–8 and March 24–27, van der Stoel met with Prime Minister Crvenkovski and Foreign Minister Frčkovski and with the leaders of the PPD, the PPDsh, the NPD, VMRO, the Democratic Party, and the mayors of Tetovo and Gostivar to obtain firsthand information as to what triggered the crisis and to discuss how such incidents could be prevented in the future (OSCE Secretariat 1997e, 6). The high commissioner made a follow-up visit, from September 28 to October 1, 1997, largely to investigate the Gostivar unrest of July 1997 and to look into the severity of the mayor of Gostivar's sentence—13 years and 8 months imprisonment (OSCE Secretariat 1997c).

It is of course difficult to measure exactly what the precise effects of van der Stoel's recommendations have been on policy changes initiated by the Macedonian government, especially because other actors, such as the ICFY Working Group, engaged in a similar dialogue on many of the same issues.[8] In some cases, the high commissioner's recommendations were simply acknowledged and no policy changes implemented, for example, the issue of Tetovo University. Even though the illegal university represents a de facto parallel institution—an outcome the Macedonian government always feared—van der Stoel's "compromise formula" for creating a multilingual institution has never been acted upon, partly because of lack of enthusiasm on the part of the Macedonian authorities, but also because of the immense capital costs involved. It is questionable whether such an institution would have satisfied ethnic Albanians' demands for higher education. These demands are strongly motivated by the often expressed need for recognition of a separate culture—a need that will not be fulfilled by incorporating ethnic Albanians into a Macedonian curriculum. Indeed, it is because ethnic Albanians express their demands for

8. There are as yet no studies specifically assessing the influence of the HCNM on policy changes in various OSCE Mission countries. Currently, the Institute for Peace Research and Security Policy at the University of Hamburg, Germany, is planning to initiate such a study.

higher education in a larger cultural framework that the Tetovo University issue has been so difficult to resolve.

On other issues, however, van der Stoel's recommendations have met with considerable progress. The Macedonian government has shown the political will to accommodate a number of significant minority demands. The number of ethnic Albanians in the police and military has increased substantially; access to print and broadcasting media for ethnic Albanians, and for other ethnic minorities is significant, given that Macedonia is a small country with limited resources; the law on local self-government has been passed.

Van der Stoel's influence clearly contributed to the accommodation of minority demands and to the defusing of ethnic tensions in Macedonia. He provided an outside voice, insisting that there be progress in managing interethnic conflicts. Equally important, van der Stoel fulfilled the letter and the spirit of the HCNM mandate, identifying sources of potential conflict, bringing these to the attention of the Macedonian government, and publicizing them in a wider regional forum. In short, van der Stoel's visits to Macedonia helped establish and maintain a political dialogue that resulted in significant, incremental changes.

THE OSCE AND MACEDONIA'S EUROPEAN OPTION

The OSCE is also able to exercise long-term conflict prevention in Macedonia by virtue of its role as a major European institution. The importance of belonging to Europe is a recurring theme in Macedonia's foreign policy orientation. The OSCE was one of the first international organizations to which the newly independent Macedonia sought access. After repeated rejections, Macedonia finally succeeded in becoming a full member of the OSCE in October 1995.

As every one of the politicians interviewed for this project made clear, becoming part of Europe is a top priority in Macedonia's foreign policy. Pursuit of the "European option" has led the Macedonian government to establish and maintain close political and economic ties with a number of European institutions, including NATO's Partnership for Peace Program, the Council of Europe, the European Union, and the Central European Initiative (Crvenkovski 1996; Frčkovski 1996; Gligorov 1996).

In the view of Macedonia's political leaders, membership in European institutions offers three significant advantages. First, integration with Europe facilitates Macedonia's transition to democracy and a free-market economy. Second, it helps fill the security vacuum created by the Yugoslav wars. Although the 1995 Dayton Peace Accords restored a measure of regional stability, the area is still far from secure. Albania continues to be domestically unstable; Kosovo is wracked by war; and the limited success of postconflict peacebuilding efforts in Bosnia depends largely on the continued presence of the NATO Stabilization

Force. Thus the sentiment that membership in the OSCE and in NATO's Partnership for Peace provides an institutional framework to ensure Macedonia's security is widespread.

As a third significant advantage, Macedonia's European association promises, by promoting a European rather than a Macedonian outlook, to keep in check an emergent, divisive nationalism. Even the more nationalist ethnic Albanian leaders in Macedonia emphasize the need to identify with Europe. In pursuit of their own cultural and political aims, they embrace Europe's pluralist structures and values and the importance Europe attaches to the protection of minority rights (Xhaferi 1996a; Ibrahimi 1996a).

The Spillover Mission and the Kosovo Conflict

Although the mission's activities in 1996 were less demanding because fact-finding, dialogue facilitation, and mediation had made an impact on managing divisive interethnic issues, and there were rumors that the mission's mandate would terminate after it expired in 1997, sporadic outbreaks of civil disobedience and unrest in March and July 1997 proved otherwise. The protests and student hunger strike in March 1997 over the use of the Albanian language at the Pedagogical Institute and the killing of an ethnic Albanian in July 1997 during a demonstration justified a continued monitoring role for the mission and the continued involvement of the HCNM. During the 1997 trial of the Gostivar major, for example, the Spillover Mission assumed once more one of its traditional monitoring roles (OSCE Secretariat 1997a, 9). Moreover, in 1998, High Commissioner van der Stoel visited the country four times, impressing on the government the need to strengthen dialogue, communication, and tolerance among ethnic groups and exploring the ongoing issues of the Albanian language university and for ethnic Albanians' higher education (OSCE Secretariat 1998a, 12).

The most critical challenge posed to the OSCE mission has been the Kosovo conflict, which escalated throughout 1998 and seriously affected Macedonia because of a steady influx of Kosovar refugees. Already on March 11, 1998, in a special session on the Kosovo crisis, the OSCE's Permanent Council decided to enhance temporarily the monitoring capacity of the Spillover Mission for "adequate observation of the borders with Kosovo, FRY, and prevention of possible crisis spillover effects" (cited in "The OSCE Spillover Monitor Mission to Skopje" 1999). Because NATO intervention in Serbia and the spillover of refugees led to the destabilization of Macedonia, the mission's monitoring capabilities were adjusted to address this new conflict potential. For one, the mission was engaged in the assessment of the refugee crisis's impact on Macedonia, which involved monitoring and close cooperation with humanitarian organizations, especially their ability to accommodate vast numbers of refugees. The mission's second task was to monitor the effects of the refugee crisis on interethnic relations. And third, the mission was involved in security issues such as the monitoring of Kosovo Liberation Army (KLA) movements within Macedonia (Troni 1999).

To master some of these tasks, the mission received additional staff support from the OSCE Kosovo Verification Mission (KVM),which was created on October 25, 1998, to oversee the return of refugees and displaced persons within Kosovo. Established under an OSCE Permanent Council decision, the unarmed verifiers were deployed to Kosovo in late October, but withdrawn on March 19, 1999, following a decision by the OSCE Chairman-in-Office, Norwegian foreign minister Knut Vollebaek, after their safety could no longer be guaranteed. After their evacuation from Kosovo, the KVM, with a remaining staff of 334—seventy of whom were sent to Albania—worked with the United Nations High Commissioner for Refugees (UNHCR) on coordinating various humanitarian organizations, assisting in refugee camps and border crossings, and conducting interviews with refugees on human rights violations ("OSCE Contributes to Relief Efforts" 1999; "The Involvement of the OSCE" 1999).

Although the Spillover Mission remains the most successful of the OSCE's many preventive diplomacy missions, its presence in Macedonia might be long-term depending on the outcome of the Kosovo conflict and the repatriation of refugees.

7

NONGOVERNMENTAL ORGANIZATIONS AND LONG-TERM CONFLICT MANAGEMENT

OVER THE LAST twenty to thirty years, nongovernmental organizations have proliferated on the international scene and expanded their scope of operations. To humanitarian relief and developmental assistance—their more traditional roles—they have added human rights monitoring, refugee advocacy, and conflict management and resolution. Moreover, there is growing interest in assigning NGOs two other, more formidable roles—early warning and conflict prevention. Advocates generally note that NGOs are better equipped to approach community and religious leaders, and that a significant number of NGOs are already either directly or indirectly involved in building civil society. Because they operate on the grassroots level and are considered to be impartial, and because they are less politically constrained, more focused on the implementation of projects, and more flexible than their regional and international counterparts, NGOs are more likely to obtain the trust of local populations. In many cases, NGOs also work with indigenous groups or have local partners, and therefore enjoy access to local cultures and local leaders. Oriented toward serving the needs of local communities, NGOs also have a better knowledge of sources of conflict and impending crises. In addition, NGOs often find themselves in the midst of intergroup or interstate violence when providing developmental, emergency relief, or refugee assistance. In short, advocates argue, NGOs are uniquely positioned to play a powerful role in early warning and conflict prevention (see, for example, Rupesinghe 1995b, 112–14; Aall 1996, 433–43; Anderson 1996, 343–54; Boulding 1991, 789–805; Loescher 1993; MacFarlane 1996; Ross 1996; Hackett 1996, 269–84; Weiss and Gordenker 1996).

One way to provide NGOs with a voice in early warning is to give them better access to third parties who can muster the political will to avert impending violence. This would mean greater cooperation and coordination among

NGOs, international organizations, and individual states, however, something difficult to achieve because NGOs differ from other entities in their structure, mandate, and mission. To faciliate coordination, it has been suggested that international and regional organizations as well as donor agencies determine which NGOs are best suited for preventive action and peacebuilding programs.

Many NGOs, on the basis of their mission and the specific projects they implement, are already in a position to effectively participate in conflict prevention. For example, several volunteer groups have had a long and distinguished record in unofficial mediation and conflict management. This includes the Quakers, who have mediated in violent conflicts such as the war in Biafra (Dahlen, Westas, and Wood 1988). John Lederach, director of the International Conciliation Service of the Mennonite Central Committee, a religious group with a long-standing tradition in dispute resolution, acknowledges that NGOs understand that there is a continuum between short-term humanitarian efforts and long-term projects directed toward sustainable peace (Aall 1996, 442–43). What Lederach seems to suggest here is that NGOs can play an active role in preventing the outbreak of conflicts by tailoring their programs specifically toward peacebuilding, be it after periods of violence or in previolent stages of conflict.

Kenneth Hackett (1996, 272), who sees preventing conflict not only as addressing the causes of conflict but also as "repairing relationships and changing systemic problems in society," has suggested that preventive projects (1) facilitate mechanisms within the local community for dialogue, relationship building, and healing; (2) assist in building an "indigenous institutional capacity to manage conflict"; and, (3) engage local actors and organizations, particularly those overlooked in the peacebuilding process in war-torn societies (Hackett 1996, 272). NGOs can undertake conflict prevention in all three of these ways.

They can carry out educational and training projects designed to bring members of conflicting groups together, focusing on different age groups and social and professional groups. Moreover, NGOs, especially indigenous ones, can adjust conflict prevention and long-term conflict management projects to the particular cultural setting in which the preventive action takes place.

Although much has been written on NGOs in the last decade, and although the literature on NGOs is beginning to advocate that they play a stronger role in conflict prevention and conflict management, there are few empirical studies of NGOs that have already proceeded in that direction. Such studies require extensive fieldwork; many NGOs have neither the personnel nor the resources to provide written summaries of their activities, much less to conduct long-term follow-up studies on the impact of those activities. Moreover, empirical research into the effectiveness of NGOs in the implementation of conflict prevention projects is hampered by the dearth both of precise data and of effective instruments for measuring the success of particular projects.

The Republic of Macedonia is host to an impressive number of nongovernmental organizations, both international and indigenous, to include the Red Cross of Macedonia, CARITAS (serving especially the Rom community), the Helsinki Committee for Human Rights, Catholic Relief Services, the Young European Federalists, and the Open Society Institute. These NGOs carry out activities in three principal areas: (1) humanitarian relief and development assistance; (2) democratization, human rights, women's issues, and the environment; and (3) facilitation of interethnic dialogue through education and training. This chapter will focus on the third area.

Catholic Relief Services (CRS), with headquarters in the United States, is a good example of an NGO that has complemented its traditional humanitarian and refugee programs with conflict management. Arriving in Macedonia in 1992 with the outbreak of war in Bosnia, CRS first concentrated on relief work with Bosnian refugees, coordinating its efforts with the UNHCR.[1] Given the catastrophic state of Macedonia's economy in the early years of independence, CRS also provided humanitarian assistance to the wider population, and began to implement development programs (Chen 1995; Saraqini 1995). In 1995, CRS launched a major preventive project, "Peace and Reconciliation," designed to increase exchange among members of ethnic groups by bringing together community and religious leaders, and by creating parent-teacher associations in multiethnic schools (Saraqini 1995).

Indigenous NGOs in Macedonia which represent diverse issue areas, from human rights and democratization to environmental, youth, and women's issues, face several problems when it comes to conflict prevention. First, they tend to be divided along ethnic lines, reflecting much of the segregation that characterizes Macedonian society (Beška 1996b, 133–46). For example, the humanitarian and cultural organization El-Hilal, is composed almost entirely of Muslims, either ethnic Albanians or ethnic Turks, although it has cooperated in the past with CRS (Pruthi 1995). Other indigenous NGOs represent single ethnic groups, such as the League of Albanian Women, the League of Vlachs, or the Union of Rom. Few indigenous NGOs have managed to organize themselves around issue-areas that are in the interest of members of all ethnic groups.

Second, indigenous NGOs tend to lack the leadership needed for conflict prevention—individuals who "are brave enough to disclose opinions that are different [from] and even opposite [to] the ones expressed by the majority of their ethnic group"(Beška 1996b, 139). Because of this, both the scope of their

1. Not all Bosnians who came to Macedonia remained there; many only used Macedonia as a transit country. At the height of the war, there were about 30,000 refugees from Bosnia; in the summer 1996, only about 5,000 to 6,000 remained.

activities and their influence on policy makers in the area of conflict prevention are limited. Third, largely because Macedonia is still a very young democracy in the process of developing a civil society, indigenous NGOs have a low status in Macedonian society. Fourth, they face widespread skepticism about the possibility of improving relations between ethnic groups. A prevailing attitude, left over from the Communist days, is that ordinary citizens have little power to contribute to changes in society. And finally, given the ethnic divisions in Macedonian society, few indigenous NGOs are willing to engage in projects that facilitate interethnic dialogue at the risk of being accused of favoring one side over the other (Beška 1996b; Beška and Saraqini 1995).

Against the background of these constraints, this chapter will discuss the preventive activities of two NGOs in the Republic of Macedonia—Search for Common Ground in Macedonia (SCGM), an American nongovernmental organization based in Washington, D.C., and the Ethnic Conflict Resolution Project (ECRP), an indigenous organization located at the St. Cyril and Methodius University in Skopje. Both organizations are exclusively engaged in activities directed toward conflict prevention in Macedonia. Considerable time was spent with the directors of both NGOs to obtain information on their respective missions and projects to facilitate interaction between ethnic groups, as well as on the success they have achieved—and the limits they face—in preventing and managing conflict. By adapting a long-term conflict management approach to the cultural values of the social environment in which they operate, SCGM and ECRP have implemented programs that explicitly reflect the needs of the citizens of Macedonia and that have encouraged Macedonians to take a more constructive and active role in mitigating the conflict between ethnic groups.

CITIZEN DIPLOMACY: SEARCH FOR COMMON GROUND IN MACEDONIA

Founded in 1982 by John Marks, the author of a critical account of CIA operations, Search for Common Ground (SCG) provides "a framework within which people can solve their own problems," and in which conflicting parties can "approach problems in a non-adversarial manner while looking for win-win scenarios" (Vangelova 1995, 15). This "common ground approach" rests on multiple elements, including conflict resolution, negotiation, facilitation, and collaborative problem solving, where the highest, not the lowest, common denominator serves as the basis for interaction among adversaries. Accordingly, SCG strongly roots its programs on the grassroots level and in the belief that "once adversaries recognize that they share interests and problems, they can often work together and become partners in satisfying mutual needs" (SCG 1995, 4).

The first major activity of the newly established organization was to assist in improving U.S.-Soviet relations, a task that could not have come at a more appropriate time given the still strained relations between the two countries during the early years of the Reagan administration. However, as relations between the Soviet Union and the United States became more amiable, Marks began to shift SCG's focus to the Middle East, which culminated with the establishment of the Initiative for Peace and Cooperation in the Middle East, centered on the idea that nongovernmental organizations should always be proactive, that is, they should act ahead of governmental initiatives and not be "a cheerleader for government policy" (Vangelova 1995, 15).

In this spirit, SCG also founded offshoots in countries that required immediate attention—in Russia, in Burundi, in South Africa, and in Macedonia. Conflict prevention became the organization's most critical objective, especially in Macedonia but also in Burundi. In January 1995, SCG opened its office in Burundi's capital, Bujumbura, in cooperation with Refugees International and the U.N. secretary-general's special representative in Burundi (SCG 1995, 15). The organization did not take similar measures in Rwanda because ethnic hatreds had already killed close to half a million Tutsis and moderate Hutus there, and it was judged to be more expedient to prevent a similar outcome in Burundi, where ethnic violence also threatened to erupt into mass murder. This is consistent with SCG's policy for conflict prevention, which is to focus on countries where some success in preventing violence is still possible.

Established in March 1994 in Skopje, Search for Common Ground in Macedonia (SCGM) has become well known for its innovative and successful approach to conflict prevention, thanks to the tireless efforts of its current director, Eran Fraenkel, a trained historian and Balkan specialist, its underlying philosophy, and its many practical projects in education, journalism, and the environment, which provide attractive training components in the prevention and management of conflicts.

SCGM's founding director was former U.S. Ambassador Robert Frowick, a career diplomat who had served as U.S. ambassador to the CSCE. Frowick played a central role in maintaining access to governmental representatives, using his good offices to mediate in the disputes between Greece and Macedonia and between ethnic Albanians and the Macedonian government. Frowick used his political influence to obtain a compromise solution regarding the instruction of Albanian-language teachers.

Given Frowick's short term as director (six months) and his top-down approach to conflict prevention, SCGM was initially little involved in practical projects intended to facilitate community building. This all changed when Fraenkel took over. A scholar of Albanian and Macedonian history and culture with a lifelong interest in the Balkans and its neighboring countries, fluent in Albanian and Macedonian, Fraenkel first came to Macedonia as a consultant for the Washington-based International Foundation for Electoral Systems before the Macedonian elections in 1994.

Because Fraenkel believed in a grassroots approach to conflict prevention, and because he lacked the kind of access to the Macedonian political elite that Frowick had, SCGM shifted its emphasis in the direction of a more bottom-up approach. Fraenkel's goal was to change not just the behavior of groups and individuals but also their attitudes and values, a process that would require much more time and effort. Only then could long-term, enduring change be achieved. The underlying philosophy of SCGM was to assist Macedonian society in their resistance to the escalation of ethnic conflict into violence (Fraenkel 1995a, 1995b).

Fraenkel soon realized that, proceeding strictly from a culturally based perspective on conflict, SCGM could not address all the problems it needed to address. He therefore shifted his emphasis from long-term cultural projects that dealt principally with the issues of a particular ethnic group to projects that dealt with more immediate issues affecting all segments of the population, regardless of ethnic group. Fraenkel concluded that SCGM should have "multiple programs that touch[ed] on multiple aspects of society and its problems, that [were] geared at different paces" (Fraenkel 1995b), and that were deeply rooted in the common needs of all Macedonians. Fraenkel was convinced that Macedonians shared common needs, for which common solutions were essential. To understand the nature and importance of NGOs and their contribution to conflict prevention and management on the grassroots level, we will explore several concrete projects SCGM has implemented in Macedonia.

In the beginning, SCGM followed much in the footsteps of other NGOs engaged in dialogue building in Macedonia. This entailed creating a neutral environment where members of various groups could meet and discuss issues of common concern without fear. Fraenkel soon realized that dialogue building, although a basic and widely employed tool in conflict management and conflict prevention, would not, by itself, assure long-term conflict prevention. Consequently, he initiated a series of projects that dealt with specific issues and problems, and that were geared to finding specific solutions. Fraenkel realized that long-term conflict prevention required, most of all, some form of practical exposure to working collectively in the search for commonly acceptable solutions.

The list of projects that SCGM has undertaken thus far and that are specifically geared to prevention on a grassroots level is quite impressive, given the relatively short time that the organization has been in Macedonia. From 1996 to 1997, two major programs were a journalism project; and cross-ethnic environmental cooperation projects.

The underlying goal of each project is to identify problems as common problems requiring common efforts for solution. According to SCGM's philosophy, the needs of citizens are generally the same, which invites an approach to find common solutions acceptable to all sides. Such an approach is intended, first, to counteract certain psychological processes whereby members of one ethnic group tend to blame another ethnic group for their problems. Second, this approach prevents conflicts that are not necessarily ethnic in nature from becoming ethnicized. Because citizens' needs have priority and because these needs reflect the socioeconomic and political conditions of the country, SCGM's projects are never static but adapt to changing circumstances.

This working philosophy also allows SCGM to remain deeply rooted in the principle of citizen diplomacy, which underlies Search for Common Ground in all its worldwide programs. According to Fraenkel, the essence of citizen diplomacy is "that when you want to prevent the . . . escalation of conflict you have to explore the needs of citizens within societies and work towards meeting these needs rather than working towards meeting the needs of states and governments" (Ackermann and Chatterjee 1997).

SCGM's projects are all designed to involve members of different ethnic groups, although some are specifically directed toward ethnic Albanians and Slavic Macedonians. Because projects are based on a shared need or problem and a shared solution, participants are encouraged to feel they form part of one society. To help these projects succeed, SCGM has entered into partnerships with organizations having specific expertise in particular issue areas. In the past, these partners have included the Boston-based Balkan Peace Project, the Center for War, Peace, and the News Media of New York University, Catholic Relief Services, and the Skopje-based Ethnic Conflict Resolution Project.

Journalism Project

Among the earliest programs undertaken by SCGM—and the longest running—the journalism project has included a variety of different activities, from workshops to cross-ethnic reporting projects that provide participants with practical training in what is referred to as "inclusive journalism." In 1994, SCGM also produced its own television series, "Paths to Agreement," which investigated a number of public interest issues, some highly controversial, such as Tetovo University, the educational rights of ethnic Albanians, and access of ethnic minorities to media in their own language.

SCGM has concentrated on the training and education of journalists because journalists can make a difference in how they report an event involving other ethnic groups. SCGM's goal was to provide journalists with practical instruction in unbiased, noninflammatory reporting. The emergence of multilingual media has both a positive and a negative side. One the one hand, it demonstrates that Macedonia has made remarkable strides toward providing media access to all its ethnic communities. On the other, it has resulted in the segregation of the media by ethnic group. Because most ethnic Albanians are also proficient in Macedonian, they can avail themselves of both Macedonian- and Albanian-language publications and broadcasts, whereas Slavic Macedonians, most of whom do not know Albanian, are limited to their own language media. As a consequence of this asymmetrical access to the media, there is little shared information between the two ethnic groups. To address this problem, SCGM added an active training component to its journalism project.

The journalism project has been organized and carried out with SCGM's partner, the New York University Center for War, Peace, and the News Media. Its first phase was launched in July 1994, when the center's associate director, Robert Levitt, conducted a field assessment to determine what kinds of journalistic activity would be beneficial to Macedonia. The assessment led to the creation of two workshops, for journalists and editors repectively. Held on November 2–4, 1994, Journalism and Social Responsibility: The Role of the Media in Inter-Ethnic Relations was designed to train journalists in how to cover ethnic issues without resorting to familiar stereotypical images and language. The workshop sought to raise awareness of the role of journalists in perpetuating ethnic stereotypes. It also sought to teach journalists how they could assume greater responsibility in providing a more balanced and objective account of ethnically driven events.

Conducted by a team of Belgian journalists and two American editors (from daily newspapers in Seattle, Washington, and Providence, Rhode Island) who had considerable experience in the coverage of racial and ethnic affairs, directed by ABC News journalist Deborah Amos, the workshop was attended by fifteen print and broadcasting journalists from the ethnic Macedonian, Albanian, Turkish, and Rom communities. This was one of the few occasions in which Macedonian journalists from different ethnic groups actually had the opportunity to make contact with each other. Many of the participants also joined the Journalists' Club for Inter-Ethnic Dialogue, which was specifically created as a meeting place for journalists from different ethnic groups. The journalists' workshop was followed, on March 29–31, 1995, by a workshop directed toward newspaper and magazine editors, which included editors from Macedonia's Albanian-, Macedonian-, and Turkish-language newspapers and magazines. The workshop focused on training editors how to cover ethnic issues in a more unbiased way and how to support journalists on their staffs who practiced inclusive journalism.

An important, hands-on initiative to emerge from the workshops, the cross-ethnic feature-reporting projects have made a significant contribution to the community-based prevention of ethnic violence. Under the direction of *Los Angeles Times* staff writer Denise Hamilton, who spent four months as a

Fulbright Scholar teaching journalism at Skopje's St. Cyril and Methodius University, the first of these projects, "How we Survive," concentrated on economic issues and consisted of a team of four journalists—two Slavic Macedonians, one from the Macedonian-language daily *Nova Makedonija* and one from the Macedonian-language radio station Radio NoMa; one ethnic Albanian, from the Albanian-language daily *Flaka e vëllarzërimit;* and an ethnic Turk, from the Turkish-language newspaper *Birlik*.

"How We Survive" fulfilled its two immediate objectives: the production of a story by a multiethnic team of reporters, something never before attempted in Macedonia, and the introduction of Macedonian journalists to U.S. reporting styles. For one month, the journalists worked in multiethnic teams of two, conducting interviews throughout the various ethnic communities of Macedonia. All the reports were coauthored, with a joint byline. There were four stories in all: one on the overall economic situation in Macedonia; a second on the role of women in the economy; a third on the effects of tobacco; and a fourth on the economic plight of young people. To make the stories available to all ethnic groups, they were published in the Macedonian-, Albanian-, and Turkish-language press simultaneously, an agreement SCGM had worked out with the editors of the various newspapers by contacting editors who had participated in an earlier SCGM workshop.

"How we Survive" also fulfilled two larger objectives, however. First, reporters and the reading public became aware that economic problems are not intrinsic to just one ethnic community but affect Macedonian society as a whole. Second, by working cooperatively in multiethnic teams, reporters got to know and report on the problems of another ethnic community. Although they had grown up in the diverse ethnic communities of Macedonia, most of them had never crossed ethnic lines. One reporter told of the change of attitude that came with this cross-ethnic reporting exercise: "You know, I am a human being as well as a reporter. I care about the people here. And I realize that only if [ethnic] Albanians get along with [Slavic] Macedonians can we stay at peace here" (SCG 1995, 4). Denise Hamilton (1996, 82) described the project's impact on the journalists: "The breadth and depth of our reporting . . . forced them to confront and shatter stereotypes they might have held about the poor gypsy, the rich Albanian or the lazy Macedonian bureaucrat."

Fraenkel noted that the language barrier poses a very real problem for ethnic Macedonian journalists and their readership, one that affects what journalists report and what readers get to know about the other ethnic communities:

> So [ethnic] Albanians cross the linguistic line, [Slavic] Macedonians don't, and consequently these lines define the line of knowledge about each other. Knowledge that is largely perpetuated through the media;

> knowledge that might or might not be true or accurate information. Information which is largely based on prejudice or stereotypes or other misconceptions. So the question is, in this type of multicultural society, whether you want to call it that officially or not, how do you function as a member of the mass media? Whom do you serve? Do you serve your own community, that is, your language community, or do you serve society as a whole? (Fraenkel 1995b)

Cross-ethnic reporting has sought to overcome this language, thus cultural, barrier. Although the journalism project operates on a small scale, it has the potential for making significant changes in how ethnic communities report events about each other, in how issues and problems can be presented to a wider public as being shared by all groups, and in how empathy can be created toward individuals of all groups who currently suffer from the hardships of economic transition. The cross-ethnic reporting project on economic issues was so successful that SCGM has undertaken three other such projects, on health care, on water and air pollution, and on women's issues.

Environmental Cooperation Projects

SCGM has also implemented a number of cross-ethnic environmental cooperation projects.

"Adopt-a-Monument." Launched in the spring 1996, Adopt-a-Monument brings together children from ten different schools in three Macedonian cities and towns. In this project, school children from the various ethnic communities share a collective responsibility for cleaning up cultural and historical monuments, including those in Skopje, Tetovo, and Štip. Even in ethnically mixed schools, children often do not know members of the other ethnic community because classes are taught in separate languages. Adopt-a-Monument exposes children to those from other ethnic groups, allowing them to make contacts they otherwise would not have made.

The project has five principal goals, all of which make some contribution to conflict prevention on the grassroots level: (1) to "instill some sense of common ecological awareness among the children," something completely absent in Macedonia as a whole; (2) to "instill the sense of a common cultural and historical legacy so that regardless of whether you are [Slavic] Macedonian or [ethnic] Albanian or Turkish . . . you feel a sense of ownership of the cultural or historical legacy, whether it is a mosque or a church or a bridge or a monastery"; (3) "to stimulate in the children some sense of proactive civic initiative," something that did not exist in Yugoslavia, where citizens were used to letting the government take responsibility; (4) "to increase interethnic dialogue and . . . to have that dialogue lead to concrete projects in the community"; and (5) "to promote interethnic cooperation and to diminish the tendency of Macedonia's communities to blame each other rather than addressing their common concerns" (Fraenkel 1996c, 1996d, 3).

Accompanying Fraenkel and the school children for a day (see Ackermann and Chatterjee 1997), one acquires a sense of how Adopt-a-Monument is carried out in practice. Meeting the children on a school yard in one of Tetovo's schools, Fraenkel provides on-site instructions on what is to be done. The cleanup then proceeds around one of the oldest mosques in town, while Fraenkel distributes pamphlets in Albanian and Macedonian to bypassers and shopkeepers, which explain the project and the childrens' efforts on behalf of their communities. Every month, between 30 and 40 students participate in the project. During the summer months, when school is in recess, "ecopatrols" follow up once a week to ensure that the adopted areas remain litter-free. Environmental workbooks are provided as teaching tools for classroom use to support the project and to retain students' interest. Adopt-a-Monument has also attracted considerable attention from the media and from ethnic community leaders who favor such cooperative projects. Most important, children are learning that positive changes can be accomplished through interethnic cooperation.

Cleaning up Lake Prespa. A second environmental project has sought to create a similar learning experience for two ethnically mixed villages, Arvati and Krani, near Lake Prespa, in western Macedonia. Because none of the villages has any waste disposal systems, all waste is dumped into a river, from where it then pollutes Lake Prespa. After several meetings with villagers in which each group blamed and accused the other for not taking action, for lacking cleanliness, and for being impossible to work with, SCGM staff succeeded in persuading citizens to take constructive action rather than blaming each other's group for the existing condition. As a result, villagers from the two ethnic communities arranged a cleanup of their river and lake. Following this example, other community leaders have also expressed an interest in imitating the initiative (Fraenkel 1996d).

How then does SCGM differ from other international NGOs engaged in the Republic of Macedonia? According to Fraenkel (1996b), there is a significant difference that derives from the organization's unique philosophy: "We look for various entries into Macedonian society to design programs whose long-term effort is conflict prevention. This includes journalism projects, conflict management training, and environmental projects. All projects have the same goal. We hope that goal becomes internalized by the individuals who participate." Rather than approaching problems with Western-style solutions, SCGM adapts its conflict resolution approach to local cultural values (Fraenkel 1995b).[2]

Applied Psychology: The Ethnic Conflict Resolution Project

A voluntary organization of a different type is that directed by Violeta Beška, a psychologist at the St. Cyril and Methodius University in Skopje. Having done graduate work at Columbia University, Beška was influenced by American concepts of conflict resolution, a good example of how educational exchanges can facilitate innovations elsewhere. After receiving her doctorate in psychology from the University of Belgrade, Beška began teaching at the St. Cyril and Methodius University, where she founded the Ethnic Conflict Resolution Project (ECRP), basing it on some of the very same techniques of conflict resolution she had become familiar with in the United States. A voluntary group with only a small staff drawn primarily from the psychology and sociology departments of the university, a psychologist from one of the public schools and a political scientist from an adult education institution in Tetovo, the ECRP adopted conflict resolution techniques to fit the conflictive environment of ethnic groups in Macedonia.

Realizing that ethnic conflict constitutes the greatest threat to the country and that there are no institutions that provide public education on conflict resolution techniques or awareness as to the relevant problems of ethnic minorities, Beška and her colleagues set out to create an organization that would teach Macedonians from all ethnic groups to take an active approach to the resolution of conflicts. Because the conflict between ethnic Albanians and Slavic Macedonians is the most volatile, the ECRP focuses primarily on bringing members of these two groups together. Moreover, the ECRP does not try to work out the more divisive issues between the two ethnic groups, such as the Tetovo University issue. Rather, it adopts a more overarching approach: by educating members of ethnic groups in conflict management techniques it hopes to create a culture of nonviolence, one that stresses win-win situations for all participants concerned.

The ECRP takes a practical approach to conflict prevention and conflict management through three kinds of interactive projects: education in conflict management, research in conflict management, and direct mediation between members of groups in conflict. Education in conflict management techniques is primarily conducted through workshops, many specifically geared to the train-

2. SCGM's conflict prevention projects are also described in Lumsden 1997.

ing of educators, psychologists, social workers, and students. Occasionally, even senior government officials have participated in such workshops, as did the former Education Minister Emilija Simovska, who took a more accommodative approach to the educational demands of ethnic Albanians.

Because many ethnic stereotypes develop at an early age and can flourish in a school system where ethnic groups do not necessarily attend classes in the same language, the ECRP has since January 1990 targeted children, teaching conflict management in primary and secondary schools. School children learn about the various needs of members of different ethnic groups, and how conflicts can be resolved in cooperative and nonviolent ways. They attend ECRP workshops that focus on how conflicts are provoked, how the spiral of escalation works, and how conflict management techniques can resolve conflicts nonviolently and achieve win-win outcomes. There are already several pilot schools with an ethnically mixed student population where such workshops take place. Children also participate in ECRP conflict management games once a week in a year-long program for fourth graders that has been incorporated into the regular curriculum. Because the objective of these programs is to create and eventually spread a culture of conflict management, the ECRP also has developed a teacher's handbook to train more teachers and school psychologists in conflict management, with the hope that they will train still others.

Like Search for Common Ground in Macedonia, the ECRP also targets journalists, who have the power to promote—or to abate—the escalation of conflict. Here as elsewhere, the objective of the ECRP is to "educate people [to] see conflicts in a different manner, to help them understand how to act in situations of conflict between individuals or between groups, and how to obtain an active relationship to conflict management" (Beška 1996a).

Because there were no textbooks on conflict analysis and conflict resolution in Macedonian or Albanian, Beška also wrote and designed a bilingual, and more general, conflict management handbook for the many audiences she trains. Published in 1995, the book is divided into two language sections, with the front cover introducing the Macedonian section of the book and the back cover the Albanian section—or vice versa, however the reader chooses to approach the book. In 1997, an English version of the handbook was also published with the financial assistance of Search for Common Ground. In its introduction, Eran Fraenkel notes that "among all communities in the Balkans, making *muabet* is a refined art: Regardless of language, people skillfully talk with each other but are much less adept at communicating TO [*sic*] each other" (Beška 1997, iii). Through the handbook and those trained by it and by ECRP's programs, Beška hopes that members of different ethnic groups will learn to communicate to each other about their conflicting needs and interests.

Although the ECRP is not a nongovernmental organization in the traditional sense, being located within the Faculty of Philosophy at the St. Cyril and Methodius University in Skopje, its activities are in many ways those of an NGO. It is also closely involved with international NGOs, sharing scarce resources and expertise as well as expanding the scope of projects. Because it lacks the resources to finance projects and programs in the long term, the ECRP has various project partners who provide financial assistance and with whom it often engages in cooperative projects. Among these are Search for Common Ground in Macedonia, Soros's Open Society Institute in Macedonia, and Catholic Relief Services, NGOs that share similar objectives in their approach to conflict management at the grassroots level.

IMPACT OF NGOS ON CONFLICT PREVENTION

That the two NGOs described at length in this chapter have adjusted their instruments of prevention to the specific cultural environment in which they operate seems to account for the relative success of their work. As in the case of the preventive efforts of regional and international organizations, it is of course difficult to measure quantitatively what impact SCGM and the ECRP had in changing the attitudes of members of ethnic groups toward each other or in teaching conflict management skills. Because their preventive activities are directed toward small groups over the long term, we cannot as yet judge their success. One way to obtain data on the effectiveness of long-term preventive projects therefore is to undertake appropriate long-term assessment studies for NGOs such as SCGM and the ECRP.

The experience of SCGM and the ECRP has much to tell us about opportunities for early warning and conflict prevention by NGOs in countries where there are interethnic tensions but where violence is low or nonexistent. One of these opportunities is to design programs that actively help people to understand conflicts both within themselves and between their and other ethnic groups. Another is to make training in conflict resolution techniques available on the grassroots level. Moreover, working directly with members of ethnic groups allows SCGM and the ECRP to monitor signs of deterioration in interethnic relations and thus to play a role in early warning.

My interviews of Violeta Beška and Eran Fraenkel also provide insight into the limits that NGOs face in conflict prevention. Although some of these limits apply specifically to indigenous or to international NGOs, others are common to both.

In addition to the five principal constraints discussed in this chapter's introduction, indigenous NGOs in Macedonia face two others, which bear directly on their capacity for early warning and conflict prevention: (1) they have little or no access to government officials and the media; and (2) few of their members have training in conflict management skills, an essential prerequisite for understanding which projects are needed to address ethnic conflicts (Beška 1996a, 1996b; Beška and Saraqini 1995; Beška and Popovski 1996).

According to Fraenkel most international NGOs in Macedonia also lack access to government officials. American NGOs in particular, especially because they are often associated with the U.S. government, arouse suspicion on the part of not only some government officials but also of the wider public. Moreover, they are often regarded by indigenous NGOs as "fund providers" rather than as cooperative partners in the building of civil society. Fraenkel also noted the absence of strong networks between international and indigenous NGOs and between NGOs and international organizations, although SCGM has been much more successful in establishing such cooperative linkages because of its unique philosophy and its individual leadership (Fraenkel 1996a, 113–32; 1995a, 1995b, 1996b, 1996c).

The activities of SCGM and the ECRP, exemplify the new proactive role that NGOs can play in early warning and conflict prevention. What distinguishes the preventive work of these two NGOs from that of official preventive actors, is however, that, despite the difficulties they face, SCGM and the ECRP have adapted long-term conflict resolution approaches aimed at changing both attitudes and behavior to local cultural values. The long-term individual and group-based changes they have achieved through education, exchange programs, and cooperative community projects linking ethnic neighborhoods will far outlive the efforts of their regional and international counterparts. The principal preventive role of NGOs, therefore, is one of long-term conflict prevention and conflict management, continuing long after official actors have brought their mandates to a close.

8

THE ART OF CONFLICT PREVENTION

If peace, like war, is something that individuals and groups learn, then the prevention of war and violent conflicts is also something that can be learned. As was demonstrated in this study, conflict prevention does not come automatically, effortlessly, or through good will alone. In other words, conflict prevention, like peace, is not something that just happens. It entails the conscious implementation of preventive measures before the outbreak of violence. It requires the tireless efforts and hard work of many actors, on many different, overlapping levels. A principal lesson to be learned from the case of Macedonia, is that violent conflict can be prevented—through design rather than by accident.

But how can a world in which the literature on the art of war has filled the shelves of most libraries for centuries, learn to engage in the "art of prevention"? The case studies of preventive diplomacy presented in this book yield some possible answers to this question.

LESSONS FROM THE CASE STUDIES

It was argued at the beginning of this book that, among the cases of preventive diplomacy, Macedonia is unique. Several reasons were cited for this "uniqueness": Macedonia's location in a war zone, within an historically unstable region; the strong linkage between its external and internal sources of conflict; its position as a small, democratizing state, without a viable defense capability, but with posturing, even militant neighbors; its economic fragility and high level of interethnic tension; its role as bone of contention, over which the middle powers of the region fought two costly and cruel wars at the beginning of the twentieth century. Yet Macedonia is unique in another respect. It is the best working case study on the successful application of timely, multifaceted preventive diplomacy. From the positive and negative cases we have examined, we can extract several general—and in many ways intertwined—factors necessary to the success of conflict prevention.

Timely Involvement

Because preventive action must take place in the early or formative stages of conflict when there is no or only sporadic violence and when contending parties have not mobilized yet to use force, the early involvement of third parties is vital. This is critical in cases where spillover of violent conflict across borders is imminent or where discontent within a country has already reached high levels. In the case of Macedonia, for example, measures were taken immediately for the preventive deployment of U.N. peacekeepers along the Serbian-Macedonian border following the outbreak of war in Bosnia-Hercegovina—to prevent Serbian aggression against Macedonia and the much-feared spillover of armed confrontations into the wider region. Preventive initiatives were also immediately taken to provide a forum in which the grievances and demands of ethnic groups—particularly those of ethnic Albanians and ethnic Serbs—could be voiced and subsequently dealt with through compromise and accommodation. In the cases of Croatia and Bosnia, but also of Rwanda, regional actors failed to respond in timely fashion, either because of their inability to muster the necessary political will for preventive involvement, their indifference to the conflict, or the lack of support from major actors outside the region.

Support of Major International Actors

Successful preventive action is also largely dependent on the support of at least one major country or international/regional organization outside the region of the conflict. Because of the hesistancy of the international community to become involved in the internal affairs of states, political will must be mustered for preventive action to be initiated. This often means that a dominant international actor must either initiate preventive diplomatic efforts or be supportive when domestic players request third-party involvement. In all successful cases previously discussed, either the United States or international/regional institutions were vital to the initiation and the subsequent continuation of preventive measures. Macedonia had the strong backing of the United States and the United Nations in its attempts to avoid armed confrontations. The inclusion of a contingent of U.S. soldiers in the preventive force provided UNPREDEP with much-needed additional "deterrent value." Washington was also the driving force in jump-starting Greek-Macedonian negotiations after efforts for a settlement sponsored by the United Nations had broken down. Estonia, on the one hand, and Slovakia and Hungary, on the other, both benefited from the timely and concerted actions of the OSCE and the HCNM.

It also must be emphasized that the role of individuals representing international and regional organizations and their leadership and personal commitment to preventive diplomacy is important for successful prevention. That was the case for UNPREDEP's chief of mission, Henryk Sokalski, and the Working Group's chairman, Geert Ahrens, in Macedonia. Their personal investment in preventive action was, among other factors, crucial for the two organizations to complement each other without the organizational rivalries that can occur when there is an overlapping of mandates.

The support of major international actors was missing in the case of Rwanda, but also in the cases of Croatia and Bosnia. In Rwanda, the United Nations sought to stop the escalation of the genocide but did not get sufficient backing from the United States to have the appropriate coercive instruments to do so. In Croatia, the conflicting positions among the major European states and between the United States and its European allies made adoption of a coordinated preventive action plan impossible. Instead, the conflicting positions, national agendas, and interests resulted in a piecemeal and ad hoc approach to the crisis. Prime responsibility for mediation was left to the European Community, which resorted to traditional diplomatic means, such as the Troika mechanism, but was unable to get the warring parties to engage in political dialogue.

Coordinated, Varied, and Multifaceted Intervention

The successful cases of preventive diplomacy, and Macedonia in particular, also demonstrate that coordinated, varied, and multifaceted actions, instruments, and strategies are needed to prevent conflict, especially in environments of impending violence. In Macedonia, official and unofficial actors applied a number of instruments, from preventive deployment, to the use of good offices and mediation, to grassroots activities designed to induce behavioral changes among members of the contending groups. In none of the other successful cases discussed was there such a significant presence of regional and international actors as well as non-governmental organizations. Where mandates overlapped, as in the case of the CSCE/OSCE Spillover Mission and UNPREDEP, actors were able to coordinate and even complement their preventive efforts.

An important part in this wide-ranging network of preventive actors was played by the ICFY Working Group, under the long-standing and able leadership of Ambassador Ahrens, who knew the region well, had a personal interest in the Balkans, and had a strong personal belief in preventive diplomacy. Ahrens was particularly able to draw in ethnic Albanian factions seeking a more radical solution to the ethnic Albanian problem within Macedonia. Operating behind the scenes, the Working Group provided a nonthreatening forum for negotiations on diverging positions and interests and influenced parties to adopt compromise solutions, as for example was the case in the disputes over the wording of the constitution.

Although neither Estonia nor Slovakia and Hungary saw multiple and varied preventive efforts on the scale of Macedonia, several different preventive instruments were used in both cases, especially on the part of the CSCE and the HCNM. OSCE missions were established in various parts of Estonia; a special representative was appointed to deal with the contentious issue of former Soviet pensioners once employed in the military and security forces in Estonia; CSCE expert teams were dispatched as consultants on educational and language policies in Slovakia and Hungary; and, of course, High Commissioner van der Stoel made frequent visits to Estonia, Slovakia, and Hungary, inducing the respective governments to address the demands and grievances of their ethnic minorities, and to seek some form of political dialogue and accommodation.

By contrast, in the cases of the former Yugoslavia and Rwanda, not only were too few instruments employed but a wide-ranging network of third-party actors was also lacking. The inability of the CSCE/OSCE to attend to the crisis because of the Yugoslav veto, the lack of support from the United States, the bickering among regional states as to how to respond to the conflict, and the failure of the EC/EU to avert the escalation of violence resulted in a diplomatic vacuum. In Rwanda, for example, the United Nations sought to muster support for stopping the genocide through a preventive force, but failed to obtain the backing of significant players, such as the United States or some of the regional actors. French intervention, after the genocide had already killed tens of thousands, was driven more by historical, geopolitical, and national than by preventive considerations.

Moderate Behavior of Domestic Leaders

Although preventive efforts can be initiated without the support of one or the other contending faction, this study has illustrated that preventive diplomatic efforts are more likely to succeed if they are supported by domestic leaders willing to moderate their behavior. Moderate behavior can mean, on the one hand, abstention from the pursuit of nationalist, exclusionary agendas, from the use of hate rhetoric, from the falsification and misuse of historical events, symbols, and myths, and from extreme expressions of victimization; and a willing openness to political accommodation and power sharing, on the other, which may be expressed in governmental coalitions, a veto power on legislation for all or the major ethnic groups, a system of proportionality in parliament or in administrative and other professions, or some degree of local or regional autonomy, however incremental or limited at first. Political leaders must also be able to convince their followers that such accommodative measures work to the benefit of all segments of society.

Again, the case of Macedonia is an excellent example to illustrate the importance of moderate leadership to the peaceful outcome of conflicts. Macedonia's government and ethnic leaders continue to maintain a balanced, moderate approach, where political dialogue, power sharing, coalition building, conciliatory gestures, and abstention from extreme nationalist or ethnic rhetoric provide a framework for finding solutions acceptable to both sides.

Such moderate behavior was absent in the case of Croatian and Serbian leaders, who deliberately appealed or reinvented historical myths to advance their personal political ambitions. In the case of Serbia, political leaders frequently appealed to their supporters to avenge the defeat of the Serbian kingdom in the fourteenth century by the Ottoman Turks, associating this historical tragedy with the victimization of present-day Serbs in the secessionist Yugoslav republics. It was also absent in Rwanda, where hateful rhetoric was spread throughout the mass media to incite communal violence and to legitimize the murder and dismemberment of "the other" group—the Tutsi.

In the cases of Estonia and of Hungary and Slovakia, although political leaders sometimes resorted to policies considered harsh and discriminatory by their ethnic minorities, they were willing, at least in many incidents, to modify such policies in response to minority protests or to the involvement of third parties. For example, Estonia changed its citizenship requirements after a massive outcry on the part of ethnic Russians, and the preventive involvement of the CSCE and the HCNM. Hungarian and Slovakian authorities have engaged in consistent bilateral efforts to arrive at more acceptable policies on divisive educational and language issues affecting their ethnic minorities, largely at the urging of the OSCE and its high commissioner.

Group-Specific Factors

As noted in the previous discussion, there are certain factors intrinsic to societies that make peaceful outcomes more likely, such as the moderate behavior of political leaders. Related to this are psychological factors, largely rooted in the collective unconscious of nations and ethnic groups, that are much more difficult to address through preventive efforts. These include the images ethnic groups hold of themselves and the images they have of each other, as well as the presence or absence of traumatic historical experiences, such as genocide, mass expulsion, or forceful assimilation. Our case studies strongly suggest that the absence of a history of extreme individual and collective victimization and the presence of a peaceful self-image for ethnic groups are vital to the prevention of violence.

The case of Rwanda is illustrative. Given the "divide and conquer" approach of its colonizers, it comes as no surprise that Rwanda has had a long history of interethnic animosities and has failed to develop a culture of cooperation and accommodation. Moreover, the absence of serious attempts to account for past abuses and to seek ethnic and national reconciliation has hampered efforts to prevent violent conflicts and contributed to conditions that made genocide all the more likely.

Although Estonia experienced the traumatic occupation of its territory and the subsequent deportation of many of its citizens, both vividly recalled by Estonia's older generation, this national trauma has not prevented Estonia's leaders from seeking bilateral negotiations or from moving toward conciliatory accommodation of its ethnic Russian population.

Again, Macedonia presents a unique case. Although atrocities were committed on the part of the Ottoman Turk rulers over the span of several centuries, these events do not figure into the historical repertoire of contemporary Macedonians, be they ethnic Albanians or Slavic Macedonians. In fact, neither group bears any animosity toward ethnic Turks, who are descended from the Ottoman Turk colonizers. To the contrary, Slavic Macedonians and ethnic Albanians I interviewed all pointed to a shared positive historical experience—that of having lived together for centuries under Ottoman rule. Moreover, those interviewed from each group thought of their group as the more peaceful of the two, but did not attribute a "warrior image" to the other, whereas members of both groups associated Serbs with the image of "the fighter" or "the warrior." When asked why there was no war in Macedonia, each group claimed responsibility for itself.

Country-Specific Factors

Although the study did not explicitly focus on these factors or test their validity in the Macedonian case study, they warrant mention for possible inclusion in my proposed analytical framework. Country-specific factors include population and country size, the relative size of ethnic groups, the geographical distribution of ethnic groups, and the economic strength of the country.

One can draw some conclusions and insights from the Macedonian case study with regard to at least two of these factors. For one, Macedonia is a relatively small country, only the size of Vermont, which made it easier to engage in widespread preventive action. For another, ethnic Albanians are mostly concentrated in a single geographic region, along Macedonia's border with Albania and Kosovo, which allowed preventive actors to use their limited resources and personnel to maximum effect. What remains to be explored, however is the relative importance of country-specific factors to the success of conflict prevention.

LIMITS TO PREVENTIVE DIPLOMACY

Although preventive diplomacy provides hope to those with a strong belief in peace, a cautionary note is in order. First, despite the most effective, concerted, and multifacted efforts, preventive diplomacy may not entirely succeed or may even fail. One reason for such an outcome is that conflicts have their own dynamics. Because they cannot always be manipulated by outside parties, nor entirely controlled by the leaders of contending groups, factors intrinsic to a particular conflict, such as the psychological factors mentioned above, can inhibit peaceful outcomes.

Second, because preventive diplomacy is an ongoing process, it is never entirely complete, as the cases of Macedonia, of Estonia, and of Hungary and Slovakia demonstrate. It is essential therefore to follow up on initial preventive efforts with long-term conflict management strategies and instruments.

Third, although preventive diplomatic efforts are generally less costly than massive reconstruction projects after protracted wars, it may be difficult to muster the necessary resources to engage in preventive activities. Fourth, preventive diplomacy raises a number of troublesome questions. What is the appropriate length of preventive missions, such as those of the United Nations or the OSCE? How do third parties know when to withdraw? And what if the withdrawal is followed by armed hostilities? Who ultimately pays for these preventive missions? And which countries are eligible for preventive diplomatic action? What criteria should be used and which third-party actors should decide whether they are met?

Finally, it is vital not to have exaggerated expectations as to what preventive diplomacy can accomplish. Successful prevention, warns Kriesberg (1998b), does not seek to achieve "utopian perfection." Nor should we expect preventive diplomacy to lead to the complete settlement of conflict. Preventive diplomacy may, however, result in the eventual transformation of conflict, perhaps over many years, provided a culture of political dialogue, accommodation, power sharing, proportional representation, and coexistence is able to develop.

AN ANALYTICAL FRAMEWORK FOR CONFLICT PREVENTION

On the basis of this study, I have developed an analytical framework, which describes the various actors, methods, and approaches that appear to be necessary for successful conflict prevention (see table 2). Systematic single case studies are needed to determine what accounts for the success or failure of preventive diplomacy; when and where to use it—how to muster the necessary political will to use it in serious conflictive situations, such as impending genocide; how to make it part of the foreign policy of major regional and international actors; and finally, how to institutionalize preventive diplomacy over the long term.

What is crucial as we near the beginning of a new millennium is that we focus, not on the failures, but on the successes of preventive diplomacy, so that we may learn how we can make peace prevail.

Table 2
Conflict Prevention Model:
Prevention at the Emerging Stages of Conflict

Actors	Preventive approaches/policies
Level I: Top leadership (Political elite)	Initiate dialogue; accommodation and power sharing; coopting; allow for formation of ethnic parties; abstain from nationalist rhetoric; foster willingness to consider compromise solutions; adopt moderate behavior and approach vis-à-vis leaders of contending groups.
Level II: Leaders of ethnic groups and political movements (Mid-level)	Willingness toward dialogue, negotiation, and power sharing; adopt moderate behavior; abstain from nationalist rhetoric/ agendas; rephrase demands as "access" rather than "exit"; maintain nonviolent approach.
Level III: International/regional organizational (Third-party actors)	Mediation; facilitation of political dialogue through creation of special forum (e.g., trilateral forum in Macedonia); fact-finding missions; monitoring missions; economic, developmental, and humanitarian assistance; establish confidence-building measures; maintain dialogue with all political and civic groups in the country; preventive deployment; provide noninflammatory information to all parties; support institution building and civil society building; provide retraining for military and police forces; assist in the development of legal and human rights norms.

Table 2—*Continued*

Level IV: NGOs and other grassroots organizations (e.g., religious, civic, humanitarian, university) (Societal level)	Provide education in conflict management; conduct training projects (e.g., for journalists, children, students, social workers, government officials); initiate community-building projects centered on common problems; conduct projects in prejudice reduction and reframing techniques; organize problem-solving workshops with representatives from contending groups; provide training in "inclusive" and noninflammatory journalism; teach nonviolent action; write and publish conflict resolution textbooks for schools; reexamine history and social science textbooks for ethnic stereotypes.

EPILOGUE

Making Peace Prevail is the story of a former Yugoslav republic that seceded peacefully in 1991 without the violence and bloodshed that accompanied secession elsewhere in Yugoslavia. Since then, Macedonia has been successful in building a democracy and a viable state, and in managing relations with its ethnic minorities and its regional neighbors. From the previous discussions it is evident that Macedonia's political and ethnic leaders and several third parties made a considerable investment in preventing violent conflict. Although some minority issues, like that of Tetovo University and the use of the Albanian language as an official language, remain unresolved, considerable progress has been made toward proportional representation and power sharing, and the representation of ethnic Albanians on many professional levels.

The composition of the Macedonian government is indicative of the advancements toward interethnic coalition-building. On November 19, 1998, after two rounds of parliamentary elections on October 18 and November 2, the VMRO, the Democratic Alternative (DA), and the Democratic Party of the Albanians (PDsh) formed a coalition government after a landslide victory. The VMRO won 49, the DA 13, and the PDsh under Xhaferi, together with the National Democratic Party (NDP), won 11 of the 120 seats in the National Assembly. Giving five cabinet posts to the PDsh—thirteen went to the VMRO and eight to the DA—Ljubco Georgievski, Macedonia's new prime minister, emphasized that the reasons for the PDsh inclusion in the coalition, even though the VMRO and the DA had secured enough votes to form a government, demonstrated to the international community Macedonia's commitment to internal stability and peace (Ministry of Information 1999, 1–3).

Since constituting a coalition government, Georgievski and Xhaferi, once ardent nationalist leaders, have emerged as pragmatic statesmen who have toned down their more radical political positions of previous years. For example, Georgievski, who had always strongly criticized the Crvenkovski government and President Gligorov for "giving in" to the Greeks on the Macedonian flag and the name FYROM, continues to build constructive relations with Greece (Ministry of Information 1999, 4). Xhaferi, a representative in the

National Assembly, in speaking about internal self-determination, stresses the loyality of ethnic Albanians to the Macedonian state (FBIS 1999d).

In spring 1999, the Kosovo refugee crisis and NATO's intervention in the Federal Republic of Yugoslavia put the country at risk. There was considerable concern that Macedonia was becoming destabilized by external forces, primarily the refugee spillover, a concern shared by Macedonia's political elite and international observers like the OSCE. The epilogue explores the refugee crisis and its impact on Macedonia.

THE REFUGEE CRISIS

The Kosovo conflict had already produced thousands of refugees and internally displaced persons throughout 1998 and the first two months of 1999 as Serbian police, paramilitary units, and Yugoslav army troops fought the Kosovo Liberation Army (KLA).[1] The crisis worsened following NATO's air strikes launched on March 24, 1999, after President Milošević refused to sign the Rambouillet agreement on Kosovo.[2] In the early weeks, following NATO military intervention, Kosovar refugees fled in the hundreds of thousands to neighboring Macedonia, Albania, and the Yugoslav republic of Montenegro, bringing their total number to more than 780,000 by late May 1999. Albania took in most of the refugees, about 440,000, followed by Macedonia with 250,000, and Montenegro with 68,000; about 20,000 fled to Bosnia-Hercegovina.[3]

Macedonia's reaction to the massive influx of Kosovar refugees in the early weeks was one of panic, after Georgievski issued a statement on March 23 saying that Macedonia was staying out of the conflict and that NATO troops would not be allowed to stage attacks from Macedonian territory ("Macedonia Seeks to Stay Out of Conflict" 1999, 6).[4] Fearing Serbian retaliation, and that

1. For more recent literature on the Kosovo crisis, see Caplan 1998, 745–61, and Weller 1999, 211–51.

2. The Rambouillet Agreement, known by its official name, the Interim Agreement for Peace and Self-Government, was negotiated at Rambouillet, France, in February 1999. The agreement entailed political and military provisions for a settlement of the Kosovo conflict, including a 26,000-strong NATO peacekeeping force to police the agreement. The United States and Western Europe threatened President Milošević with NATO air strikes if he failed to sign.

3. The number of Kosovars in Albania, Macedonia, and Montenegro changed daily with the arrival of more refugees and their evacuation to third countries. The refugee population estimates cited in the epilogue are from June 1, 1999. See the United Nations High Commissioner for Refugees 1999. Also about 10,000 Rom fled from Kosovo to Macedonia, most of them because of NATO bombing, and several thousand Croatian refugees.

4. The decision not to let NATO use Macedonian territory for attacks on Serbia was made by the Macedonian National Security Council, chaired by President Gligorov. During a television inter-

ethnic relations within Macedonia would become destabilized, officials adopted several confusing, highly controversial policies to respond to the refugee crisis. Some of these specified the number of refugees Macedonia was willing to admit; others regulated the opening and closing of borders along the Kosovo-Macedonia divide. All of them stirred up international criticism, especially on the part of humanitarian organizations and the media.

On March 23, the day the first 4,000 refugees arrived, officials announced they would close the border to holders of Yugoslav passports, only to reopen them on March 24 (Troni 1999; "Reopens Border to Refugees" 1999, 6). By the end of March, the government's policy that it would only admit 20,000 refugees was overturned when it announced that Macedonia would accept another 10,000, and talks were held to determine what neighboring countries could accommodate the refugees. Meanwhile border patrols had virtually shut down the border by delaying the processing of papers ("Kosovars Continue to Flee" 1999, 6). In an interview with Bosnia-Hercegovina Radio on April 3, President Gligorov emphasized that Macedonia, with almost 140,000 refugees, could probably cope somehow, provided there was international assistance, but that it "could not accept any more refugees because this would have additional economic, social, and national repercussions." He asked the European Union and NATO countries to accept Kosovar refugees as well (Foreign Broadcast Information Service 1999b).

In spite of Gligorov's statement, Macedonia found itself unable to cope. From April 6 to April 9, the continued influx of refugees overwhelmed authorities. There were countless incidents of maltreatment of refugees by the Macedonian police; there were 85,000 refugees stranded in a muddy no-man's land between Kosovo and Macedonia; and there were allegations of "forced" resettlement to Albania, Greece, and Turkey in which families became separated ("Where Are the Refugees?" 1999, 5). That the strain was too much became evident in Georgievski's statement on April 6 in which he accused NATO of having acted irresponsibly by ignoring the government's predictions that air strikes could trigger a humanitarian disaster ("Georgievski Blasts NATO" 1999, 6). By mid-April, the government felt that the international community had not done enough to help Macedonia in coping with this massive influx of refugees.

Meanwhile, Georgievski's coalition partner, the ethnic Albanian leader Arbën Xhaferi, pursued a policy that contradicted that of the government. Besides coming out strongly on the side of the use of NATO ground forces in Kosovo, Xhaferi

---

view, when he was asked what the Macedonian government would do if attacked by Serbia, Prime Minister Georgievski responded that Macedonia would not provide any pretext for such hostile action. See Foreign Broadcast Information Service 1999b.

also called on all ethnic Albanians to take Kosovars into their homes, insisting that all refugees remain in neighboring areas rather than be resettled to third countries. In an interview on April 7, Xhaferi spoke of "a plan to accommodate and take care [of] about 100,000 people," to draw people "out of that mud over there at the border between Kosovo and Macedonia," and to provide them "with accommodation in houses and various categories of public facilities, including churches, sports halls, schools, and such" (FBIS 1999d). Xhaferi's advocacy for placing refugees within private homes was succcessful, but it created two types of refugees. About 130,000 Kosovars shared homes with ethnic Albanians in Macedonia, many with relatives, and some with as many as forty or fifty people in apartments in Skopje, Tetovo, and Gostivar. There were more than 45,000 refugees in Tetovo, and 30,000 in Skopje (Troni 1999). Entire villages took in refugees. In Malina, which is close to the Kosovo border, up to one hundred people out of several thousand lived in each home, after having crossed the border illegally ("Relief Workers Reach Stranded Refugees" 1999, 6).

The remaining refugees were distributed among ten camps, some holding more than 30,000 refugees, for example Cegrane, near Tetovo with a camp population of more than 32,000 as of May 7, 1999. The United Nations High Commissioner for Refugees (UNHCR) administered the camps in cooperation with several humanitarian organizations such as Oxfam, which was responsible for providing water supplies throughout the camp; CARE International, which was responsible for the distribution of food; or the International Rescue Committee, which was responsible for sanitation. There were repeated disagreements with the UNHCR over Macedonia's border policy because it was not consistent and led to arbitrary openings and closings of borders, often forcing refugees to return to Kosovo. On May 20, however, Prime Minister Georgievski issued a statement to United Nations Secretary-General Kofi Annan, promising to keep borders open ("Georgievski Pledges Open Border" 1999, 5).[5]

IMPACT OF THE REFUGEE CRISIS

Anxiety that Macedonia was being destabilized by refugees prevailed. There was growing concern about the potentially serious consequences of the refugee crisis for interethnic relations and for Macedonia's long-term internal and external security prospects. The presence of so many refugees had affected Slavic Macedonian–ethnic Albanian relations, although how much is not yet entirely

5. In several press conferences I attended in early May 1999, Macedonian government officials insisted that the borders were open and that it was not Macedonian policy to close them; instead they noted that Serbian patrols had been blocking border crossings.

clear. Violeta Beška, the psychology professor, whom I interviewed in 1995 and 1996, and then again in May 1999, thought that the refugee crisis had affected interethnic relations, especially on the people's level. She argued that politicians had moved much closer together and that there was more harmony on a political level than ten years ago. Among the general population, however, fear of the "other" and misperceptions were running more rampant. Beška noted the positive aspects to the refugee crisis: ethnic Albanians have become more loyal to the Macedonian state, and they see their place within it and that they need to take an active approach toward preventing its deterioration. Unfortunately, it is the Slavic Macedonians who have widened the gap the ethnic Albanians have been trying to close, making it harder for ethnic Albanians to be "Macedonians" (Beška 1999).

What divided Slavic Macedonians and ethnic Albanians was the question of what to do with the refugees, with Xhaferi and other ethnic Albanian politicians arguing that they should stay in the region, that they should be better treated by the police and border patrols, and that ethnic Albanian families sheltering refugees should receive financial assistance. The government's position, on the other hand, was that refugees should be relocated to third countries to avoid a destabilization of Macedonia; therefore they were in favor of the air bridge that began to operate on April 5. Because most ethnic Albanians in Macedonia have relatives or friends in Kosovo, they did not support the repatriation of Kosovar Albanians to third countries. Also, ethnic Albanians had conflicting views over NATO intervention, with many favoring the use of ground forces, even from Macedonian territory.

The OSCE Spillover Mission and High Commissioner van der Stoel supported the removal of refugees out of fear that interethnic relations would be seriously affected if they continued to stay for a prolonged time. The UNHCR was also in favor of relocating refugees to other countries because of concerns over camp overcrowding, inadequate facilities, and possible health risks. One particular incident where overcrowding caused unrest occurred on May 9 at the Stenkovic refugee camp near Skopje. Chanting pro-KLA slogans, about 3,000 camp inhabitants protested against the lack of freedom of movement and demanded that ethnic Albanian police guard the camp—a request that was granted—and that the operation of the air bridge be accelerated. The investigating Spillover Mission called it a "minor incident," but nevertheless it warned of a potentially volatile situation because all refugee camps were large and continued to grow with the flow of refugees (Troni 1999). By June 1, under the UNHCR and the International Organization for Migration humanitarian evacuation program, 73,000 Kosovar Albanian refugees had already departed to Germany, Austria, France, the Netherlands, Switzerland, Norway, Sweden, and the United States. By that time forty countries had made offers allowing for the potential evacuation of 137,000 refugees (UNHCR 1999, 3).

What was positive about the refugee crisis was that some of the old and unresolved issues such as nation status and the Albanian-language university in Tetovo were sidestepped, overshadowed by a more pressing question: Would the refugees be able to return? And if not, what was to be done with them? Although the refugee crisis affected interethnic relations negatively, it was fortunate for Macedonia that its government is a coalition of two former radical parties and that each leader realized the need to appeal for harmony to not exacerbate the situation. A good example is Xhaferi, who in the wake of police excesses at border crossings called on ethnic Albanians not to let themselves be provocated because that would play into the hands of Milošević.

The refugee crisis, however, triggered concerns over changing demographics, the intentions of one ethnic group versus the other, and the economic consequences of the refugee crisis. One fear was that if Kosovar Albanians stayed in Macedonia for long, the percentage of ethnic Albanians would rise to 30 or 40 percent, the number always claimed by Macedonian Albanians. Refugees made up ten percent of the total population—according to both Slavic Macedonians and government officials—which was going to change Macedonia. Misperceptions among the two ethnic groups were rampant. Slavic Macedonians, for example, feared that an independent Kosovo might lead to the secession of Western Macedonia, and ethnic Albanians held the view that the government was trying to make Macedonia part of a Greater Bulgaria.

The negative effects on the economy were particularly burdensome. With an unemployment rate of 30 percent, and perhaps as high as 40 percent, and with the building and maintenance of camps, the Macedonian government had few resources and little time to make good on its election promise to improve the sluggish economy. An OSCE Spillover Mission report in April 1999 stated that "optimistic forecasts of 6.5 percent GDP-growth, growing trade and foreign direct investments have been rendered obsolete by the events" (OSCE Spillover Monitor Mission to Skopje 1999, 2)

The crisis in Kosovo affected the economy in two ways: in costs related to refugees, and in costs related to the interruption of trade with the Federal Republic of Yugoslavia. The Macedonian government repeatedly stated that the international community was responsible for the refugee camps but did not provide enough support. In spite of such statements, international aid was forthcoming, although it was difficult to obtain exact numbers because some of the assistance came in the form of pledges from bilateral and international donors. At the Paris Donors' Conference on May 5, 1999, for example, international agencies pledged $252 million, and bilateral donors $60 million (OSCE Spillover Mission 1999, 1–2). There was also considerable delay in the transfer of funds because international donors such as the European Union have slow-working bureaucracies, making a more timely release of financial assistance difficult.[6] On the other hand, the Macedonian government had difficulty demonstrating to international organizations what expenses actually had been incurred, in part because Macedonia initially provided for the building of camps.[7]

Interruption of trade was another problem Macedonia had to struggle with during the refugee crisis. Again estimates of losses are difficult to obtain because trade with the Federal Republic of Yugoslavia is on a barter basis. However, the Macedonian Chamber of Commerce has estimated that at least 70 percent of export contracts with the Federal Republic of Yugoslavia were canceled. There were also rerouting problems because most of the exports to the EU and other Central European countries went through the Federal Republic of Yugoslavia. Export goods had therefore to be rerouted through Bulgaria and Romania or shipped through Thessaloniki, all of which was expensive and time consuming. The April 1999 OSCE Mission's report on the economic spillover effects pointed out that transportation costs had gone up by 30 percent; that trade and investment agreements had been postponed or canceled; and that the textile, metals, and chemical industries had also experienced serious losses.

The social effects of this economic spillover were equally disturbing as the number of unemployed, estimated at 320,000, was "for the first time higher than the number of employed"; and "that 40,000 employees are on so called forced leave and that 120,000 workers have not received their salaries for the last two months." There were also lapses in paying social benefits to at least 100,000 employees; food prices and other cost-of-living expenses increased; and families were forced to live off their savings (OSCE Spillover Monitor Mission 1999, 5). The economic spillover effects from the Kosovo crisis therefore held the potential of negatively affecting interethnic relations, not only because Slavic Macedonians were blaming Kosovar Albanians for draining the economic system, but also because in times of economic stress existing interethnic divisions become magnified as ethnic groups are forced to compete over the allocation of scarce resources.

Macedonia also faced three other worries—Serbia, the KLA, and NATO. Prime Minister Georgievski and President Gligorov explicitly put the blame for the destabilization of Macedonia on President Milošević, accusing him of pro-

6. Emma Bonino, the acting European commissioner, European Commission of Humanitarian Affairs, made this comment during her briefing with representatives from the international humanitarian organizations on May 8, 1999, while visiting the Cegrane refugee camp.

7. The UNHCR paid the Macedonian government $3.5 million for the construction of camps (United Nations High Commissioner for Refugees 1999, 3).

voking ethnic tensions in Macedonia with the mass expulsion of refugees ("Georgievski: Milosevic Trying to Destabilize Macedonia" 1999, 5; "Gligorov Says Serbia Destabilizing Macedonia" 1999, 6). But Macedonia's security continues to depend on a democratic transition in Serbia, and on a political settlement for Kosovo. Resolving the Kosovo conflict will also reduce some of the Macedonian anxieties over the extent of KLA activities on Macedonian territory. In April 1999, Macedonian police located a weapons depot in Kumanovo, alleged to belong to the KLA. Information on KLA operations in Macedonia is sketchy. The Macedonian authorities have responded mostly with preventive rather than repressive measures, such as the monitoring of the movements of KLA members. Ethnic Albanian politicans have also taken a cautious tone. Xhaferi, for example, expressed to international representatives that "we [PDsh and KLA representatives] have taken the political decision for the KLA not to take any actions that will destabilize the country" (Troni 1999). But whether there will be a continued KLA activities again depends on finding a political solution for Kosovo (Troni 1999).

Macedonians, although not directly anti-NATO, were critical of NATO's use of Macedonian territory and air space and feared that Macedonia would be drawn into armed confrontations with Serbia. In particular, they were concerned about how many more NATO troops the government would allow into Macedonia. Slavic Macedonians also believed that the refugee crisis had been a direct result of NATO bombings rather than Serbia's forced expulsion policy. Among Macedonia's intellectuals, considerable anger was expressed over what was perceived as NATO's insensibilities toward Macedonia's security needs and Macedonia's long-term security dependence on NATO. Ethnic Serbs held much stronger anti-NATO sentiments, which found their expression in the numerous protests and demonstrations with the beginning of the NATO air strikes. Macedonia's Albanian population, including Kosovar refugees, were generally in support of NATO because of what they perceived as NATO's intervention in a humanitarian cause that was stopping Serbia's genocide against Kosovar Albanians.

Macedonia's government often shifted between being a victim and an active supporter of NATO. One the one hand, Macedonian authorities felt that NATO had not sufficiently appreciated the support it provided for NATO troops. On the other hand, Macedonia was eager to present itself as a "reliable, potential NATO ally," hoping that its efforts would lead eventually to NATO membership. Much of NATO public relations efforts were spent changing Macedonia's self-image as being victimized by NATO: reinforcing how much Macedonia's efforts were appreciated, supporting the air bridge, and promising long-term economic assistance and security guarantees. When NATO Secretary-General Javier Solana visited Macedonia on May 12, he took with him a comprehensive European Union plan for the stabilization of the country, addressing economic and security aspects and political institution-building, a plan President Gligorov said would "stop the nationalisms of the regions."[8] Without doubt Macedonia remains dependent on NATO because NATO will have to provide long-term stability in the region.

A FINAL WORD ON PREVENTIVE DIPLOMACY IN MACEDONIA

In spite of some degree of destabilization that has come as the result of the Kosovo conflict, the case study on successful prevention in Macedonia presented in this book is significant because it documents Macedonia's considerable efforts and those of the international actors in resolving ethnic conflict peacefully from its independence in 1991 to the present. The destabilization that befell Macedonia in March 1999 is not of its own making. It was not triggered by internal circumstances such as ruthless, nationalist politicians, repressive laws on ethnic minorities, or revoking long-established interethnic coexistence, dialogue, and power sharing. It was the work of external forces, primarily Serbia's forced expulsion of Kosovar Albanians, which placed all of southeastern Europe at risk, and, indirectedly, the rest of Europe as well. The recent events support one of the conclusions reached in this study: that it is imperative for conflict prevention to be long-term, particularly in regions with considerable instabilities because of unresolved territorial and ethnic problems such as in Kosovo or precarious peace settlements as in Bosnia-Hercegovina. Of all the international preventive actors engaged in Macedonia, only the OSCE and its high commissioner are still active; and it was the high commissioner who, on May 12, 1999, submitted an early report on the situation in Macedonia to the OSCE's Permanent Council, warning of Macedonia's destabilization.[9]

Once more, Macedonia has held on to peace. However, there is a continued need for preventive engagement as long as the region is affected by the conflict in Kosovo and the growing physical unrest in the Federal Republic of Yugoslavia.

8. The press conference was held on May 12, with NATO Secretary-General Solana and President Gligorov at the National Assembly, Skopje (notes taken by the author).

9. The early warning was issued at the 229th Plenary Meeting of the Permanent Council (see OSCE, *PC Journal No. 229*, 12 May 1999). The report (HCNM.GAL/2/99) is classified and has not been made public as of June 1, 1999. Between April and June 1999, Ambassador Geert Ahrens was also on a fact-finding mission in Macedonia at the request of the German government. The author conducted several interviews with Ambassador Ahrens.

APPENDIX
REFERENCES
INDEX

APPENDIX: ACRONYMS

ADU-LP	Albanian Democratic Union—Liberal Party
ASMN	Association of Serbs and Montenegrins
CDR	Coalition pour la défense de la république
CSCE	Conference on Security and Cooperation in Europe
CSO	Committee of Senior Officials
DA	Democratic Alternative
DPSM	Democratic Party of Serbs in Macedonia
EC	European Community
ECHO	European Community Humanitarian Office
ECMM	European Community Monitor Mission
ECRP	Ethnic Conflict Resolution Project
EU	European Union
FBIS	Foreign Broadcast Information Service
FYROM	Former Yugoslav Republic of Macedonia
HCMN	High Commissioner on National Minorities
ICFY	International Conference on the Former Yugoslavia
ICOM	International Census Observation Mission
KLA	Kosovo Liberation Army
KVM	Kosovo Verification Mission
LP	Liberal Party
MPMA	Movement for Pan-Macedonian Action
NATO	North Atlantic Treaty Organization
NGO	Nongovernmental organization
NORDBAT	Nordic Battalion
NPD	National Democratic Party
OAU	Organization of African Unity
ODIHR	Office for Democratic Institutions and Human Rights
OEEC	Organization for European Economic Cooperation
OSCE	Organization for Security and Cooperation in Europe
PDD	Presidential Decision Directive
PDsh	Democratic Party of the Albanians

PPD	Party for Democratic Prosperity
PPD-A (PPDsh)	Party for Democratic Prosperity of Albanians
RPF	Rwandan Patriotic Front
RP	Republican Party
RFM-LP	Reformist Forces of Macedonia-Liberal Party
SAM	Sanctions Assistance Mission
SCG	Search for Common Ground
SCGM	Search for Common Ground in Macedonia
SPM	Socialist Party of Macedonia
SDSM	Social Democratic Alliance of Macedonia
SDUM	Social Democratic Union of Macedonia
UNAMIR	United Nations Assistance Mission in Rwanda
UNCRO	United Nations Confidence Restoration Operation
UNCIVPOL	United Nations Civilian Police
UNHCR	United Nations High Commissioner for Refugees
UNICEF	United Nations International Children's Education Fund
UNMO	United Nations Military Observer
UNOMUR	United Nations Observer Mission Uganda-Rwanda
UNPF	United Nations Peace Forces
UNPREDEP	United Nations Preventive Deployment
UNPROFOR	United Nations Protection Force
USBAT	United States Battalion
VMRO-DP	Internal Macedonian Revolutionary Organization-Democratic Party
VMRO-DPMNE (VMRO)	Internal Macedonian Revolutionary Organization-Democratic Party for Macedonian National Unity
WEU	Western European Union
YNA	Yugoslav National Army

REFERENCES

Aall, Pamela. 1996. "Nongovernmental Organizations and Peacemaking." In *Managing Global Chaos: Sources of and Responses to International Conflict,* edited by Chester A. Crocker and Fen Osler Hampson, with Pamela Aaal, 433–43. Washington, D.C.: United States Institute of Peace Press.

Ackermann, Alice. 1993. "Conflict Management in Regional Settings: Estonia-Russia-Ukraine: A Preventive Conflict Management Approach." Paper presented at the WIIS Conference on "The Role of the Ethnic Factor in Russian-Ukrainian and Russian-Estonian Relations," Tallinn, Estonia.

———. 1994. "Reconciliation as Peace-building Process in Postwar Europe: The Franco-German Case." *Peace and Change* 19, no. 3: 229–50.

———. 1995. "The European Union, Germany, and the Politics of Recognition of the Former Yugoslav Republics." Paper Prepared for the International Studies Association Annual Conference, Chicago.

———. 1996. "The Former Yugoslav Republic of Macedonia: A Relatively Successful Case of Conflict Prevention in Europe." *Security Dialogue* 27, no. 4: 409–24.

———. 1997. "Mazedonien und die OSZE: Präventive Diplomatie in der Praxis." In *OSZE Jahrbuch 1997,* edited by the Institut für Friedensforschung und Sicherheitspolitik, 73–80. Baden-Baden, Germany: Nomos Verlag.

———. 1998a. "Macedonia and the Kosovo Conflict." *International Spectator* 33, no. 4: 41–48.

———. 1998b. "The Republic of Macedonia and the OSCE: Preventive Diplomacy in Practice." In *OSCE Yearbook 1997,* edited by the Institute for Peace Research and Security Policy at the University of Hamburg, 69–76. Baden-Baden, Germany: Nomos Verlag.

Ackermann, Alice, and Antonio Pala. 1996. "From Peacekeeping to Preventive Deployment: A Study of the United Nations in the Former Yugoslav Republic of Macedonia." *European Security* 5, no. 1: 83–97.

Ackermann, Alice, and Sanjeev Chatterjee. 1997. *From the Shadow of History:*

A Video Documentary on Preventive Diplomacy in the Republic of Macedonia. Coral Gables, Florida.

Adelman, Howard, and Astri Suhrke. 1996. "Early Warning and Response: Why the International Community Failed to Prevent the Genocide." *Disasters* 20, no. 4: 295–304.

"Albania to Reconsider Its Macedonian Policy." 1995. *MILS News.* 23 Feb. (online source).

"Amerikanische Initiative im Mazedonienzwist." 1995. *Neue Züricher Zeitung.* 5–6 Aug., 7.

Anderson, Benedict. 1991. *Imagined Communities: Reflections on the Origin and Spread of Nationalism.* Rev. ed. London and New York: Verso.

Anderson, Mary B. 1996. "Humanitarian NGOs in Conflict Intervention." In *Managing Global Chaos: Sources of and Responses to International Conflict,* 343–54. Washington, D.C.: United States Institute of Peace Press.

Andov, Stojan. Former President of the Macedonian Assembly, and Former President of the Council for Ethnic Relations. 1995. "Interview with the Author (Audio)." 5 May. Skopje, Republic of Macedonia.

Andrejevich, Milan. 1991a. "Retreating from the Brink of Collapse." *RL/RFE Report on Eastern Europe* 2, no. 15: 25–30.

———. 1991b. "Republican Leaders Reach Compromise Accord on Country's Future." *RL/RFE Report on Eastern Europe* 2, no. 26: 33–37.

Antonovska, Svetlana. Director, Statistical Office of Macedonia. 1995. "Interview with the Author." 5 May. Skopje, Republic of Macedonia.

Archer, Clive. 1994. "Conflict Prevention in Europe: The Case of the Nordic States and Macedonia." *Cooperation and Conflict* 29, no. 4: 367–86.

Arifi, Teuta. Journalist. 1995. "Interview with the Author (Audio)." 8 May. Skopje, Republic of Macedonia.

"Athen erweitert Blockade Mazedoniens." 1994. *Frankfurter Allgemeine Zeitung.* 19 Feb., 2.

Aydini, Gazmend. Editor-in-Chief, TV ERA. 1999. "Interview with the Author." 4 May. Skopje, Republic of Macedonia.

Ayoob, Mohammed. 1996. "State Making, State Breaking, and State Failure." In *Managing Global Chaos: Sources of and Responses to International Conflict,* edited by Chester A. Crocker and Fen Osler Hampson, with Pamela Aall, 37–52. Washington, D.C.: United States Institute of Peace Press.

Barrington, Lowell W. 1995. "Nations, States, and Citizens: An Explanation of the Citizenship Policies in Estonia and Lithuania." *Review of Central and East European Law,* no. 2: 103–48.

"Beharren auf Bundesstaat könnte zum endgültigen Zerfall führen." 1991. Radio Jugoslawien, 4 June; *Deutsche Welle Monitor Dienst Osteuropa,* 5 June.

Bercovitch, Jacob, and Jeffrey Z. Rubin, eds. 1992. *Mediation in International Relations: Multiple Approaches to Conflict Management.* New York: St. Martin's.

Beška, Violeta Petroska. 1996a. "Interview with the Author (Camera and Audio)." 6 June. Skopje, Republic of Macedonia.

———. 1996b. "NGOs, Early Warning, and Preventive Action: Macedonia." In *Vigilance and Vengeance: NGOs Preventing Ethnic Conflict in Divided Societies,* edited by Robert I. Rotberg, 133–46. Washington, D.C.: Brookings Institution Press.

———. 1997. *Conflicts: What They Are and How to Resolve Them.* Skopje: Faculty of Philosophy, 1997.

———. 1999. "Interview with the Author." 5 May. Skopje, Republic of Macedonia.

———. n.d. "Non-Governmental Organizations, Early Warning, and Preventive Diplomacy—The Case of Macedonia." Unpublished Paper.

Beška, Violeta Petroska, Director, Ethnic Conflict Resolution Project, and Nafi Saraqini, Project Manager, Catholic Relief Services. 1995. "Interview with the Author (Audio)." 8 May. Skopje, Republic of Macedonia.

Beška, Violeta Petroska, and Mihajlo Popovski, Ethnic Conflict Resolution Project. 1996. "Interview with the Author (Audio)." 13 March. Skopje, Republic of Macedonia.

Birckenbach, Hanne-Margret. 1996a. "Die erfolgreiche Einhegung eines gewaltträchtigen Konflikts: Hypothesen aus der Analyse der Konflikte in den baltischen Staaten." *Die Friedenswarte* 71, no. 4: 442–54.

———. 1996b. "Fact-Finding: Gewaltprävention in Estland und Lettland." In *Jahrbuch Frieden 1995,* edited by Hanne-Margaret Birckenbach et al., 75–85. Munich: Verlag C. H. Beck.

———. 1997. *Preventive Diplomacy Through Fact-Finding: How International Organizations Review the Conflict over Citizenship in Estonia and Latvia.* New Brunswick, N.J.: Transaction Publisher.

Blacker, Coit D. 1994. "A Typology of Post-Cold War Conflicts." In *U.S. Intervention Policy for the Post-Cold War World,* edited by Arnold Kanter and Linton F. Brooks, 42–62. New York: W. W. Norton.

Blais, Giorgio. 1994. "Experiences with CSCE Monitoring in the Former Yugoslav Republic of Macedonia." In *Verification after the Cold War: Broadening the Process,* edited by Jürgen Altmann, Thomas Stock, and Jean-Pierre Stroot, 302–7. Amsterdam: VU University Press.

———. Deputy Chief of Mission, OSCE Spillover Mission to Skopje. 1995. "Interview with the Author (Audio)." 4 May. Skopje, Republic of Macedonia.

Bloed, Arie, ed. 1993. *The Conference on Security and Cooperation in Europe:*

Analysis and Basic Documents, 1972–1993. Dordrecht, Netherlands: Martinus Nijhoff.
Bøgh, Tore. OSCE Head of Mission. 1996. "Interview with the Author." 11 June. Skopje, Republic of Macedonia.
Borger, Julian, and Helena Smith. 1994. "Caught on the Edge of a Balkan Abyss." *The Guardian Weekly*. 24 July, 6.
"Bosnia Appeals to U.N." 1991. *New York Times*. 24 Dec., A3.
Bothe, Michael, Natalino Ronzitti, and Allan Rosas, eds. 1997. *The OSCE in the Maintenance of Peace and Security: Conflict Prevention, Crisis Management and Peaceful Settlement of Disputes*. The Hague: Kluwer Law International.
Boulding, Elise. 1991. "The Old and New Transnationalism: An Evolutionary Perspective." *Human Relations* 44, no. 8: 789–805.
Boutros-Ghali, Boutros. 1992. *Agenda for Peace: Preventive Diplomacy, Peacemaking and Peacekeeping*. Report of the Secretary-General, adopted by the Summit Meeting of the Security Council on 31 Jan. 1992. A/47/277-S/24111, 17 June. New York: United Nations.
———. 1995. *An Agenda for Development 1995*. New York: United Nations, Department of Public Information.
———. 1996. "Challenges of Preventive Diplomacy: The Role of the United Nations and Its Secretary-General." In *Preventive Diplomacy: Stopping Wars Before They Start*, edited by Kevin M. Cahill, 16–34. New York: Basic Books.
Brown, Michael E., and Richard N. Rosecrance, eds. 1999. *The Costs of Conflict: Preventing and Cure in the Global Arena*. Lanham, Md.: Rowman and Littlefield.
Bugajski, Janusz. 1994. *Ethnic Politics in Eastern Europe: A Guide to Nationality Policies, Organizations, and Parties*. Armonk, N.Y.: M. E. Sharpe.
———. 1996. *Nations in Turmoil: Conflict and Cooperation in Eastern Europe*. Boulder, Colo.: Westview.
Burci, Gianluca. 1997. "Division of Labour Between the UN and the OSCE in Connection with Peace-keeping." In *The OSCE in the Maintenance of Peace and Security: Conflict Prevention, Crisis Management and Peaceful Settlement of Disputes*, edited by Michael Bothe, Natalino Ronzitti, and Allan Rosas, 289–314. The Hague: Kluwer Law International.
Burg, Steven L. 1995. "The International Community and the Yugoslav Crisis." In *International Organizations and Ethnic Conflict*, edited by Milton J. Esman and Shibley Telhami, 235–74. Ithaca, N.Y.: Cornell Univ. Press.
Burkhalter, Holly. 1994. "A Preventable Horror?" *Africa Report*, Nov.–Dec., 17–21.
———. 1995. "The Question of Genocide: The Clinton Administration and Rwanda." *World Policy Journal* 11, no. 4: 44–54.

Cahill, Kevin M., ed. 1996. *Preventive Diplomacy: Stopping Wars Before They Start.* New York: Basic Books.

Camus, Albert. 1986. *Neither Victims Nor Executioners.* Philadelphia: New Society.

Caplan, Richard. 1998. "International Diplomacy and the Crisis in Kosovo." *International Affairs* 74, no. 4: 745–61.

Chen, Julie, Country Representative, Catholic Relief Services. 1995. "Interview with the Author." 4 May. Skopje, Republic of Macedonia.

Chigas, Diana. 1996. "Preventive Diplomacy and the Organization for Security and Cooperation in Europe: Creating Incentives for Dialogue and Cooperation." In *Preventing Conflict in the Post-Communist World,* edited by Abram Chayes and Antonia Handler Chayes, 25–97. Washington, D.C.: Brookings Institution Press.

"China Vetoes Extension of UN Force's Mandate in Macedonia." 1999. *RFE/RL Newsline* 3, no. 40, part 2, 26 Feb., 6.

Clinton, William J. 1996. "The President's Radio Address, 3 June 1995." In *Public Papers of the Presidents of the United States: William J. Clinton 1995,* Book I: *January 1 to June 30, 1995,* 804–5. Washington, D.C.: United States Government Printing Office.

Cohen, Lenard J. 1993. *Broken Bonds: The Disintegration of Yugoslavia.* Boulder, Colo.: Westview.

Commission on Security and Cooperation in Europe. 1992. *The Referendum on Independence on Bosnia-Hercegovina, February 29–March 1, 1992.* Washington, D.C.: Commission on Security and Cooperation in Europe.

CSCE (Conference on Security and Cooperation in Europe). 1992a. "CSCE Helsinki Document 1992: The Challenges of Change." Helsinki Summit 1992.

———. 1992b. "Drittes Treffen des Rates, Zusammenfassung der Schlussfolgerungen, Beschluss Friedliche Beilegung von Streitigkeiten," Stockholm.

CSCE Secretariat. 1992. "CSCE Spillover Monitor Mission to Skopje." CSCE Communication No. 282, 16 Sept., Prague, Czech Republic.

———. 1993. "HCNM Recommendations Concerning Inter-ethnic Relations in FYR of Macedonia." CSCE Communication No. 305, 28 Nov., Rome.

Constitution of the Republic of Macedonia. 1994. Skopje, Republic of Macedonia.

"Controversy over Macedonia." 1993. *UN Chronicle* 30, no. 2: 12.

Cottey, Andrew. 1995. *East-Central Europe After the Cold War.* New York: St. Martin's.

Craig, Gordon A., and Alexander L. George. 1995. *Force and Statecraft: Diplomatic Problems of Our Time.* 3d ed. New York: Oxford Univ. Press.

Cranna, Michael, ed. 1994. *The True Cost of Conflict.* London: Earthscan.

Crvenkovski, Branko. Prime Minister of the Republic of Macedonia. 1996. "Interview with the Author (Notes)." 14 Mar. Skopje, Republic of Macedonia.

Csepeli, György, and Antal Örkény. 1992. "Conflicting Loyalties of Citizenship and National Identity in Eastern Europe." In *Minorities in Politics: Cultural and Language Rights,* edited by Jana Plichtová, 45–51. Bratislava: European Cultural Foundation.

Dahlen, Olle, Bo Westas, and Duncan Wood. 1988. *Peaceful Resolution of Conflicts: Non-governmental Organizations in the International System.* Life and Peace Reports No. 1. Uppsala, Sweden: Life and Peace Institute.

Danforth, Loring M. 1995. *The Macedonian Conflict: Ethnic Nationalism in a Transnational World.* Princeton: Princeton Univ. Press.

"Dangerously Escalated Serbian Provocation." 1994. *MILS News,* 20 June (online source).

Davies, John L., and Ted Robert Gurr, eds. 1998. *Preventive Measures: Building Risk Assessment and Crisis Early Warning Systems.* Lanham, Md.: Rowman and Littlefield.

Destexhe, Alain. 1994/95. "The Third Genocide." *Foreign Policy* 97: 3–17.

———. 1995. *Rwanda and Genocide in the Twentieth Century.* New York: New York Univ. Press.

"Die Präsidenten der sechs jugoslawischen Teilrepubliken treffen sich im mazedonischen Ochrid." 1991. *Frankfurter Allgemeine Zeitung.* 19 Apr., 8.

"Die UNO-Vermittlung in der Mazedonienfrage." 1994. *Neue Züricher Zeitung.* 22 Apr., 5.

Dimovska, Dosta. Vice President, VMRO-DPMNE. 1995. "Interview with the Author." 31 July. Skopje, Republic of Macedonia.

Dowty, Allan, and Gil Loescher. 1996. "Refugee Flows as Grounds for International Action." *International Security* 21, no. 1: 43–71.

Duncan, W. Raymond, and G. Paul Holman, eds. 1994. *Ethnic Nationalism and Regional Conflict: The Former Soviet Union and Yugoslavia.* Boulder, Colo.: Westview.

Durch, William J., ed. 1993. *The Evolution of UN Peacekeeping: Case Studies and Comparative Analysis.* New York: St. Martin's.

Edwards, Gwyneth. 1996. "Early Warning and Preventive Diplomacy." *The RUSI Journal* 141, no. 5: 42–46.

Engelbrekt, Kjell. 1994. "Papandreou Sets Conditions for Talks with Macedonia." *RFE/RL Daily Report,* no. 11: 4.

Engström, Juha. Brigadier-General, UNPREDEP Commander. 1995. "Interview with the Author (Audio)." 8 May. Skopje, Republic of Macedonia.

Errington, R. Malcolm. 1990. *A History of Macedonia.* Berkeley: Univ. of California Press.

Estébaniez, Maria Amor Martin. 1997. "The High Commissioner on National Minorities: Development of the Mandate." In *The OSCE in the Maintenance of Peace and Security: Conflict Prevention, Crisis Management and Peaceful Settlement of Disputes,* edited by Michael Bothe, Natalino Ronzitti, and Allan Rosas, 123–66. The Hague: Kluwer Law International.

"Ethnische Spannungen in Mazedonien." 1995. *Neue Züricher Zeitung,* 19 Feb., 5.

Evans, Gareth. 1993. *Cooperating for Peace.* St. Leonards, Australia: Allen and Unwin.

Eyal, Jonathan. 1994. "No Prophylactic Against War." *The Spectator,* 1 Oct., 16.

Feil, Scott R. 1998. *Preventing Genocide: How the Early Use of Force Might Have Succeeded in Rwanda.* New York: Carnegie Cooperation of New York.

Feldman, Lily Gardner. 1999. "The Principle and Practice of 'Reconciliation' in German Foreign Policy: Relations with France, Israel, Poland, and the Czech Republic." *International Affairs* 75, no. 2: 1–22.

Fetscher, Iring. 1972. *Modelle der Friedenssicherung.* Munich: Piper.

Fisher, Ronald J. 1995. "Pacific, Impartial Third-Party Intervention in International Conflict: A Review and an Analysis." In *Beyond Confrontation: Learning Conflict Resolution in the Post-Cold War Era,* edited by John Vasquez et al., 39–59. Ann Arbor: Univ. of Michigan Press.

Fisher, Sharon. 1996. "Making Slovakia More 'Slovak.'" *Transition* 2, no. 24: 14–17.

Fitzmaurice, John. 1996. *Damming the Danube: Gabcikovo and Post-Communist Politics.* Boulder, Colo.: Westview.

Foreign Broadcast Information Service (FBIS). 1997a. "FYROM: Albania: Aliti on US Visit, Interethnic Relations." *FBIS Daily Report.* FBIS-EEU-97-216. 26 Oct. (on-line source).

———. 1997b. "FYROM: EU Officials Express Concerns about Ethnic Protests." *FBIS Daily Report.* FBIS-EEU-97-071. 12 March (on-line source).

———. 1997c. "FYROM: Foreign Minister Favors Extension of UNPREDEP Mandate." *FBIS Daily Report.* FBIS-EEU-97-3111. 7 Nov. (on-line source).

———. 1997d. "FYROM: Number of Albanian Students Growing Each Year." *FBIS Daily Report.* FBIS-EEU-97-035. 19 Feb. (on-line source).

———. 1997e. "FYROM: Parliament Adopts Language Law on School of Pedagogy." *FBIS Daily Report.* FBIS-EEU-97-022. 31 Jan. (on-line source).

———. 1997f. "FYROM: Students Continue Protest Outside Parliament Building." *FBIS Daily Report.* FBIS-EEU-97-076. 17 Mar. (on-line source).

———. 1997g. "FYROM: Students to Protest Law on Albanian University Classes." *FBIS Daily Report.* FBIS-EEU-97-010. 13 Jan. (on-line source).

———. 1999a. "Gligorov Tells U.N.'s Annan: Kosovo Threatens to Escalate." *FBIS Daily Report.* FBIS-EEU-99-0315. 17 Mar. (on-line source).

———. 1999b. "Macedonia Can Accept No More Refugees." *FBIS Daily Report,* FBIS-EEU-99-0410. 10 Apr. (on-line source).

———.1999c. "Security Council—FYROM Cannot Be Used for NATO Action." *FBIS Daily Report.* FBIS-EEU-99-0323. 23 Mar. (on-line source).

———. 1999d. "Xhaferi: Pro-Serb Faction Obstructs Aid." *FBIS Daily Report,* FBIS-EEU-99-0409. 7 Apr. (on-line source).

Foundation on Inter-Ethnic Relations, ed. 1997a. *Bibliography on the OSCE High Commissioner on National Minorities: Documents, Speeches and Related Publications.* The Hague: Foundation on Inter-Ethnic Relations.

———. 1997b. *The Role of the High Commissioner on National Minorities in OSCE Conflict Prevention: An Introduction.* The Hague: Foundation on Inter-Ethnic Relations.

Fraenkel, Eran. Executive Director, Search for Common Ground in Macedonia. 1995a. "Interview with the Author (Audio)." 10 May. Skopje, Republic of Macedonia.

———. 1995b. "Interview with the Author (Audio)." 25 July. Skopje, Republic of Macedonia.

———. 1996a. "International NGOs in Preventive Diplomacy and Early Warning: Macedonia." In *Vigilance and Vengeance: NGOs Preventing Ethnic Conflict in Divided Societies,* edited by Robert I. Rotberg, 113–32. Washington, D.C.: Brookings Institution Press.

———. 1996b. "Interview with the Author (Audio)." 24 May. Skopje, Republic of Macedonia.

———. 1996c. "Interview with the Author (Camera)." 28 May. Skopje, Republic of Macedonia.

———. 1996d. "Search for Common Ground in Macedonia, Spring Quarter Report, 1996." Washington, D.C.: Search for Common Ground.

Frankland, Erich. 1995. "Struggling with Collective Security and Recognition in Europe: The Case of the Macedonian Republic." *European Security* 4, no. 2: 354–79.

Frčkovski, Ljubomir. Foreign Minister, Republic of Macedonia. 1996. "Interview with the Author (Camera)." 10 June. Skopje, Republic of Macedonia.

Friedman, Victor. 1993. "Language Policy and Language Behavior in Macedonia: Background and Current Events." In *Language Contact—Language Conflict,* edited by Eran Fraenkel and Christina Kramer, 73–106. New York: Peter Lang.

———. 1996. "Observing the Observers: Language, Ethnicity, and Power in the 1994 Macedonian Census and Beyond." In *Toward Comprehensive Peace in*

Southeast Europe: Conflict Prevention in the South Balkans, edited by Barnett R. Rubin, 91–128. New York: Twentieth Century Fund Press.

Gaer, Felice D. 1993. "The Former Yugoslavia." In *A Global Agenda: Issues Before the 48th Global Assembly of the United Nations,* edited by John Tessitore and Susan Woolfson, 6–40. Lanham, Md.: Univ. Press of America.

Gagnon, V. P. 1994/95. "Ethnic Nationalism and International Conflict: The Case of Serbia." *International Security* 19, no. 3: 130–66.

———. 1995. "Historical Roots of the Yugoslav Conflict." In *International Organizations and Ethnic Conflict,* edited by Milton J. Esman and Shibley Telhami, 179–97. Ithaca, N.Y.: Cornell Univ. Press.

George, Alexander L., ed. 1983. *Managing U.S.-Soviet Rivalry: Problems of Crisis Prevention.* Boulder, Colo.: Westview.

George, Alexander L., and Jane E. Holl. 1997. *The Warning-Response Problem and Missed Opportunities in Preventive Diplomacy.* New York: Carnegie Corporation of New York.

Georgieva, Lidija. Professor, St. Cyril and Methodius University. 1999. "Interview with the Author." 1 May. Skopje, Republic of Macedonia.

Georgievski, Ljupco. Party Leader, VMRO-DPMNU. 1996a. "Interview with the Author (Notes)." 21 May. Skopje, Republic of Macedonia.

———. 1996b. "Interview with the Author (Camera)." 3 June. Skopje, Republic of Macedonia.

"Georgievski Blasts NATO." 1999. *RFE/RL Newsline* 3, no. 67, part 2, 7 Apr., 6.

"Georgievski: Milosevic Trying to Destabilize Macedonia." 1999. *RFE/RL Newsline* 3, no. 73, part 2, 15 Apr., 5.

"Georgievski Pledges Open Border." 1999. *RFE/RL Newsline* 3, no. 98, part 2, 20 May, 5.

Geroski, Branko. Journalist, *Večer.* 1995a. "Interview with the Author (Audio)." 28 July. Skopje, Republic of Macedonia.

———. 1995b. "Tetovo Trials." *War Report,* May, 15–16.

Geroski, Branko. Editor-in-Chief, *Dnevnik.* 1996. "Interview with the Author (Camera)." 28 May. Skopje, Republic of Macedonia.

———. 1999. "Interview with the Author." 7 May. Skopje, Republic of Macedonia.

Giersch, Carsten, and Daniel Eisermann. 1994. "Die westliche Politik und der Kroatien-Krieg, 1991–1992." *Südosteuropa* 43, no. 3–4: 91–125.

Glenny, Misha. 1993. "Is Macedonia Next?" *The New York Times,* 30 July, A27.

———. 1994. *The Fall of Yugoslavia: The Third Balkan War.* Rev. ed. New York: Penguin Books.

———. 1995a. "The Birth of a Nation." *The New York Review of Books.* 16 Nov., 24–28.

———. 1995b. "Heading Off War in the Balkans." *Foreign Affairs* 74, no. 3: 98–108.

Gligorov, Kiro. 1991. "In Jugoslawien ist nur eine Kompromißlösung möglich." *Fernseh-/Hörfunkspiegel Ausland,* 25 July.

———. President of Macedonia. 1996. "Interview with the Author (Camera)." 6 June. Skopje, Republic of Macedonia.

"Gligorov Says Serbia Destabilizing Macedonia." 1999. *RFE/RL Newsline* 3, no. 74, part 2, 16 Apr., 6.

Goodman, Anthony. 1995. "Greece Ends Feud with Macedonia. *The Independent,* 6 Sept., 13.

Gordenker, Leon. 1992. "Early Warning: Conceptual and Practical Issues." In *Early Warning and Conflict Resolution,* edited by Kumar Rupesinghe and Michiko Kuroda, 1–14. New York: St. Martin's.

Goulding, Marrack. 1993. "The Evolution of United Nations Peacekeeping." *International Affairs* 69, no. 3: 451–64.

"Griechisch-mazedonische Normalisierung." 1995. *Neue Züricher Zeitung,* 15 Sept., 1.

Gurr, Ted R. 1993a. "The Internationalization of Protracted Communal Conflicts since 1945: Which Groups, Where, and How." In *The Internationalization of Communal Strife,* edited by Manus L. Midlarsky, 3–26. New York: Routledge.

———. 1993b. *Minorities at Risk: A Global View of Ethnopolitical Conflicts.* Washington, D.C.: United States Institute of Peace Press.

———. 1994. "Peoples Against States: Ethnopolitical Conflict and the Changing World System." *International Studies Quarterly* 38, no. 3: 347–77.

———. 1995. "Transforming Ethno-political Conflicts: Exit, Autonomy, or Access?" In *Conflict Transformation,* edited by Kumar Rupesinghe, 1–30. New York: St. Martin's.

———. 1996. "Minorities, Nationalists, and Ethnopolitical Conflict." In *Managing Global Chaos: Sources and Responses to International Conflict,* edited by Chester A. Crocker and Fen Osler Hampson, 53–77. Washington, D.C.: United States Institute of Peace Press.

Gurr, Ted R., and Barbara Harff. 1994. *Ethnic Conflict in World Politics.* Boulder, Colo.: Westview.

Hackett, Kenneth. 1996. "The Role of International NGOs in Preventing Conflict." In *Vigilance and Vengeance: NGOs Preventing Ethnic Conflict in Divided Societies,* edited by Robert I. Rotberg, 269–84. Washington, D.C.: Brookings Institution Press.

Hamilton, Denise. 1996. "Multi-Ethnic Reporting in Macedonia." *Nieman Reports* 50, no. 2: 82.

Hampson, Fen Osler. 1996. *Nurturing Peace: Why Peace Settlements Succeed or Fail.* Washington, D.C.: United States Institute of Peace Press.

Heraclides, Alexis. 1993. *Helsinki-II and Its Aftermath: The Making of the CSCE into an International Organization.* London: Pinter.

Hobsbawm, Eric J. 1990. *Nations and Nationalism since 1780.* New York: Cambridge Univ. Press.

Holsti, Kalevi J. 1991. *Peace and War: Armed Conflict and International Order, 1648–1989.* New York: Cambridge Univ. Press.

———. 1996. *The State, War, and the State of War.* New York: Cambridge Univ. Press.

Hope, Karin. 1995. "Ethnic Divisions Deepen in Macedonia." *Financial Times,* 27 Feb., 4.

Horowitz, Donald L. 1985. *Ethnic Groups in Conflict.* Berkeley: Univ. of California Press.

Höynck, Wilhelm. 1994. "CSCE Missions in the Field as an Instrument of Preventive Diplomacy—Their Origin and Development." In *The Challenge of Preventive Diplomacy: The Experience of the CSCE,* edited by Ministry for Foreign Affairs, 55–72. Stockholm: Ministry for Foreign Affairs.

Huber, Konrad. 1993. "Preventing Ethnic Conflict in the New Europe: The CSCE High Commissioner on National Minorities." In *Minorities: The New Europe's Old Issue,* edited by Ian M. Cuthbertson and Jane Leibowitz, 285–310. New York: East-West Institute.

Human Rights Watch/Helsinki. 1996. *A Threat to "Stability:" Human Rights Violations in Macedonia.* New York: Human Rights Watch.

Huntington, Samuel P. 1993. "The Clash of Civilizations?" *Foreign Affairs* 72, no. 3: 22–49.

Ibrahimi, Sami. Parliamentarian, PPDsh/NPD. 1996a. "Interview with the Author (Audio)." 24 May. Skopje, Republic of Macedonia.

———. 1996b. "Interview with the Author (Camera)." 28 May. Skopje, Republic of Macedonia.

International Conference on the Former Yugoslavia (ICFY) Source. 1996. (anonymous)

———. 1999. (anonymous)

International Institute for Strategic Studies, ed. 1997. *The Military Balance 1997/98.* London: Oxford Univ. Press.

"Involvement of the OSCE in the Kosovo Crisis, The." 1999. OSCE on-line source, http://www.osceprag.cz.

Ivanov, Branko. Assistant Minister of Industry, Ministry of Economics. 1995. "Interview with the Author." May. Skopje, Republic of Macedonia.

Jehl, Douglas. 1994. "Officials Told to Avoid Calling Rwanda Killings 'Genocide.'" *New York Times,* 10 June.

Jentleson, Bruce W. 1996. "Preventive Diplomacy and Ethnic Conflict: Possible, Difficult, Necessary." Policy Paper #27, IGCC. Davis: Univ. of California.

Judah, Tim. 1992. "Wolves of War Circle Their Macedonian Prey." *The Times,* 11 Nov., 12.

"Jugoslawiens Vielvölkerstaat am Scheideweg?" 1990. *Neue Züricher Zeitung,* 14 July, 5.

Kaplan, Cynthia S. 1995. "Political Culture in Estonia: The Impact of Two Traditions on Political Development." In *Political Culture and Civil Society in Russia and the New States of Eurasia,* edited by Vladimir Tismaneanu, 227–68. Armonk, N.Y.: M. E. Sharpe.

Kask, Peet. 1996. "Institutional Development of the Parliament of Estonia." In *The New Parliaments of Central and Eastern Europe,* edited by David M. Olson and Philip Norton, 193–212. London: Frank Cass.

Kasriel, Ken. 1992. "Danube Dam Spurs Hungary's Ire." *The Christian Science Monitor,* 30 Oct., 2.

Kaufman, Stuart J. 1996. "Preventive Peacekeeping, Ethnic Violence, and Macedonia." *Studies in Conflict and Terrorism* 19: 229–46.

Kaufmann, Chaim. 1996. "Possible and Impossible Solutions to Ethnic Civil Wars." *International Security* 2, no. 4: 136–37.

Kelman, Herbert. 1972. "The Problem-Solving Workshop in Conflict Resolution." In *Communication in International Politics,* edited by Richard L. Merritt, 168–204. Hobson, Ill.: Univ. of Illinois Press.

Kende, Istvan. 1989. "The History of Peace: Concept and Organization from the Late Middle Ages to the 1870s." *Journal of Peace Research* 26, no. 3: 233–47.

"Keynote Speech by Ambassador Max van der Stoel, CSCE High Commissioner on National Minorities." 1994. In *CSCE Seminar on Early Warning and Preventive Diplomacy, Consolidated Summary.* Office for Democratic Institutions and Human Rights, 19–21 Jan., Warsaw.

Kirch, Aksel. 1992. "Russians as a Minority in Contemporary Baltic States." *Bulletin of Peace Proposals* 23, no. 2: 205–12.

Kirch, Marika. 1994. "Identification Diversity in Estonia: Grounds for Integration or Grounds for Disintegration? In *Changing Identities in Estonia: Sociological Facts and Commentaries,* edited by Marika Kirch and David D. Laitin, 11–24. Tallinn, Estonia: Akadeemia Trükk.

Kirch, Marika, and Aksel Kirch. 1995. "Search for Security in Estonia: New Identity Architecture." *Security Dialogue* 26, no. 4: 439–48.

Kitanovski, Lazar. Parliamentarian, SDSM. 1995. "Interview with the Author (Audio)." 27 July. Skopje, Republic of Macedonia.

Kolodziej, Edward A., and I. William Zartman. 1996. "Coping with Conflict: A Global Approach." In *Coping with Conflict after the Cold War,* edited by Edward A. Kolodziej and Roger E. Kanet, 3–34. Baltimore: Johns Hopkins Univ. Press.

"Kosovars Continue to Flee." 1999. *RFE/RL Newsline* 3, no. 63, part 2, 31 Mar., 6.

"Kosovars Flee to Macedonia." 1999. *RFE/RL Newsline* 3, no. 41, part 2, 1 Mar., 5.

Kraft, Ekkehard. 1995. "Der 'makedonische Faktor' in der griechischen Außen- und Innenpolitik: Ursachen und Auswirkungen." *Südosteuropa* 44, no. 6–7: 385–412.

Krause, Stefan. 1995. "First Greek-Macedonian Talks on Name Issue." *OMRI Daily Digest,* 19 Dec., 6.

Kriesberg, Louis. 1989. "Transforming Conflicts in the Middle East and Central Europe." In *Intractable Conflicts and Their Transformation,* edited by Louis Kriesberg, Terrell A. Northrup, and Stuart J. Thorson, 109–31. Syracuse: Syracuse Univ. Press.

———. 1995. "Applications and Misapplications of Conflict Resolution Ideas to International Conflicts." In *Beyond Confrontation: Learning Conflict Resolution in the Post-Cold War Era,* edited by John A. Vasquez et al., 87–102. Ann Arbor: Univ. of Michigan Press.

———. 1996a. "Coordinating Intermediary Peace Efforts." *Negotiation Journal* 12, no. 4: 341–52.

———. 1996b. "Varieties of Mediating Activities and Mediators in International Relations." In *Resolving International Conflicts: Theory and Practice of Mediation,* edited by Jacob Bercovitch, 219–33. Boulder, Colo.: Lynne Rienner, 1996.

———. 1997. "Preventing and Resolving Destructive Communal Conflicts." In *Wars in the Midst of Peace: The International Politics of Ethnic Conflict,* edited by David Carment and Patrick James, 232–51. Pittsburg: Univ. of Pittsburgh Press.

———. 1998a. *Constructive Conflicts: From Escalation to Resolution.* Lanham, Md.: Rowman and Littlefield.

———. 1998b. "The Phases of Destructive Conflicts: Communal Conflicts and Proactive Solutions, edited by David Carment and Patrick James, 33–62. Columbia: Univ. of South Carolina Press, 1998.

Kuperman, Alan J. 1996. "The Other Lesson of Rwanda: Mediators Sometimes Do More Damage." *SAIS Review* 16, no. 1: 221–40.

Kürti, Lázló, and Juliet Langman, eds. 1997. *Beyond Borders: Remaking Cultural Identities in the New East and Central Europe.* Boulder, Colo.: Westview.

Lahelma, Timo. 1994. "The Role of the CSCE Missions in Preventive Diplomacy—The Case of Estonia (Aug. 1993–June 1994)." In *The Challenge of Preventive Diplomacy: The Experience of the CSCE,* edited by the Ministry for Foreign Affairs, 87–99. Stockholm: Ministry for Foreign Affairs.

Langman, Juliet. 1997. "Expressing Identity in a Changing Society: Hungarian Youth in Slovakia." In *Beyond Borders: Remaking Cultural Identities in the New East and Central Europe,* edited by László Kürti, and Juliet Langman, 111–31. Boulder, Colo.: Westview.

Lauren, Paul Gordon. 1983. "Crisis Prevention in Nineteenth-Century Diplomacy." In *Managing U.S. Soviet Rivalry: Problems of Crisis Prevention,* edited by Alexander L. George, 31–64. Boulder, Colo.: Westview.

"Law on the Pedagogical Faculty Practically Enforced Yesterday." 1997. *MILS News,* 21 Feb. (on-line source).

Leatherman, Janie. 1994. "The CSCE's (Im)possibilities for Preventive Diplomacy in the Context of Ethnic Conflict." *International Journal on Group Rights* 2, no. 1: 35–54.

Leatherman, Janie, William DeMars, Patrick D. Gaffney, and Raimo Väyrynen. 1999. *Breaking Cycles of Violence: Conflict Prevention in Intrastate Crises.* West Hartford, Conn.: Kumarian Press.

Lefebvre, Stephanie. 1994. "The Former Yugoslav Republic of Macedonia (FYROM): Where To?" *European Security* 3, no. 4: 711–33.

Lemarchand, René. 1994. "Managing Transition Anarchies: Rwanda, Burundi, and South Africa in Comparative Perspective." In *Journal of Modern African Studies* 32, no. 4: 581–604.

Lewis, Paul. 1997. "How U.N. Keeps Pace as Fewer Keep Peace." *New York Times,* 4 May, A4.

Lijphart, Arend. 1977. *Democracy in Plural Societies.* New Haven: Yale Univ. Press.

Loescher, Gil. 1993. *Beyond Charity: International Cooperation and the Global Refugee Crisis.* New York: Oxford Univ. Press.

Lowenthal, Mark M. 1993. "Preventive Diplomacy: Prospects and Issues." In *CRS Report for Congress,* 25 Mar. 1993. Washington, D.C.: Congressional Research Service.

Lumsden, Malvern. 1997. *Peacebuilding in Macedonia: Searching for Common Ground in Civil Society.* Stockholm: PRIO.

Lund, Michael. 1996a. *Preventing Violent Conflicts: A Strategy for Preventive Diplomacy.* Washington, D.C.: United States Institute of Peace Press.

———. 1996b. "Toward a Framework for Diagnosing and Designing Conflict Prevention in Europe." Paper presented at the Joint IAI/SWP Project Conference on "Preventing Violent Conflict in Europe," 22–23 Nov. Stiftung Wissenschaft und Politik, Ebenhausen, Germany.

Macedonian Information Center. 1994. *Republic of Macedonia: Basic Data.* Skopje, Dec.

"Macedonia Seeks to Stay Out of Conflict." 1999. *RFE/RL Newsline* 3, no. 58, part 2, 24 Mar., 6.

MacFarlane, S. Neil. 1996. "Non-Governmental Organizations and Conflict Prevention." Paper presented at the Joint IAI/SWP Project Conference on "Preventing Violent Conflict in Europe," 22–23 Nov. Stiftung Wissenschaft und Politik, Ebenhausen, Germany.

Maleski, Ognen. 1996. Assistant to the Foreign Minister, Ljubomir Frčkovski, Macedonian Foreign Ministry. "Interview with the Author." 15 Mar. Skopje, Republic of Macedonia.

"Mazedonien erkennt Staatspräsidium nicht mehr an." 1991. *Süddeutsche Zeitung,* 17 Oct., 1.

"Mazedoniens behutsame Jugoslawien-Politik." 1991. *Neue Züricher Zeitung,* 31 Oct., 3–4.

"Mazedonien zu Grenzvertrag mit Athen bereit." 1995. *Neue Züricher Zeitung,* 10 Apr., 4.

McKinley, James C., Jr. 1997. "New Rwanda Killings Dim Hopes for Amity." *New York Times,* 15 Jan., A1 and A6.

McKinley, James C., Jr., with Howard W. French. 1997. "Uncovering the Guilty Footprints Along Zaire's Long Trail of Death." *New York Times,* 14 Nov., A1 and A12.

Meier, Viktor. 1991a. "Jetzt entscheiden die Republiken." *Frankfurter Allgemeine Zeitung,* 23 Apr., 6.

———. 1991b. "Mazedonien macht sich keine Illusionen." *Frankfurter Allgemeine Zeitung,* 28 Nov., 14.

Mickey, Robert W., and Adam Smith Albion. 1993. "Success in the Balkans? A Case Study of Ethnic Relations in the Republic of Macedonia." In *Minorities: The New Europe's Old Issue,* edited by Ian M. Cuthbertson and Jane Leibowitz, 53–98. New York: Institute for East-West Studies.

Midlarsky, Manus L., ed. 1993. *The Internationalization of Communal Strife.* New York: Routledge.

Milcin, Vladimir, Executive Director, Open Society Institute. 1995. "Interview with the Author (Audio)." 31 July. Skopje, Republic of Macedonia.

———. 1996. "Interview with the Author (Audio)." 25 May. Skopje, Republic of Macedonia.

Ministry of Information, Republic of Macedonia. 1999. *Political Mosaic.* February. Skopje, Republic of Macedonia.

"Mission Observes Worrying Trends in the Former Yugoslav Republic of Macedonia." 1997. *OSCE Newsletter* 4, no. 3: 9.

Mitchell, Christopher R. 1993. "The Process and Stages of Mediation." In *Making War and Waging Peace: Foreign Intervention in Africa,* edited by David R. Smock, 139–60. Washington, D.C.: United States Institute of Peace Press.

Mitchell, Christopher R., and K. Webb, eds. 1988. *New Approaches to International Mediation.* New York: Greenwood.

Moeller, Wolfgang. 1997. "Makedonien: Konfliktverhütung durch präventive Stationierung von UN-Blauhelmen." In *Der gelungene Frieden: Beispiele und Bedingungen erfolgreicher friedlicher Konfliktbearbeitung,* edited by Volker Matthies, 278–305. Bonn: Verlag J.H.W. Dietz.

Moore, Patrick. 1991. "Where Is Yugoslavia Headed?" *Radio Liberty/Radio Free Europe Reports on Eastern Europe* 2, no. 36: 33.

———. 1997. "Macedonian Students Keep Up Protest Against Albanian-Language Instruction." *OMRI Daily Digest,* no. 39, 25 Feb. (on-line source).

———. 1998. "Three Questions for Macedonia." *RFE/RL Newsline* 2, no. 208, part 2, 28 Oct., 8–9.

Moore, Will H., and Ted Robert Gurr. 1997. "Assessing Risks of Ethnorebellion in the Year 2000: Three Empirical Approaches." Paper Prepared for the Synergy in Early Warning Conference, York Univ., Toronto, 15–18 Mar., and the International Studies Association Annual Meeting, Toronto, 18–22 Mar.

Mueller, John. 1994. "The Catastrophe Quota: Trouble After the Cold War." *Journal of Conflict Resolution* 38, no. 3: 355–75.

Munuera, Gabriel. 1994. *Preventing Armed Conflict in Europe: Lessons from Recent Experience.* Paris: Institute for Security Studies, Western European Union.

"Nach Sarajewo ist Jugoslawien auf dem Weg zur Staaten-Allianz." 1991. *Frankfurter Allgemeine Zeitung,* 8 June, 2.

"Neue Vermittlungsmission in der Mazedonienfrage." 1994. *Neue Züricher Zeitung.* 10 June, 4.

"Neuer Vermittlungsanlauf der USA im Mazedonienstreit." 1994. *Neue Züricher Zeitung.* 20 Dec., 4.

"Neuer Vermittlungsanlauf im Mazedonienzwist." 1994. *Neue Züricher Zeitung.* 10 Nov., 5.

Nicolaïdis, Kalypso. 1996. "International Preventive Action: Developing a Strategic Framework." In *Vigilance and Vengeance: NGOs Preventing Ethnic Conflict in Divided Societies,* edited by Robert I. Rotberg, 23–72. Washington, D.C.: Brookings Institution Press.

NORDBAT-UNPREDEP. 1996. Pamphlet. Skopje, Republic of Macedonia: Nordbat.

Nørgaard, Ole. 1996. *The Baltic States After Independence.* Cheltenham, England: Edward Elgar.

Norkus, Renatas. 1996. "Preventing Conflict in the Baltic States: A Success Story That Will Hold." Paper presented at a Joint ISA/SWP Project Conference on "Preventing Violent Conflict in Europe." 22–23 Nov., Stiftung Wissenschaft und Politik, Ebenhausen, Germany,

O'Connor, Mike. 1996. "Officials Blame Bosnia and Themselves for Mine Clearing Delays." *New York Times,* 28 Oct., A6.

"Opinion of the Arbitration Committee." 1991. *Yugoslav Survey,* no. 4: 17–19.

Organization for Security and Cooperation in Europe (OSCE), High Commissioner on National Minorities (HCNM). 1995a. "List of HCNM Mission Travels." The Hague: Office of the High Commissioner on National Minorities.

———. 1995b. "Recommendations to Macedonia, Including Reply." HC/REF/3/95. The Hague: Office of the HCNM.

———. 1996a. "Recommendations to Estonia Dated 11 December 1995, Pursuant to a Visit on 30 November and 1 December 1995, and Response Dated February 7, 1996." HC/01/96. The Hague: Office of the HCNM.

———. 1996b. "Recommendations to the Slovak Republic Dated 13 August 1996, Pursuant to a Visit on 22–24 May 1996 with Response Dated 21 October 1996." HC/12/96. The Hague: Office of the HCNM.

"OSCE Contributes to Relief Efforts." 1999. OSCE on-line source: http://www.osce.org/e/docs.

OSCE Mission to Bosnia and Herzegovina, Refugee Elections Steering Group (RESG). 1996. *Final Report on Bosnia and Herzegovina National and Cantonal Elections Abroad,* Vienna, 11 Oct. 1996. REF. SEC/622/96, 21 Oct., 23.

OSCE Permanent Council. 1996. "Interpretative Statement Under Paragraph 79 (Chapter 6) of the Final Recommendations of the Helsinki Consultations." PC.DEC/144/144. 21 Nov., Annex.

OSCE Secretariat. 1995a. *OSCE Handbook: 20 years of the Helsinki Final Act, 1975–1995.* Vienna: OSCE.

———. 1995b. *OSCE Newsletter* 2, no. 1: 7.

———. 1995c. "Report by the OSCE High Commissioner on National Minorities on His Most Recent Visit to the Former Yugoslav Republic of Macedonia and the Comments by the Government of the Former Yugoslav Republic of Macedonia Thereon." 13 January, Prague, Czech Republic.

———. 1996a. *OSCE Handbook 1996.* 2d. ed. Vienna: OSCE Secretariat.

———. 1996b. *OSCE Newsletter* 3, no. 1: 5.

———. 1996c. *OSCE Newsletter* 3, no. 7: 3.

———. 1996d. *OSCE Newsletter* 3, no. 10: 4.

———. 1997a. "Mission Observes Worrying Trends in the Former Yugoslav

Republic of Macedonia." *OSCE Newsletter* 4, no. 3: 9.
———. 1997b. "News Briefs from OSCE Missions: Mission to Estonia Notes Positive Developments in Citizenship Issue." *OSCE Newsletter* 4, no. 2: 5.
———. 1997c. "News Briefs from OSCE Missions: Spillover Monitor Mission to Skopje Follows Security Situation." *OSCE Newsletter* 4, no. 9: 12.
———. 1997d. "Report from the HCNM: Estonia." *OSCE Newsletter* 4, no. 4: 7.
———. 1997e. "Report from the HCNM: The Former Yugoslav Republic of Macedonia." *OSCE Newsletter* 4, no. 3: 9.
———. 1997f. "Report from the HCNM: Hungary." *OSCE Newsletter* 4, no. 2: 6.
———. 1997g. "Report from the HCNM: Slovakia." *OSCE Newsletter* 4, no. 4: 7.
———. 1997h. "Survey of OSCE Long-Term Missions and Other OSCE Field Activities." SEC.GAL/13/97, 7 October, Vienna, Austria.
———. 1998a. "Report from the HCNM: The Former Yugoslav Republic of Macedonia." *OSCE Newsletter* 5, no. 5: 12.
———. 1998b. "Report from the HCNM: Slovakia." *OSCE Newsletter* 5, no. 3: 8.
OSCE Secretary-General. 1994. *Annual Report 1994 on OSCE Activities.* Vienna: OSCE.
———. 1995. *Annual Report 1995 on OSCE Activities.* Vienna: OSCE.
OSCE Source, Macedonian Delegation (Vienna). 1997. "Interview with the Author (Telephone)." 4 Apr. Miami, Florida.
"OSCE Spillover Monitor Mission to Skopje, The." 1999. OSCE on-line source, http://www.osceprag.cz/e/docs.
OSCE Spillover Monitor Mission to Skopje. 1999. *Background Report on the Economic Spillover Effects From the Crisis in Kosovo.* April. Skopje, Republic of Macedonia.
Ott, Attiat F., Aksel Kirch, and Marika Kirch. 1996. "Ethnic Anxiety: A Case Study of Resident Aliens in Estonia (1990–1992)." *Journal of Baltic Studies* 27, no. 1: 21–37.
Owen, David. 1995. *Balkan Odyssey.* New York: Harcourt, Brace and Company.
Palmer, Stephen E., and Robert R. King. 1971. *Yugoslav Communism and the Macedonian Question.* Hamden, Conn.: Archon Books.
Park, Andrus. 1994. "Ethnicity and Independence: The Case of Estonia in Comparative Perspective." *Europe-Asia Studies* 46:69–87.
Peck, Connie. 1993. "Improving the U.N. System of Preventive Diplomacy and Conflict Resolution: Past Experiences, Current Problems and Future Perspectives." In *Blauhelme in einer turbulenten Welt,* edited by Winrich Kühne, 401–21. Baden-Baden, Germany: Nomos.
———. 1996. *The United Nations as a Dispute Settlement System: Improving Mechanisms for the Prevention and Resolution of Conflict.* The Hague: Kluwer Law International.

Perry, Duncan M. 1992. "Macedonia: A Balkan Problem and a European Dilemma." *RFE/RL Research Report* 1, no. 5: 35–45.

———. 1993a. "Diplomatic Events Concerning Macedonia." *RFE/RL Daily Reports: Central and Eastern Europe,* no. 230: 3.

———. 1993b. "Macedonia and the UN." *RFE/RL Daily Reports: Central and Eastern Europe,* no. 4: 3.

———. 1993c. "Politics in the Republic of Macedonia: Issues and Parties." *RFE/RL Research Report* 4, no. 23: 31–37.

———. 1994a. "Crisis in the Making? Macedonia and Its Neighbors." *Südosteuropa* 43, no. 1–2: 31–58.

———. 1994b. "Macedonia." *RFE/RL Research Report* 3, no. 16: 83–86.

———. 1995. "On the Road to Stability—or Destruction?" *Transition,* 25 Aug., 40–48.

———. 1996. "Macedonia: Balkan Miracle or Balkan Disaster?" *Current History.* March, 113–17.

———. 1997. "The Republic of Macedonia: Finding Its Way." In *Politics, Power, and the Struggle for Democracy in South-East Europe,* edited by Karen Dawisha and Bruce Parrott, 226–81. Cambridge, England: Cambridge Univ. Press.

Pettai, Vello. 1996. "Estonia's Controversial Language Policies." *Transition* 2, no. 4: 20–22.

Pettifer, James. 1992. "The New Macedonian Question." *International Affairs* 68, no. 3: 475–86.

Poulton, Hugh. 1994. "The Rest of the Balkans." In *Minority Rights in Europe: Prospects for a Transnational Regime,* edited by Hugh Miall, 66–86. New York: Council on Foreign Relations Press and The Royal Institute of International Affairs.

———. 1995. *Who Are the Macedonians?* Bloomington: Indiana Univ. Press.

Pribichevich, Stoyan. 1982. *Macedonia: Its People and History.* University Park: Pennsylvania State Univ. Press.

Prunier, Gérard. 1995. *The Rwanda Crisis: History of a Genocide.* New York: Columbia Univ. Press.

Pruthi, Abdurauf. President of the NGO, El Hilal. 1995. "Interview with the Author." 26 July. Skopje, Republic of Macedonia.

Ramet, Sabrina P. 1992. *Nationalism and Federalism in Yugoslavia: 1962–1991.* Bloomington: Indiana Univ. Press.

———. 1996. *Balkan Babel: The Disintegration of Yugoslavia from the Death of Tito to Ethnic War.* 2d. ed. Boulder, Colo.: Westview.

Raun, Toivo U. 1994. "Post-Soviet Estonia, 1991–1993." *Journal of Baltic Studies* 25, no. 1: 73–80.

Regan, Patrick M. 1996. "Conditions of Successful Third-Party Intervention in Intrastate Conflicts." *Journal of Conflict Resolution* 40, no. 2: 336–59.
"Relief Workers Reach Stranded Refugees." 1999. *RFE/RL Newsline* 3, no. 77, part 2, 23 Apr., 6.
"Reopens Border to Refugees." 1999. *RFE/RL Newsline* 3, no. 58, part 2, 24 Mar., 6.
"Report of Ambassador G. Norman Anderson, Head of Mission, CSCE Mission, Skopje." 1993. CSO Meeting, Rome, 27–29 Nov.
"Report of Ambassador William B. Whitman, Head of Mission, CSCE Spillover Mission, Skopje." 1993. CSO Meeting, Prague, 2 Feb.
Republic of Macedonia Secretariat of Information. 1996. "Government of the Republic of Macedonia." Skopje, Republic of Macedonia.
Republic of Macedonia, State Census Commission. 1995. "Report on the Work of the State Census Commission." Feb. Skopje, Republic of Macedonia.
Republic of Macedonia Statistical Office. 1994a. *Census '94: Data for the Present and the Future.* 14 Nov., Skopje, Republic of Macedonia.
Republic of Macedonia Statistical Office. 1994b. *Macedonia Basic Economic Data.* Skopje, Republic of Macedonia.
Reuter, Jens. 1995. "Interview mit dem Präsidenten der Republik Makedonien Kiro Gligorov." *Südosteuropa* 44, no. 8: 508–12.
Reychler, Luc. 1994. "The Art of Conflict Prevention: Theory and Practice." In *The Art of Conflict Prevention,* edited by Werner Bauwens and Luc Reychler, 1–21. London: Brassey's.
Rieff, David. 1995. "The Lessons of Bosnia: Morality and Power." *World Policy Journal* 12, no. 1: 75–78.
"Rising Stakes in Macedonia: Beware of a Full-Blown War." 1992. *The International Herald Tribune,* 14 Dec.
Robinson, Anthony, and Kerin Hope. 1995. "Washington Eager to Mediate Between Battling Neighbors." *Financial Times,* 11 Sept., 2.
Rogel, Carole. 1998. *The Breakup of Yugoslavia and the War in Bosnia.* Westport, Conn.: Greenwood.
Ross, Marc Howard. 1996. "Evaluating Success and Failure in Non-Governmental Ethnic Conflict Interventions." Paper Presented at the International Workshop on Ethnic Conflict and Ethnic Conflict Management and Resolution, Hotel Castle Szirák, Hungary, 15–17 May.
Rotberg, Robert I., ed. 1996. *Vigilance and Violence: NGOs Preventing Ethnic Conflict in Divided Societies.* Washington, D.C.: Brookings Institution Press.
Rotfeld, Adam Daniel. 1996. *From Helsinki to Budapest and Beyond: Analysis and Documents of the Organization for Security and Co-operation in Europe 1973–1995.* Oxford: Oxford Univ. Press.

Rubin, Barnett R., ed. 1996. *Toward Comprehensive Peace in Southeast Europe: Conflict Prevention in the South Balkans.* New York: Twentieth Century Fund Press.

Rubin, Jeffrey Z., ed. 1981. *Dynamics of Third Party Intervention: Kissinger in the Middle East.* New York: Praeger.

Rüb, Matthias. 1995. "Künftig kein Streit mehr unter dem Stern von Vergina?" *Frankfurter Allgemeine Zeitung,* 12 Sept.

Rummel, Reinhard. 1996. "The European Union's Politico-Diplomatic Contribution to the Prevention of Ethno-National Conflicts." In *Preventing Conflict in the Post-Communist World,* edited by Abram Chayes and Antonia Handler Chayes, 197–235. Washington, D.C.: Brookings Institution Press.

Rupesinghe, Kumar. 1992. "The Disappearing Boundaries Between Internal and External Conflicts." In *New Agendas for Peace Research: Conflict and Security Re-examined,* edited by Elise Boulding, 43–64. Boulder, Colo.: Lynne Rienner.

———. 1995a. "Conflict Transformation." In *Conflict Transformation,* edited by Kumar Rupesinghe, 65–92. New York: St. Martin's.

———. 1995b. "Towards a Policy Framework for Preventive Diplomacy." *Security Dialogue* 26, no. 1: 112–14.

Rupesinghe, Kumar, and Michiko Kuroda, eds. 1992. *Early Warning and Conflict Resolution.* New York: St. Martin's.

Rusi, Iso. 1995. "Ethnic Trouble Brews in Macedonia." *International Herald Tribune,* 7 Mar., 8.

Salla, Michael. 1995. "Kosovo, Non-violence and the Break-up of Yugoslavia." *Security Dialogue* 26, no. 4: 427–38.

Saraqini, Nafi. Project Manager, Catholic Relief Services. 1995. "Interview with the Author (Audio)." 8 May. Skopje, Republic of Macedonia.

SCG (Search for Common Ground). 1995. *Annual Report 1994.* Washington, D.C.

SCG and the Center for War, Peace, and the News Media. 1995. "How We Survive." A Journalism Project of Search for Common Ground and the Center for War, Peace, and the News Media of NYU, June–July, Skopje, Macedonia.

Schevill, Ferdinand. 1991. *A History of the Balkans.* New York: Dorset Press.

Schleicher, Harry. 1993. "Mazedonien: Droht nun der Zerfall?" *Frankfurter Rundschau,* 18 Nov., 6.

Schmidt, Fabian. 1995. "From National Consensus to Pluralism." *Transition* 1, no. 1: 22–30.

———. 1997. "Macedonian Students Protest Against Albanian-Language Education." *OMRI Daily Digest,* 18 Feb. (on-line source).

Sciolino, Elaine. 1994. "U.S. Says It Will Send 300 Troops to Balkan Republic to Limit Strife." *New York Times,* 11 June.

Shafer, Boyd C. 1972. *Faces of Nationalism.* New York: Harcourt Brace Jovanovich.

Shafir, Gershon. 1995. *Immigrants and Nationalists: Ethnic Conflict and Accommodation: Catalonia, the Basque Country, Latvia, and Estonia.* Albany, N.Y.: SUNY Press.

Shorr, David. 1995. Former Project Director, Search for Common Ground. "Interview with the Author (Audio)." 6 Mar. Washington, D.C.

Singleton, Frederick B. 1992. *Yugoslavia: The Country and Its People.* Cambridge, England: Cambridge Univ. Press.

"Skopje's Generous Gesture." 1995. *The Wall Street Journal,* 12 Sept., 6.

Smith, Graham, Aadne Aasland, and Richard Mole. 1994. "Statehood, Ethnic Relations and Citizenship." In *The Baltic States: The National Self-Determination of Estonia, Latvia and Lithuania,* edited by Graham Smith, 181–206. New York: St. Martin's.

Sokalski, Henryk. Assistant Secretary-General. Chief of Mission, UNPREDEP. 1996a. "Interview with the Author (Audio)." 11 Mar. Skopje, Republic of Macedonia.

———. 1996b. "Interview with the Author (Camera)." 26 May. Skopje, Republic of Macedonia.

"SRFY Presidency Views Regarding the Opinion of the Arbitration Committee." 1991. *Yugoslav Survey,* no. 4: 19–24.

Stanley, Alessandra. 1999. "Embassies Are Stoned as Tensions Begin to Rise." *New York Times,* 26 Mar., A8.

"Statement Issued at the Meeting of the North Atlantic Cooperation Council, Athens, Greece, 11 June 1993." 1993. *NATO Review* 41, no. 3: 23–25.

"Statement of the Head of the CSCE Spillover Monitor Mission Regarding Agreement on Understanding on Operations on the Mission." 1992 (November). Prague: OSCE Office for Documentation and Information.

Stedman, Stephen John. 1993. "The New Interventionists." *Foreign Affairs* 72, no. 1: 1–16.

———. 1995. "Alchemy for a New World Order." *Foreign Affairs* 74, no. 3: 14–20.

Steinberg, James B. 1993. "International Involvement in the Yugoslav Conflict." In *Enforcing Restraint: Collective Intervention in Internal Conflict,* edited by Lori Fisler Damrosch, 27–76. New York: Council on Foreign Relations Press.

Stošic, Gordana. Director, A1 Independent Television. 1995. "Interview with the Author." Skopje, Republic of Macedonia.

"Streit um den Sonnenstern." 1993. *Frankfurter Rundschau,* 5 Apr., 7.

Sulejmani, Fadil. Rector, Tetovo University. 1996a. "Interview with the Author (Audio)." 13 Mar. Tetovo, Republic of Macedonia.

———. 1996b. "Interview with the Author (Camera)." 30 May. Tetovo, Republic of Macedonia.

Taagepera, Rein. 1993. *Estonia: Return to Independence.* Boulder, Colo.: Westview.

Tanner, Marcus. 1992. "Macedonia 'Walking Tightrope' to Avert Balkan War." *The Independent,* 11 Nov., 10.

Thompson, Gordon, and Paula Gutlove. 1994. "Preventive Diplomacy and National Security: Incorporating Conflict Prevention and Conflict Resolution as Elements of US National Security Policy." A Report Informed by a Workshop Held in the Rayburn House Office Building, Washington, D.C., 18 Mar.

Thompson, Wayne C. 1997. "Ethnic/Communal Conflict in Two Continents: Estonia and India." Paper Presented at the 1997 ISA–South Annual Conference, 17–19 Oct., Florida International Univ., North Miami.

Touval, Saadia, and I. William Zartman, eds. 1985. *International Mediation in Theory and Practice.* Boulder, Colo.: Westview.

Törnudd, Klaus. 1994. "The Role of the CSCE Missions in Preventive Diplomacy—The Case of Estonia." In *The Challenge of Preventive Diplomacy: The Experience of the CSCE,* edited by the Ministry for Foreign Affairs, 73–86. Stockholm: Ministry for Foreign Affairs.

Troebst, Stefan. 1992. "Makedonische Antworten auf die 'Makedonische Frage,' 1944–1992: Nationalismus, Republiksgründung, Nation-Building." *Südosteuropa* 41, no. 7–8: 423–42.

———. 1994. Präventive Friedenssicherung durch internationale Beobachtermissionen? Das Beispiel der KSZE-Spillover-Monitormission in Makedonien 1992–1993. In *Sicherheitspolitisches Symposium Balkankonflikt,* edited by Wolfgang Pühs, Thomas Weggel, and Claus Richter, 125–56. Baden-Baden, Germany: Nomos Verlag.

———. 1997. "An Ethnic War That Did Not Take Place: Macedonia, Its Minorities, and Its Neighbors in the 1990s." *In War and Ethnicity: Global Connections and Local Violence,* edited by David Turton, 77–103. Rochester: Univ. of Rochester Press.

Troni, Faustino. OSCE Head of Mission. 1999. "Interview with the Author." 12 May. Skopje, Republic of Macedonia.

Tupurkovski, Vasil. 1997. "The Balkan Crisis and the Republic of Macedonia." In *Crises in the Balkans: Views from the Participants,* edited by Constantine P. Danopoulos and Kostas G. Messas, 135–52. Boulder, Colo.: Westview.

U.K. See United Kingdom.

U.N. See United Nations.

United Kingdom, Foreign and Commonwealth Office. 1998. *Survey of Current Affairs* 28, no. 1: 17–21.

United Nations. 1995. "The UN and the Situation in the Former Yugoslavia." A Background Paper, 8 Jan.

United Nations, Department of Public Information. 1996a. *The United Nations and Rwanda 1993–1996*. Vol. 10. New York: United Nations.

———. 1996b. "Report of the Special Rapporteur of the Commission on Human Rights on the Situation of Human Rights in Rwanda." In *The United Nations and Rwanda 1993–1996*, 569–92. New York: United Nations.

United Nations Development Program. 1995. *Human Development Report 1994*. New York: United Nations.

United Nations, Division of Information. 1995. "UNPREDEP." Fact Sheet, Oct.

United Nations, General Assembly. 1960. *Introduction to the Annual Report of the Secretary-General of the Work of the Organization, 16 June 1959–15 June 1960*, Supplement No. 1A (A/4390/Add. 1). New York: United Nations.

United Nations High Commissioner for Refugees (UNHCR). *UNHCR News—Kosovo Crisis Update*. 1 June. UNHCR on-line source: <http://www.unhcr.cr/news/media/kosovo.htm>

United Nations, Secretary-General. 1995. *Report of the Secretary-General Pursuant to Security Council Resolution 947 (1994)*, 22 Mar.

———. 1996a. *Report of the Secretary-General Pursuant to Security Council Resolution 1027 (1995)*, S/1996/65, 29 Jan.

———. 1996b. *Report of the Secretary-General Pursuant to Security Council Resolution 1046 (1996)*, S/1996/373, 23 May.

United Nations, Security Council. 1992. "Resolution 795, Adopted by the Security Council at Its 3147th Meeting on 11 December 1992." S/RES/795 (1992), 11 Dec.

———. 1993a. "Letter Dated 26 May From the Secretary-General to the President of the Security Council." S/25855 (1993), 28 May (on-line source).

———. 1993b. "Resolution 817, Adopted by the Security Council at Its 3196th Meeting on 7 April 1993." S/RES/817 (1993), 7 Apr.

———. 1993c. "Resolution 842, Adopted by the Security Council at Its 3239th Meeting on 18 June 1993." S/RES/842 (1993), 18 June.

———. 1993d. "Resolution 845, Adopted by the Security Council at Its 3243rd Meeting on 18 June 1993." S/RES/845 (1993), 18 June.

———. 1994. "Resolution 908, Adopted by the Security Council at Its 3346th Meeting on 31 March 1994." S/RES/908 (1994), 31 Mar.

———. 1995. "Resolution 983, Adopted by the Security Council at Its 3512th Meeting on 30 March 1995." S/RES/983 (1995), 31 Mar.

———. 1997a. "Resolution 1110, Adopted by the Security Council at Its 3783rd Meeting on 28 May 1997." S/RES/1110 (1997), 28 May.

———. 1997b. "Resolution 1140, Adopted by the Security Council at Its 3836th Meeting on 28 November 1997." S/RES/1140 (1997), 28 Nov.
———. 1997c. "Resolution 1142, Adopted by the Security Council at Its 3839 Meeting on 4 December 1997." S/RES/1140 (1997), 4 Dec.
———. 1997d. "3783rd Meeting, Wednesday, 28 May 1997." S/PV. 3783 (1997), 28 May (on-line source).
———. 1997e. "Security Council Extends Preventive Force in Former Yugoslav Republic of Macedonia until 31 August 1998." Press Release SC/6451, 4 Dec.
———. 1998a. "Resolution 1186, Adopted by the Security Council at Its 3911th Meeting on 21 July 1998. S/RES/1186 (1998), 21 July.
———. 1998b. "Security Council Extends Mandate of UNPREDEP until 28 February 1999 and Increases Troop Strength." Press Release SC/6554, 21 July.
United States, Department of State. 1995. "Summary of the Interim Accord Between Greece and FYROM." Sept.
United States, Department of State. 1995 (anonymous source).
United States Mission to the United Nations. 1995. *Global Humanitarian Emergencies, 1995*. New York, January.
Van der Stoel, Max. 1994a. "Preventive Diplomacy in Situations of Ethnic Tensions: The Role of the CSCE High Commissioner." In *Weltweite und europäische Sicherheit im Spannungsfeld von Souveranität und Minderheitenschutz,* edited by E. Hetzke and M. Donner, 43–51. Berlin: Mittler.
———. 1994b. "The Role of the CSCE High Commissioner on National Minorities in CSCE Preventive Diplomacy." In *The Challenge of Preventive Diplomacy: The Experience of the CSCE,* edited by the Ministry for Foreign Affairs, 33–54. Stockholm: Ministry for Foreign Affairs.
Van Evera, Stephen. 1994. "Hypotheses on Nationalism and War." *International Security* 18, no. 4: 5–39.
Vangelova, Luba. 1995. "Focusing on Solutions: John Marks' Search for Common Ground." *Washington International* 8, no. 4: 15.
Varvaroussis, Paris. 1995. "Mazedonien als Brennpunkt der griechischen Balkan-Politik." *Aussenpolitik* 46, no. 4: 358–64.
Väyrynen, Raimo. 1995. "The United Nations and Preventive Diplomacy: The Need of New Approaches." Paper Presented at the Conference on "The United Nations: Beyond Sovereignty and Global Governance," LaTrobe University, Melbourne, Australia, 2–6 July.
Vetik, Raivo. 1993. "Ethnic Conflict and Accommodation in Post-Communist Estonia." *Journal of Peace Research,* 30, no. 3: 271–80.
———. 1994. "Russians in Estonia: New Development Trends." In *Changing Identities in Estonia: Sociological Facts and Commentaries,* edited by Marika

Kirch and David D. Laitin, 72–79. Tallinn, Estonia: Akadeemia Trükk.
Völkl, Katrin. 1993. "Makedonien/Mazedonien." In *Der ruhelose Balkan: Konfliktregionen Südosteuropas,* edited by Michael W. Weithmann, 218–25. Munich: Deutscher Taschenbuch Verlag.
Wallensteen, Peter, and Karin Axell. 1994. "Conflict Resolution and the End of the Cold War, 1989–93." *Journal of Peace Research* 31, no. 3: 333–49.
"We Do Not Guarantee Safety to Americans in Macedonia." 1995. *MILS News,* 25 Aug., 1–2. (on-line citation)
Weiner, Myron. 1996. "Bad Neighbors, Bad Neighborhoods: An Inquiry into the Causes of Refugee Flows." *International Security* 21, no. 1: 5–42.
Weiss, Thomas G., David P. Forsythe, and Roger A. Coate. 1994. *The United Nations and Changing World Politics.* Boulder, Colo.: Westview.
Weiss, Thomas G., and Leon Gordenker, eds. 1996. *NGOs, the UN, and Global Governance.* Boulder, Colo.: Lynne Rienner.
Weller, Marc. 1999. "The Rambouillet Conference on Kosovo." *International Affairs* 75, no. 2: 211–51.
Weltman, John J. 1995. *World Politics and the Evolution of War.* Baltimore: Johns Hopkins Univ. Press.
"Where Are the Refugees?" 1999. *RFE/RL Newsline* 3, no. 67, part 2, 7 Apr., 4.
Williams, Abidoun. UNPREDEP Civil Affairs Officer. 1995. "Interview with the Author." 8 May. Skopje, Republic of Macedonia.
Woodward, Susan L. 1995. *Balkan Tragedy: Chaos and Dissolution After the Cold War.* Washington, D.C.: Brookings Institution Press.
World Bank. 1996. *Bosnia and Herzegovina: Toward Economic Recovery.* Washington, D.C.: World Bank.
Wren, Christopher. 1995. "Greece to Lift Macedonia Trade Ban." *New York Times,* 14 Sept., A6.
Xhaferi, Arbën. Leader, PPDsh. 1995. "Interview with the Author (Audio)." 28 July. Tetovo, Republic of Macedonia.
———. 1996a. "Interview with the Author (Audio)." 13 Mar. Tetovo, Republic of Macedonia.
———. 1996b. "Interview with the Author (Camera)." 30 May. Tetovo, Republic of Macedonia.
Yates, Julian Peel. OSCE Deputy Head of Mission. 1996. "Interview with the Author." 12 Mar. Skopje, Republic of Macedonia.
Young, Oran R. 1967. *The Intermediaries.* Princeton: Princeton Univ. Press.
Zaagman, Rob. 1994. "The CSCE High Commissioner on National Minorities: An Analysis of the Mandate and the Institutional Context." In *The Challenges of Change: The Helsinki Summit of the CSCE and Its Aftermath,* 113–75. Dordrecht, Netherlands: Martinus Nijhoff.

Zametica, John. 1992. *The Yugoslav Conflict.* Adelphi Paper No. 270. London: Brassey's.

Zartman, I. William. 1983. "The Strategy of Preventive Diplomacy in Third World Countries." In *Managing U.S.-Soviet Rivalry: Problems of Crisis Prevention,* edited by Alexander L. George, 341–64. Boulder, Colo.: Westview.

———. 1989. "Prenegotiation: Phases and Functions." In *Getting to the Table: The Process of International Prenegotiation,* edited by Janice Gross Stein, 1–17. Baltimore: Johns Hopkins Univ. Press.

———. 1992. *Ripe for Resolution: Conflict and Intervention in Africa.* New Haven: Yale Univ. Press.

———. 1993. "Internationalization of Communal Strife: Temptations and Opportunities of Triangulation." In *The Internationalization of Communal Strife,* edited by Manus L. Midlarsky, 27–44. New York: Routledge.

Zimmermann, Warren. 1995. "The Last Ambassador." *Foreign Affairs* 74, no. 2: 2–20.

"Zum Aufkeimen des serbischen Nationalismus in Mazedonien." 1993. *Fernseh-/Hörfunkspiegel Ausland,* 18 Jan., 7.

"Zunehmende Spannungen in Mazedonien." 1995. *Neue Züricher Zeitung,* 22 Feb., 5.

INDEX